TURBULENCE

Barry Litherland

Copyright 2017 Barry W Litherland (Bleaknorth Publishing)
All Rights Reserved
ISBN: 978-0-9955588-3-0

Turbulence

Chapter 1

Hannah stood by the kitchen window, her hands resting on the polished granite worktop. It was her second spring in the house and the silver birches she planted were breaking into leaf. Daffodils flourished below them and beside a path which curved between shrubs and lawns. There were vegetables too, by the fence to her right, though not growing yet - just shoots. The lawns were fresh from their first cut. A child's empty swing hung motionless.

Joe stood behind her next to the door which led to the hallway and the front door, ready to leave, an old canvas backpack beside him on the floor.

'I've got to go,' he said.

'I know.'

She didn't look at him. She stared out through the window at nothing in particular, vaguely aware of cattle steaming in the field away to her right beyond the fence. The pasture rose towards a copse of trees. Beyond lay a farm, a lane and a distant horizon.

'What will you tell the children?' he asked.

'I don't know. I'll think of something.'

'Tell them I'm sorry. Tell them I wish...'

She turned around and looked at him.

'No, I won't tell them that. Maybe I'll just tell them the truth. Maybe it's time. Maybe they're old enough now.'

'Which truth is that?'

She shrugged. 'The simple one maybe.'

But seven and nine years old; could that ever be old enough to know?

She shook her head to drive away the thought. 'I'll think of something.'

The sun emerged from behind the clouds. Mottled foliage was shadowed on the wall; on her face too.

'Tell them I'm sorry I couldn't say goodbye. Say I kissed them while they were asleep.'

'Where will you go?'

'I'll just keep on the move. I'll drift up towards my brother's cottage in the north. Alan will take me in for a while. Maybe they'll get tired and leave us alone.'

'You think so?'

'No, but I hope so.'

'I'm tired, Joe, really tired. We've got the children to think of. We've got a home. My father says we can live here as long as we like but we can't always be running away. They said it would be okay when the trial was over and they were sentenced - but it wasn't. Then they told us that things would settle if you went away so you left and we were alone. We moved here and we waited and waited and eventually they said we were safe again so you came home. But now...'

'I know.'

'How did they find you?'

'Someone told them.'

'Someone always tells them.'

'People believe the lies they tell.'

'Why won't they leave us alone?'

She turned and looked back into the garden at the side of the house. A gentle breeze rippled the leaves. He crossed the kitchen and stood behind her. He put his hands on her shoulders and she leaned back against him.

'The phone call was awful. I knew it was him - Caine - the way he laughed.' She shuddered. 'He knew you were here.'

'I'll phone from Alan's. I've got to go, Hannah, before the girls wake. There'd be too much explaining – and tears.'

'Why do they hate us so much?'

He kissed her hair and spoke to her gently. 'You know why.' He paused for a moment. 'It's like we were walking down a country lane – all of us together. The sun was out and there was a cool breeze and it was just right, you know. There were birds and butterflies in the hedgerow and deer across the field over by the trees' edge. That was our life. Everything was perfect, just perfect.

'Then we came to a junction and suddenly we were scared. We could turn left or just go straight on. We knew that left was the harder way but it was the way we ought to choose, even though it was tangled and overgrown and we couldn't see where it led. Straight on it looked like nothing would change, just the same country lane going on forever.'

'You turned left, Joe. You always turn left.'

'I know. I'm sorry.'

'Don't be sorry. I'm not. It'll be over one day, though, won't it? Promise me.'

'One day,' he said, 'I promise.'

She turned towards him and rested her head on his chest.

'This time they're really close, aren't they? They know you're alive and they know you're here.'

'Yes.'

'It was worth it, Joe, wasn't it?'

She raised her eyes to look at him, wanting reassurance. Round eyes, overflowing, blue beneath the tears like sky reflected in ice.

'Sometimes I wish I'd taken the easy path.'

'Me too.'

He held her close for a minute, and then another, harder minute, and then he took her arms and pushed her gently away.

'If I don't go now, I'll never.'

He walked to the door and picked up his backpack, slinging it over his shoulder and turning the handle of the kitchen door.

'If they catch you, will they kill you?'

He tried a smile. 'They've got to catch me first.'

'I know, but will they?'

'You know the answer.'

'We've got to be honest, always. It's the only way I can manage.'

He paused. 'Yes. Yes, they will. They'll never forgive me for what I did or what I am. But they won't catch me and sooner or later they'll stop and then I'll come home. See if I don't.'

'Promise?'

'Cross my heart.'

'Don't say it if you don't mean it.'

'I've got to go. I'll phone when I can.'

She turned back to the window and the garden, the child's swing moving gently now in a sudden breeze as if recently vacated, the honeysuckle, not yet in fragrant bloom, twining round the fence. She heard the door close.

Chapter 2

Joe walked down the narrow lane to the village. From there he took a bus the few miles to the centre of Dowlheim, the old market town where he would catch the intercity coach north. The village bus was quiet, just a handful of old people from Audron going shopping. He didn't speak. If you begin a conversation, you never know where it might end - maybe with difficult questions and even more difficult answers. Better to say nothing. He nodded and smiled and sat alone near the back of the bus.

Once in the town he crossed a grey car park and followed other pedestrians between high buildings and down a narrow lane which opened into a wide main street lined with wild cherry trees with pink blossom. The trees segregated the traffic from the pedestrians, the footpath and the shops. They created a rural arcade where he walked on pink petals. He barely noticed. Nor did he see the benches beneath the trees, black wrought iron with the town's coat of arms on their sides and the blossom drifting down and settling around them. He paced on through a dark world of his own, where there were no flowers.

Familiar buildings marked his progress. The jeweller's shop, established in 1849, might have been replaced by a chain chemist, the butchers, a family business in its tenth generation, by a convenience store and the old post office by a charity outlet, but the 18th Century facade was unchanged. The Old Coaching Inn might advertise a restaurant, Sky Sports and wifi, but it too was rooted in antiquity. At the end of the road, the 14th Century church stood sentinel behind defensive walls, rising on solid buttresses to gaze down on the town like a resentful old man, fearful of change.

Joe felt waves of loneliness sweep over him. He turned to cross the river over a double arched stone bridge. A solitary heron hunted the still water above the weir and the tumbling foam. Downstream were trees and fields where sheep and cows grazed, like in a story book, like it was forever.

Not much had changed here during the conflict, the ceasefire and the fragile peace which followed. Dowlheim waited it out, as it had before during other wars and other conflicts. It would change at its own pace. The inhabitants read about the troubles in their conservative newspapers and they watched the television news. They were like witnesses at a car crash. They looked after refugees who dragged themselves from the carnage further north and they wrote letters to the press denouncing the outrages but mostly they just watched as the cities crumbled and everything descended into chaos.

They were grateful it was someone else and somewhere else and not them, not there. There but for the grace of God, they thought.

But fortune was kind to the residents of places like Dowlheim. History taught them that.

The unrest affected food deliveries, of course, and disrupted services and transport. It was dangerous to travel too far from home, especially north, unless on one of the infrequent buses with their armed guards. In most respects though, life for the people of Dowlheim continued unchanged. They followed the different factions like participants in a game, and they guarded their own privileges. They even had a militia – old men, young men and young women - toy soldiers playing war games.

When the riots and unrest finally ended and an uneasy truce was brokered, they watched with everyone else as the truce became a ceasefire and the ceasefire edged cautiously towards peace. Some people complained about plans for the new devolved administration, but mostly they were just relieved it was over.

Armed guards still accompanied buses and trains as they headed north. One stood by the door of Joe's coach as he queued to get on at the bus station. There was an old man behind Joe. He had wrinkled brown skin like he'd worked the land, and rough hands like sandpaper.

'Never used to have all this trouble,' he said, 'not in the old days. If someone had told me then I'd have to go through this just to get on a bus, I wouldn't have believed them.'

'Sign of the times.'

'Never thought I'd see the day; armed police to watch you get on a bus. Got no-one to blame but ourselves, I suppose.'

'Except others.'

The old man wheezed a hoarse, dry laugh. 'Yes indeed, except others; always good to have someone to blame – insurgents, whites, blacks, Asians, Muslims, Jews. I prefer to blame the politicians. It does less harm.'

'Which politicians?'

'All of them, every single one.'

'At least there's hope now – if the agreement holds. It's four months now.'

'I gave up hoping; it's not healthy. I'm just glad I'm old. I just want to be left alone to live until I die.'

They shuffled to the front of the line and reached the guard.

'Papers and tickets!' The order was peremptory, abrupt.

Joe opened a plastic wallet and held it towards the guard. He looked the officer in the eye. The guard looked at the photo, looked at Joe and nodded; dark glasses, bulletproof vest, no hint of a smile. The old man held a tattered card. He followed Joe onto the bus, breathing heavily as he climbed the steps.

'Mind if I sit with you?'

'No. You want the window seat?' Anything was better than solitude and silence and time alone with his thoughts.

'That's kind of you, very kind.' The old man shuffled in and sat down. 'I never understood it, you know - the violence. People are people. They're born, they live and they die — black, white or brown, Muslim, Christian or Hindu — all the same. If you could tell what kind of a person someone was by their colour, that'd be different — but you can't.'

The police guard was last on. He sat near the door with his gun on his lap. He glanced back down the aisle and then along the road and at the riverside. The door slid shut with a quiet hiss and the bus edged out onto the road.

'It'd be easier for him,' Joe said, 'if you knew a killer just by looking.'

'Colour and creed don't make terrorists.'

They were quiet for a moment.

'Mind if I ask you something?' the old man said.

'No.'

'Did you see the guy back at the bus station, sitting on the bench by the ticket office?'

'No, I can't say I did.'

'Slippery-looking guy, not someone I could take to, a scruffy, unwashed, unemployable sort with too much of the weasel about him.'

'No, I didn't see him.'

'He seemed to be taking special interest in you. One minute he was reading his newspaper - or looking at the pictures, maybe - the next he was staring over it right at you. He watched as we got on the coach and then he took off. He looked to be in a hurry.'

Chapter 3

Joe fought back the anxiety that surged momentarily. 'Can't imagine why he'd be looking at me,' he said. There was an annoying tremor in his voice. Were Caine and his spies really so close?

'Maybe you look like someone he knows.'

'Yes – a famous film star maybe. I've got the profile.' He turned his face sideways.

The old man grunted a laugh. 'Are you going far?'

'Far as I can.'

'Past the zone?'

'Maybe. What about you?'

'Just north of the zone; I've got family there – a sister and her husband. They got through the insurrection alright. Now they've got to get through the ceasefire. Keep staring straight ahead, I tell them. See that light? That's the end of the tunnel. Keep watching.'

'What's the road north like? Is it safe?'

'Pretty good though not as busy as it used to be; there's a bit of trouble now and then but that'll never stop. That's just a sad fact. There's no reasoning with the militants.'

'Still, with the settlement, people may suddenly find they've a future after all.'

'Maybe, maybe - you're young, so you can be optimistic. Seems to me it just puts a pleasing gloss on failure. If we hadn't failed, we wouldn't need it.'

Slats of sunlight hit them for a moment as the bus turned a steep corner and dropped down a slipway onto the motorway. It accelerated to join a convoy of traffic heading north.

'Are you from hereabouts?' the old man asked.

'Last few months, but my wife's family have lived here longer.'

Savage - that was the name Hannah had taken when he left, her maiden name and his name too now. It was another subterfuge and another failure.

'Where were you before that?'

'Somewhere else; I've spent a lot of time being somewhere else.'

The old man leaned his head against the seat and closed his eyes. 'Me too,' he said. 'Sometimes you just want to keep moving - saves thinking about the future.'

'Or the past,' said Joe quietly.

He thought of choices he'd made, of actions and consequences and he fell silent. A couple of years back, in one, fateful moment he'd stopped running, he'd turned and stood his ground and said, 'No more.' It felt good, like his life had changed, like his history had changed, like he stood there for his father, his grandfather, his great grandfather, like he'd asserted control over the persecutors. Even in the court room when he gave his evidence, he felt empowered.

But now he was running again, always running. The old fears had returned and with them the old anger and the bitterness. He was being driven like an animal, away from those he loved. He was a victim, the latest incarnation of generations of victims. It was his Jewish heritage. Now someone had seen him and they knew he was heading north. Once again, he was helpless, floating on the sea, carried by tides.

He glanced back along the bus. There were few passengers - a woman with a child, a few older men, a young couple, an Asian guy similar age to him, - no-one seemed to pay him particular regard. He tried to relax. When he got to the city, he'd disappear again and feed on the hope that one day he'd be safe. It was a shame they knew where he was headed, though.

The old man was leaning against the window and was snoring lightly, his mouth half open, his eyes closed. Joe yawned. It would be an hour at least before they hit the conurbation. He wouldn't sleep - he had too much to think about - but at least he could rest his eyes.

He wouldn't think about the future.

Or the past.

Chapter 4

Hannah's morning passed slowly under the oppressive routine of daily tasks, getting the children up and ready for school, preparing meals, tidying, cleaning, washing. She picked up a book and tried to read but she couldn't concentrate. The words disintegrated before her eyes and seemed to fall off the page. She turned on the radio and the TV just to hear human voices, just to fill the emptiness.

Only a couple of years ago she had a career, local government, but that disappeared after the court case. There was too much uncertainty and she didn't like to leave the children any more, just in case. She didn't resent it, not normally, but this morning, without Joe, everything felt unreal, a performance acted out without interest or reason. She glanced at the pendulum clock on the kitchen wall. Eleven o'clock; he'd be on the bus now heading north. The pendulum swung slowly, without pity.

'We'll stay with my sister for a few days,' she'd said to Joe, 'just for a few days. I don't want to be on my own, not without you. The girls will have their cousins for company. It'll be good for me too, with Lisa and Adam.' She paused, just for a moment. 'Sometimes I imagine they're out there, you know, watching and waiting. I hear a clock ticking and I think that when it stops the bodyguard will be gone, my father won't be able to help us and we'll be alone.'

'They won't touch you or the girls.'

'Are you sure?'

A moment's pause, just too long.

'I won't let them. I promise.'

On her own in the house, she felt vulnerable and anxious. She looked along the garden path and listened for sounds in the lane beyond the trees. A car drove by without stopping. A dog barked from a neighbour's garden, a hundred yards away. The bodyguard, hired by her father, was out there somewhere, out of sight.

Nothing bad could happen here, she told herself. This landscape was forever.

But bad things do happen, everywhere, all the time. She knew that too. History told her that, her history and Joe's.

She wasn't old, only thirty-one, but she looked older. She looked tired too. The last couple of years had been hard on her. The lustre had bleached from her eyes, and her skin was drawn thin like canvas. The fire that burned inside her had dimmed to glowing embers.

She'd never seen the men who hunted Joe, but she'd heard them and she knew what to look for because Joe had told her and they'd filled her nightmares. The tall one, Caine, had pale skin and a scar across his cheek. His short, blond hair covered his head like a coat of paint. The shorter one was darker, his beard and hair closely cropped. He was muscular and stocky, like a night club bouncer. They called him Bull on account of the broad neck and cold eyes.

She kept a handgun in locked wall cupboard in the hall. Her father insisted. Sometimes she wondered if she could use it.

'If they ever come near the girls,' she said and her lips grew tight like a bow string, and bloodless, 'if ever.'

She opened the cabinet now and took the pistol out. She held it in her hand and checked the mechanism. She pointed it at the wall but even then, her hand shook. The black grip was cold in her hand, the short barrel polished and shiny.

She put the gun back and closed and locked the door. She put the key on top of it, out of reach.

'Hopefully never,' she murmured.

She made a sudden decision. There was no point waiting for the weekend. She left the kitchen and gathered her coat and a couple of overnight bags, ready packed, from the banister at the foot of the stairs. She picked up a bunch of keys and left the house. She went to the school which the children attended and knocked on the classroom door.

'I should have telephoned. I need to collect the children. I've got to take them to my sister's – a family tragedy, a death. They'll be gone for a few days, a couple of weeks at most.'

The primary school teacher, probably her own age or maybe a couple of years younger, smiled a compassionate, professional smile. Her face was round like a doll's. She was elegant and slender and had dark hair which shone. Hannah felt a fleeting pang of envy.

'I'm so sorry. Was it someone close?'

It was a foolish question but Hannah smiled nonetheless. 'I wouldn't be going if it wasn't.'

'No, no I suppose not.' The teacher blushed gently.

'Closer to my sister than me, but that's why I've got to go. She needs me.'

'Families have to stick close at times like this.'

'Yes.'

'We'll miss the children.'

She smiled a bright-eyed, pretty sort of smile. She looked young and naive. Had she any idea what was happening out there? Probably not, Hannah thought. She was warm and friendly though, maybe even sincere. The children liked her anyway. Teachers are like gods to children their age. They can't do anything wrong; not like parents. The two girls gathered their bags and coats and, under the dead gaze of the other children, she hurried them out of the door.

'Where are we going?' Jessica demanded.

She didn't speak until they were in the car and Jessica and Meg were belted in and secure.

'Where are we going, Mum?'

Jessica never knew when to be quiet. She was two years older than Meg, nearly ten now, but she didn't read people the same. Meg was like her father. She saw everything a face could tell. She felt it too. Even now she knew something was wrong. She sat quietly while Jessica asked again and again.

'Where are we going, Mum?'

'We're going to visit your cousins for a few days; just a little break.'

'But it's school time. You can't take holidays in school time.'

'Your teacher says it's ok. It's a special holiday.'

'You said someone's died. Who's died?'

'No-one's died.'

'Then why did you say they had?'

'For Christ's sake, Jessica, give me some peace, will you?'

Jessica fell silent for a while. She opened her school bag and took out a magazine and some pencils. Meg looked through the window. A troubled little face looked back.

'Is Dad coming?' she asked.

'Dad's got some work. He'll be away for a while. You know that. He sent big kisses to you both.'

'Will he be back soon?'

She didn't answer. What could she say? It'd been tough on the kids when he went away the first time. That was over two years ago, after the trial, and he'd been gone for months. He came back for a while then left again. They'd moved house while he was away and taken a different name, Grandpa's name, Savage. Then they'd moved to Grandpa's house – the one he didn't live in any more, not since Gran died. Then Joe came home and they were together and they thought it might be forever.

The girls were four and six when it all started, too young to remember much. They'd grown up as Jessica and Meg Savage, with Hannah and Joe Savage, their mum and dad. That's who they were. They lived at Turnpike Cottage, just outside a pretty village called Audron. It was a village with a church and a school, a shop and a hotel. They went to the village school with all their friends. When they were older, they would go to the comprehensive school in the town where they went shopping with Mum. It was called Dowlheim. Their aunt and uncle and cousins lived in the countryside just outside the town but on the other side. The two families were close. The girls often visited to play with their little cousins.

'Where's he gone?' Jessica looked up from her drawing.

'He's got a job offshore, on the rigs.'

'Will he come back on holiday?'

'Maybe. Yes, yes, I'm sure he will.'

Meg was quiet. She saw that her face in the window had tears. It was an unhappy sort of face, like a storybook face in a sad story. She closed her eyes. Please, she asked, please give my story a happy ending. Please.

'We've got no games or clothes,' Jessica said.

'I've thrown a few things in the boot.'

'What things?'

'Just a few things – clothes, books and games. You can share your cousins' toys. It's only for a few days.'

'They only have baby toys. I need my tablet and phone.'

'You won't die for want of them.'

'I might.'

She fell sulkily silent and the car turned down a slip-road onto the dual carriageway. Within minutes, they were absorbed into the stream of traffic.

Chapter 5

The soporific effect of the bus gradually drove away troubling thoughts and Joe dropped into a light sleep. Sunlight flickered through the window as if through foliage. An hour passed. He felt the bus slow as it turned onto a dual carriageway near the city and then accelerate again.

He awoke suddenly to the sound of gunfire. The window beside him shattered, there were screams and muffled cries and the bus swerved to left and right, weaving crazily across the carriageway like some wounded animal. He held to the seat in front of him as the bus slid, with a tearing of metal, against the central barriers and flung him against the old man and then back towards the aisle. More glass shattered and fell. His face and hands felt warm and sticky and he looked at the blood, barely understanding what it was.

The bus veered across the carriageway and flung him back against the seat. It broke through the roadside barrier and came to a sudden stop, nose down at the road edge, steam and smoke billowing. There was a moment of silence before the gunshots started again. He crouched down, reached across and pulled the old man away from the shattered window and down to the floor behind the seats. He heard more glass shattering and then distant sirens gathering momentum as police cars sped towards the scene. The gunshots petered out. He lay still. He could hardly see for the blood in his eyes and hair. For a moment he imagined it was him they were after.

The old man lay across him as if in some hideous embrace, his arm cast limply across his chest and his head, what was left of it, resting on his shoulder. The bullet had gone in between the eye and the temple and had travelled diagonally through his head to emerge behind his ear. Blood and brain splattered Joe's coat and face.

He pushed the body away, grabbed his rucksack and scrambled into the aisle. It was littered with the detritus of the journey – plastic bottles, food packages, discarded sandwiches. He looked up and around, trying to understand. His mind was still several steps behind his body but it was catching up fast. The guard lay dead in the seat by the door, his body hanging limply into the aisle, his head to one side; the driver was slumped over the wheel. People screamed and cried. Someone in a window seat was moaning and swearing. A woman opposite cried out to him. Blood dripped from a gash in her arm. A little girl lay across her, four years old, maybe five.

'Help me,' the woman cried, 'please.'

The little girl looked up with wide, frightened eyes, like an animal.

Joe heard more gunshots. He looked along the aisle towards the door and then at the woman and the child.

'Help me.' The voice cried out again, desperate and fearful. A hand stretched towards him. With the other she clung to the girl who lay still, numbed by shock.

Joe pulled the woman to her feet and wrapped an arm round her.

'Keep low and keep going.'

Together they scrambled to the door. He pushed them forward, down the steps and out of the door

'Run,' he said. 'Run fast and don't stop.'

He fell down the steps of the bus and rolled onto the hard shoulder then staggered to his feet. He saw the woman and the child disappear across the barriers and up a low embankment towards some ruined buildings, probably destroyed during the insurrection. They'd be safe there, for the moment. He limped after her but stopped where a small group gathered beside an old tumbled down wall. From there he could look down to where drivers and passengers, caught in the carnage behind the bus, leapt from their vehicles and ran hunched, searching for any cover. Some stayed by their cars, crouched low, shaking and fearful, unable to move. Some, overcome by shock, didn't open their doors.

There was a gunshot, like some ghastly firework, and one man fell in the road by his car. He didn't move. Joe could hear children howling, unearthly, frightened cries, like some alien life form. After a few minutes, silence fell, full of menace. Nothing moved. Everyone waited. Smoke and steam rose from crashed cars and rose vertically, unmoved by any breeze.

'They're still out there,' a voice next to him whispered. 'They've not finished. They're waiting.' He had dark eyes, an olive complexion - eastern, Indian maybe, about thirty.

'What are they waiting for?'

Another man, red-haired and bearded, nodded towards the screaming sirens. 'They're waiting for *them*,' he said. 'I'm getting out of here.'

'Keep down and wait for the police,' the first voice warned. 'They'll be here any second.'

'What good will the police do? Look.'

He turned and stumbled away, crouching low. Joe nudged his new companion and indicated where, fifty metres to their left, half hidden by a crumbling wall beyond the sloping embankment, one of the gunmen stood. They watched as he emerged and took up a better position, leaning forward to rest his elbows on a broken wall. He was holding a semi-automatic machine gun.

Joe turned and looked at the other people beside him, crouching beside the rubble, as grey as the dust that covered them. A broad, heavy-looking man leaned forward holding a phone to capture the images. A wave of revulsion swept over him but before he could act, the dark-eyed Asian slapped the phone from his hands. The man swore viciously. A few more people took advantage of the lull and slipped away towards the ruined buildings, out of sight, safe.

'He's not alone,' Joe whispered, pointing towards the gunman. 'There are others, lots of them.'

Dark figures emerged like strange subterranean creatures and took up positions near the wall. One, who had the narrow, light build of a man barely out of his teens, held an improvised rocket launcher, others machine pistols or handguns. The police cars came closer, then slowed and their sirens relented.

'Now they spring the trap,' the thick set man whispered. 'This is what they want. I'm getting out of here.' He turned and stumbled away, his phone now tucked safely into a denim pocket.

There came an explosion and then another and the cars which were not hit screeched and turned and halted. The men with semi-automatics started to fire as other figures emerged from cover, rising like dark, avenging angels, hooded and walking forward. The people in the cars had no chance. Those who had not been killed by the explosions stumbled from the battered vehicles and were cut down where they stood.

Joe seethed with cold fury. He watched as one man, maybe a head taller than the rest, strode down the embankment and crossed towards the vehicles. The others gave way before him. He stared straight ahead, a handgun held loosely at his side. He raised one hand and the gunfire stopped. He peered into each car, calmly aimed and shot once, twice, into each vehicle. No-one was left alive. When he was sure there were no survivors, he looked around as if waking from a dream, and then signalled his followers to retreat.

He was about to turn and follow them when he was distracted by the sound of a car door grinding open. He paused at the roadside and watched a young man drag himself free of the wreckage and crawl, trailing a blood-soaked broken leg, towards the roadside. Every movement the young man made sent a spasm of pain across his face.

He was about forty yards from the dark, watching figure but nearer to Joe and his hidden companion. The gunman seemed to hesitate for a moment. He stared with indifference, watching the crawling figure as one might watch a writhing insect. He paused, contemplating his choices. Then he stepped towards the man, his gun raised.

Joe looked at the victim. He would never make it. The gunman was closing fast. Joe felt a lifetime of thoughts and feelings roar through his head carrying a tide of images and sounds then he stepped forward. He stumbled into the open and slid down the embankment towards the injured man. He didn't look at the killer. He couldn't. He waited for the shot that would end his life.

'What are you doing? For God's sake, you'll get us all killed.' Joe heard the voice of the one man left behind him but he paid little heed. He focused on the dusty ground at his feet. He stood upright and took one step, two steps forward and suddenly he realised he was counting his life not in years and months but in steps. Three steps, four. He reached the wounded figure and helped him heavily onto his feet.

'Thank you. Thank you.' Breath escaped painfully with the effort of speaking.

'Thank me later,' Joe muttered, 'when we get back.'

The gunshot never came. Joe glanced up and saw the gunman standing no more than fifteen metres from him. His gun lowered, he was watching the two figures struggling like wingless butterflies squirming in a futile quest for safety.

But nowhere was safe - Joe knew that — and no-one was safe. On one side were the people with guns and on the other the victims, caught between fighting factions, wanting nothing more than to live. Everyone knew where the power lay - where it had always lain.

The dark figure turned slowly and called to his colleagues to watch. He was laughing gently. At that distance, Joe could clearly see the movement of chest and head. For a second their eyes met.

Why didn't he shoot?

Joe didn't understand, but at that moment he didn't care. For the first time since he slipped down towards the wounded man he dared to hope and with that hope came a moment of terrible fear. Perhaps the killer was playing with him, allowing him a moment of optimism before delivering the coup de gras. He waited for the shot and focussed on each step because that alone was a fragile measure of success. When he glanced up again, the killer was still watching him. When their eyes met, he raised his pistol and took aim. He mouthed a gunshot and mimed firing then he lowered the pistol. Joe could hear his laughter as he walked away towards the rubble above the embankment. His companions had already gone.

The one solitary figure was still waiting for Joe by the crumbling wall. He was reaching out a dark hand, shouting encouragement now. Together they dragged the injured man to safety.

Joe fell back, breathing heavily. In the distance, a helicopter thrummed and he heard military vehicles approaching down the by-pass. He glanced round the wall towards the embankment but it was deserted.

His Asian companion dragged at Joe's arm and pulled him behind the wall. 'I don't know who you are but you live a charmed life. What were you thinking?'

'I wasn't.'

He felt suddenly cold. It was true. He wasn't thinking of anything. He wasn't thinking of Hannah or his children, his brother Alan, his friends, his family. It was as if he didn't care. But he did care; he cared so much it scared him. Only now did he think of what he might have lost, what *they* might have lost. He felt elated but he also felt ashamed. To risk his life was one thing but to ruin theirs? His companion was right. What *was* he thinking? What was wrong with him?

The wounded man mouthed his thanks and held out a hand. Joe took it.

'Alex.'

'I'm Joe. You'll be okay now, Alex.'

New vehicles ground to a halt and troops emerged and took cover behind the wrecks of cars. The helicopter drummed overhead. An armed soldier scanned the area.

'I've got to go,' Joe said. 'I can't be here when the troops arrive.' He turned to the injured man. 'You'll be alright now. They'll get you to hospital.'

They left Alex by the wall and Joe and his new companion crouched low and sped across the tarmac and past the ruined warehouse. They clambered through a gap in some tangled wire fencing hanging from rotting posts, torn into unnatural shapes like old, arthritic limbs. They crossed a narrow, deserted road and disappeared into an alleyway between red brick terraced houses.

'Jival,' his companion said as they turned onto a narrow street and slowed to a walk.

Joe held out a hand. 'I'm Joe; nice to meet you, Jival.'

'Likewise, Joe.'

Chapter 6

'I've got to ask again, Joe. What were you thinking? You could've got yourself killed.'

They were sitting at the bar of a small pub on the quiet corner of a shop-lined street. It felt a long way from the carnage of the attack, a lot further than the half mile they'd covered.

Joe shrugged. 'I'm not sure I was thinking at all.'

'I don't think I'd have done it. I've got a wife and kids.'

Joe winced. The words were like a blow.

'Me too,' he said quietly. He could see Jival watching him, his mind full of questions.

'Well, you're one lucky guy. That was as close to suicide as anything I've seen. Those bastards aren't hesitant about killing.'

'I just saw the wounded guy and I knew I could either help him or not, that's all. I didn't have a choice.'

'You nearly got killed.'

He could hear the reproof in Jival's voice. He had a choice. He could have stayed where he was.

'They killed those people like they were no more than flies. I couldn't do anything. I felt helpless and I didn't like the feeling. Then I saw the guy in the car and suddenly I could do something. That's all.'

But that wasn't all, was it? Maybe it was deeper than that, as deep as the stories his great grandfather told about the Nazis, stories retold by his grandfather and his father. The old man hadn't been reticent about his experiences, about the people he knew who were taken away, the people who died, the ghettos and the persecution. No, he'd insisted on telling the stories over and over and Joe's grandfather did the same and his father too. Some things should never be forgotten, they said. The stories gave you back power, control.

Yes, maybe it was something to do with that. But maybe it was the thought too of Hannah and his children and how he couldn't be with them that really got to him; and maybe he was angry not just at the terrorists and his own enemies but at himself. Maybe he just wanted to let out all that anger, like releasing a valve.

'Next time you get angry, I want to be somewhere else.'

'Me too.'

They leaned on the bar and drank beer from bottles. The barman glanced towards them occasionally, but said nothing. There were only a handful of other drinkers in the room, difficult to make out in the dull light. The windows were small and opaque and shared a layer of grime with the rest of the place.

'I feel conspicuous,' Joe murmured. Eyes glanced furtively towards him, momentarily bright in the dimly lit bar, lights suddenly switched off as they looked down and away.

'We don't get as many whites as we used to, not since the conflict. But it's getting back to normal, gradually. White, brown, black – it's all the same here, like it should be.'

'I'm only part white; I'm mainly Jewish, way back. My family came from Germany just before the war, escaping Nazis. Now I'm a native through and through. What about you?'

He looked at Jival - dark eyes, black hair, dark skin, casually dressed in an open-necked shirt, clean and smart, office shoes, about thirty, thirty-five maybe, same as him.

'I'm Indian, third generation,' he laughed softly, 'born in the local hospital.'

'Hindu?'

'I keep it up for the family. It does no harm. I enjoy some of it. Call me a secular Hindu.'

Joe glanced round. 'I still feel conspicuous. Are they looking at me?'

'Maybe it's the blood and brains on your clothes.'

'Yeah, I guess so. It's easy to be paranoid, especially when you've been shot at. Who were those people back there?' He gestured back as if the motorway and the carnage they had recently experienced was just beyond the bar.

'Militants, fanatics, the residue of the conflict; they're pretty unpleasant and not good to meet. The ceasefire didn't suit them and the settlement won't suit them either. They want to take over and install their own sort of government and they won't give up till they do or they're dead. They don't like my kind. They hate yours. They don't like anyone who isn't them. There used to be a few different factions but recently, one group's taken control and not much happens now without their say-so. Where are you headed?'

'North, I've got to keep on the move.'

'Better to travel in daytime.' He checked his watch. 'It's getting late. People are heading home. You need a change of clothes.'

'Do you know a decent hotel, not too expensive?'

'For a single guy covered in blood and brains? No, I doubt it. You'd better come back with me. We've got a sofa you can have for the night. I'll lend you some clothes.'

They left the bar and turned up the main road. They were about to cross towards a line of colourful food shops when two armed police officers emerged from a side street and headed towards them. Crash helmets, dark sunglasses, stocky bodies under bulletproof vests, they eyed the two men carefully, suspiciously. They didn't seem to like what they saw. One of them unfastened his holster and held the pistol grip. He motioned to Jival and Joe to stop. The other gestured towards the shop window beside them.

'What do they want?'

'Just do as they ask; it'll be okay.'

Jival turned and leaned against the window, hands high on the glass, feet spread. Joe, conscious of his murderous appearance, copied him. The guards frisked them and turned them round. One of them indicated the bloodstains on Joe's coat and in his hair. His partner had removed the pistol from his holster and stood back, watching for a false move. Both were impassive, expressionless.

'Where did you get like that?'

'I was in the bus that got ambushed.'

'Let me see your identification.'

Joe was about to reach in his pocket but he stopped suddenly as the second officer raised and pointed the pistol, two hands on the grip, his aim steady.

'It's in my pocket.'

'Use your other hand; and slowly.'

He reached for a wallet and the guard flicked it open.

'Joe Savage – what do we need to know about you, Joe?'

'You're the one with the gun and the questions.'

The officer pocketed Joe's wallet and turned to Jival. 'Now you.'

Jival repeated the procedure and handed over his card.

'Why didn't you stay at the scene, Joe, wait for the police?'

'The police got blown up. We couldn't stay.'

'More police were coming, soldiers, helicopters too. Why did you run?'

'It wasn't safe.'

'Some people waited. Why didn't you?'

Joe shrugged. 'Most people ran. Besides, I wasn't thinking all that clearly. Bullets have that effect on me.'

Jival spoke. 'Joe rescued an injured guy from a car. The militants saw him. I thought they might be coming for him so I made him leave.' He sketched the story hurriedly.

'Looks like we've got ourselves a hero, eh?'

'I just got angry.'

'You always do stupid things when you're angry?'

'It's becoming a habit.'

The officer turned to Jival. 'Does he always do stupid things when he's angry?'

'We only met today, after the bus came off the road.'

'You were on the bus too?'

Jival nodded. 'I was coming home from a job interview in Zarten. The letter's in my pocket.'

'Did you get the job?'

'No.'

The guard turned to his colleague and nodded towards Joe. 'He was angry,' he said. 'You want to die or what?' he said to Joe.

'Not today – if that's ok by you.'

The second guard stepped forward, gun still raised. 'Are you being funny? You a funny man, are you?'

'I don't know how to be funny. I've spent a day surrounded by people dying. It spoils your sense of humour.'

The other guard spoke. 'Where are you going now?'

'I'm heading north.'

'Be precise, Joe. I'm not a patient man. Where are you going?'

'Just north,' Joe said stubbornly. 'I'm not sure where.'

He couldn't trust anyone. Caine had spies everywhere, especially in the police. He was annoyed with himself. He should have said east or west – anything to hide the truth.

'Last chance, Joe, where are you going?' The guard looked menacing, his eyes obscured by dark, reflective lenses. Joe remained silent and looked away.

The second guard sighed. 'Do you want to tell him where he's going now, Jival?'

'They're taking us down to the police compound, Joe. They want to check things out. Don't worry, we'll be okay. It happens.'

'Why?' Joe resisted the hand that took his arm.

'You're standing here with someone's blood and brains on you, you won't tell us where you're going and you ask why? Are you stupid or something?'

'I explained.'

'Come on, Joe, just do as he says.'

'I'm not doing anything wrong. I was a victim of the attack, remember? Why would you want to arrest me?'

'You're not under arrest. We need to check you out. There are white extremist groups out there as well as the other fanatics.'

'Well, I'm not one of them; not me.'

'Come on Joe, I don't want any trouble. I've got a wife and kids. Please, just do as they ask. It'll be alright.'

Joe looked at him. 'Okay, okay,' he said.

The guards signalled and an unmarked car pulled up beside them, black and shining and with dark windows. The rear door opened and they were pushed inside.

Chapter 7

The police compound was a large concrete and steel structure surrounded by a high wall and razor wire. During the worst violence, the police had retreated to the security of its solid defences after forays into the unsettled streets. Here, at least, they were safe from the shells and bullets and improvised bombs which had become a constant danger to their peacetime stations.

The black car entered through a double gate, guarded by two heavily armed men in uniform who stared impassively at each occupant and checked the vehicle. No words were spoken, no greetings exchanged.

'It's like something from a war zone,' Joe murmured.

The driver laughed ironically. 'This *was* a war zone until a few months back. Where have you been?'

'Somewhere else,' Joe said. 'You forget how bad it was.'

The car crossed a courtyard and pulled up outside a building which had all the charm of a concrete cube. Small evenly spaced windows were protected by wire and metal grilles. Joe barely had time to take it all in before the officers hurried them up narrowing steps, through a security barrier and into the foyer. It was only when they passed the polished reception area and went through another door that they saw the familiar bustle of police activity, guards hurrying from one room to another, officers monitoring screens or seated at cluttered desks.

The guards led them between desks and cabinets towards a corridor. Joe was pushed forward into an empty room. Jival was directed into another. One man, obviously a senior officer, sat behind a polished desk, reading. He didn't look up.

'Give these men your shirt,' he said.

He looked up and his small, black eyes stared indolently at Joe.

'Get a DNA sample,' he said to the guards, 'and fetch Jackson. I don't want to be accused of racism. What's your name?'

Joe told him.

'Well, Joe, we'll just sit here for a while until we get a chance to check things out. Do you want to call anyone?'

'I don't know anyone.'

'No family? No friend?'

He shook his head.

'Jival is calling his wife. You got no-one?'

'I could phone Jival's wife too, I suppose.'

The inspector sat back and sighed. 'A smart mouth will get you nowhere, Joe.'

'No, really,' Joe leaned forward. 'I can explain to her that Jival nearly got killed when a bus blew up, that he helped me and led me away to safety and then got arrested because he was with me. I'd like to apologise to her. I'd like to tell her she's got a good man there who deserves better treatment.'

The inspector sighed again and tapped a pencil end against the table. A door opened and another officer entered. He wore the same high-collared black uniform, the same embroidered insignia, and he sported the same short hair and sculpted beard. He differed in one significant respect. His skin was a similar tone to Joe's, his cropped hair was brown and his eyes were dark. For a moment Joe was surprised, and his face must have registered his reaction. The inspector laughed a short, dry laugh and the new officer looked annoyed.

'Sit down, Jackson. I don't want Joe to think I'm some kind of racist. Jackson is one of my best officers and he shares your ethnicity.' He turned his eyes back on Joe. 'We're short of staff here, Joe, and my people have to work long hours and they're tired and impatient and short tempered. There's still a lot of ill feeling out there and a lot of danger and guys like Jackson here had to break with a lot of people to keep their jobs. So be nice, eh?'

The years had taken their toll on Jackson. He breathed heavily and, despite the slim fitting uniform, he showed signs of deterioration. His waistline bulged over his belt and his face flushed red. He drew out a handkerchief and mopped his forehead.

Joe smiled for a moment. The irony of the white detectives brought in to interview the person they thought of as a white suspect hadn't escaped him.

'Have you got any Jewish detectives?' he asked, 'only I'm fourth generation Jewish immigrant, lapsed of course, and as loyal as a monarchy, but you can't be too careful. We have historical differences, you and me.'

The sarcasm didn't escape the officer.

'I have enough problems without history, Joe. I just get through the days. Jackson will have to do.'

Joe was suddenly aware that Jackson was looking at him closely, too closely. He leaned forward, picked up Joe's identification card and scrutinised it and then placed it rather too casually back on the table. Joe felt a momentary discomfort. He tried to escape Jackson's eyes, but no matter where he looked, he was aware that Jackson was watching. The inspector spoke again.

'What brings you to this zone then, Joe?'

It was a good question. Shame he didn't have a good answer. He was running away, a persecuted minority of one. The first time he ran – that was after he was conveniently killed off and given a new identity - they found him a job on the rigs, out in the North Sea. It was hard, physical work but the comradeship was good and when he got time off, he stayed with a workmate in Aberdeen. When he had to run again, he got a job in East Anglia doing seasonal farm work. Then he'd worked on a ferry on the North Sea. This time he'd had to leave too quickly to make any plans other than to get to his brother's house in Cambrier.

'I'm just passing through, heading north.'

'Where in the north?'

'Anywhere, I'm not fussy; maybe Altcastle or maybe Lorvek, who knows?'

The agent sighed despondently. 'There you go again, Joe. I'm trying to be nice and friendly here and you're giving me a hard time. Why is that, Joe?'

Joe turned at looked from one officer to the other. How could he trust anyone with the truth?

'I've got friends up there. Does it matter? I've done nothing wrong here.'

A fleeting look passed between the agents, a raised eyebrow and a silent communication from Jackson. The subject changed abruptly.

'Tell me about the men you saw attacking the bus - the ones who killed my officers and friends.'

'There's not much to tell. They were masked, dressed in dark clothing, and had hoods. The only one I really noticed was pointing a gun at me.'

'What sort of gun?'

'That's not my area of expertise. It was a handgun, that's all I can tell you. He mimed shooting me and then holstered the pistol and walked away. I had a definite feeling he was laughing at me.'

'He probably was. Describe him.'

'He was about thirty-five I'd guess, quite a bit taller than the others and definitely in control. He raised a hand and everything stopped. He moved a finger and men moved forward. It was quite impressive.'

'Akmal.' The inspector glanced towards his subordinate. Jackson nodded.

'Is that all you can tell us?'

'My mind was on other things, like staying alive. He looked pretty fearless, though. Even when bullets were flying, he just stood there. It must give you an awesome sense of power to be without any fear of death.'

'You sound like you admire him?'

'He was an indiscriminate murderer. There was nothing to admire.'

'To his followers he's a hero, a role model, a single-minded man of principle and belief. Can you understand that?'

'I understand it, but the values which define him are skewed and distorted. He thinks he's wearing angel wings but really they're a straightjacket. His followers are misguided.'

'What about you, Joe? What defines you?'

'I'm too aware of my own complexity to define myself. I can't shut out all the different me's for long enough.'

'Are you a man of principle, Joe?' Jackson interrupted. He spoke slowly, as if he'd been working the words around his mouth in preparation to speak.

Joe, whose eyes had been fixed on the inspector now turned and looked at Jackson. He looked tired. He was probably a remnant of the Force as it existed before the ceasefire and the fragile settlement, before a surge of optimism brought recruits from ethnic minorities ready to help create a bright new future. In the meantime, Jackson was too weary to look for work elsewhere, too near retirement to find another job so he just hung in there, rode the changes and got on with it.

'I don't know what that means.'

'I mean, are you the sort of man who stands up to be counted when he sees things happen right in front of him that he doesn't agree with?' He didn't wait for an answer. 'I remember something a couple of years ago. It happened on the edge of the zone, in what we used to call border country.' He looked at the inspector. 'You mind if I tell a story, Chief?'

'You go ahead, Jackson, but make it pertinent to our current situation, will you? It's been a long day already and it isn't going to get any shorter.'

'The areas on the edge of the zone were bad in those days, far worse than they are now. It was dangerous enough in the daytime, but once darkness fell it just wasn't safe for ordinary, decent people to be out. Didn't matter about colour or race or religion, there was always someone out to get you, someone with a grudge. The worst of them were in gangs – one colour, one race or religion – they thought they believed in something, said they were fighting for good against evil, that sort of thing.'

He shook his head and laughed to himself.

'Well, one day a colleague of mine was patrolling out there in the border area to the south, one of the worst areas, full of vicious, nationalist types. It was early evening and a report came in about an attack on this Asian guy and his girl. My colleague and his partner headed out, got there just in time too. It was a dangerous spot, not a place for an Asian to walk in those days, especially after dark. The Asian guy was a mess, his face pounded, nose broken, eyes bruised and swollen. He had a stab wound in his gut. He was sitting in a pool of blood as if he didn't know what had happened to him. The girl had been slapped around a bit and her mouth and eyes were cut. Yeah, it was a real mess apparently. Their attackers were a couple of white thugs – supremacist types with short hair and stubble - big too - looked like their faces had been used to hammer nails, yeah, really nasty.'

'Are you going to get to the point, Jackson?'

'The point, Chief, is that these two guys, big as they were, had been disarmed and laid out flat - with their own baseball bat too. They'd thrown it down since the Asians were such easy pickings.' He turned to Joe. 'My colleague said there was this young guy there, about your height but a few years younger, a white guy too. He was standing over them and wielding this bat as if he wanted to kill someone; looked like his head was about to explode he was so angry, snorting like a bull. Somehow – God knows how – he'd got a knife off the attackers and thrown it across the road. They were lying there, bruised and bewildered, wondering what the hell had just happened to them. I tell you, it was a hell of a risk that young guy took that night. Within minutes there were other thugs gathering, looking for trouble. It was getting nasty. This guy just didn't seem to care. I guess he was a man of principle. Are you a man of principle, Joe?'

'I wouldn't want to get myself killed,' Joe said. He spoke calmly, casually. He didn't want to let them see how his heart was beating and his blood pulsing.

'This guy probably felt the same, Joe. He had a wife and two children, I recall – both of them girls. They'd have been about five or six, I guess; pretty girls too. I seem to recall his wife was a pretty, young woman. You got a family, Joe?'

Joe shook his head quickly. It felt like betrayal. 'What happened to him, the man you're talking about?' His voice was casual, maybe too casual, as if he was restraining an involuntary tremor.

'He went to court. He spoke out against the assailants. That was either brave or stupid, depending on where you look at it from. A lot of people saw him as a hero, especially when it turned out he was Jewish.' He laughed dryly, little more than a wheezing in his chest, and there was a momentary flickering in his eyes. 'Can you imagine how the Government and the press loved that, a Jewish guy rescuing a couple of Asian Muslims from cowardly white bigots? They said he was what our new country was going to be about. They dragged him onto the television and radio to create a positive spin, to help in the journey towards peace.'

'I recall something about that,' the inspector said. 'Remind me what happened to the two white thugs, Jackson?'

'From what I recall, they were found guilty of attempted murder and incarcerated. One of them got killed, I believe, right there in the prison. I can't recall the details. The other will be a lot older by the time he gets out.'

Jackson's eyes caught and held Joe's. He didn't blink. The inspector watched closely. He was sitting forward on his seat now.

'Of course, some people thought of them as martyrs to the cause. It was a pretty bad case of twisted logic in my view, but there were a lot of people who felt angry about what happened and especially that it was a Jewish guy who got them sent down. That young man found himself with a whole load of enemies. To make matters worse, it transpired too that one of the thugs was the brother of a really nasty piece of psychopathic fanaticism – influential too, and powerful. What was his name now?' He pondered for a moment. 'Caine, that was it, Nathan Caine. Our local hero was in a lot of trouble and so were his wife and daughters.'

Joe remained sullenly silent, not allowing his eyes to waver.

'What happened to him?' he asked at last.

'I heard he was killed in a road traffic accident. It was just an accident, nothing sinister, they said. His wife and daughters were left alone. They moved away. I was never sure I believed in that accident, but I guess it was probably true.'

The inspector leaned forward. 'I think the point Jackson is making, Joe, is that you should think twice before you stand up against people like these. For you, it could mean kidnap or death. For us it could mean a nasty racial incident just when we don't need one. You understand me?'

He nodded.

A uniformed officer knocked and entered. He handed over a document.

'It seems you got on the bus as you said and there's nothing to cast doubt on what you've told us, Joe. We may have to let you go.' He laid the paper on the desk top and tapped it thoughtfully. 'Things are a lot better around here, Joe, even in a short time. People are getting on pretty well, all things considered, and we've got all sorts here too, mostly Muslim of course, but Hindus like Jival and Sikhs and Christians and hell, even atheists too. What are you, Joe?'

'I think if God was all that great, he would have stopped short of giving us religion. We don't know how to handle it.'

'You haven't answered my question.'

'A non-believer through and through; if you're going to be an evil, murdering, fanatical bastard, it doesn't seem fair to blame it all on someone who doesn't exist, don't you think?'

'I don't think about things like that, Joe. I'm not paid enough. I'm just happy to get through a week with no problems. I try to stack one good day on another until they become a habit. This has been a particularly bad day.'

'Where are you staying tonight, Joe?' Jackson asked. If he'd drawled any more slowly, he wouldn't have reached the questioning inflection.

'Jival offered me a sofa.'

'Jival's gone home to his wife and family,' the inspector said. 'We let him out half an hour ago. Can we get Joe a lift to Jival's house, Jackson?'

'I'll give him a lift myself, Chief. I want to see he doesn't do anything heroic. I still think he might be a man of principle.'

And that was that. They stuffed his bloodied shirt in a bag and gave him an outsized t-shirt which had been hanging around the office for some days. He picked up his canvas rucksack and shook hands with the inspector, who broke momentarily into an unconvincing smile.

'Travel in daylight and keep travelling. Don't do anything stupid and you'll be okay.'

Five minutes later, Joe was seated beside Jackson in a black, unmarked car. Jackson eased the car slowly into traffic and waited patiently at one set of lights and then another. Eventually they broke free and their speed increased.

'The story I was telling, I guess you already knew it.' His voice emerged slowly as if from a distance.

Joe didn't speak. He looked out of the side window at the houses and shops slipping past.

'I recognised you as soon as I saw you. Different name on your ID, but that's to be expected.'

Joe looked out of the window. He was thinking fast. Jackson turned off the main road. Cars were parked on the roadside now and the houses were poorer and cheaper.

'It's my wife's family name. Did the inspector recognise me?'

Jackson glanced at Joe and then back at the road. He nodded. 'He understood what I was telling him.'

Joe hesitated. His voice betrayed an annoying weakness. 'Am I safe?'

'The Chief won't say anything and I sure as hell won't. I've got no time for those white nationalist types. You did a good thing, Joe.'

Joe grunted a dry laugh. 'Shame I had to die.'

'Indeed. I'd have sent flowers if I'd believed it.'

'What happens now?'

'Now you keep moving. You won't be safe for long. News has a habit of breaking free of the restraints we put on it, especially in my line of work. You can't trust all my colleagues. Some of them are sympathetic to Caine and his movement. It'll only take a word.'

'I'll move on tomorrow.'

The car slowed as Jackson dropped through the gears. They turned left into a narrow street of terraced houses.

'It's just down here on the right,' he said. He signalled and turned. 'Are they still after you?'

Joe nodded. 'I had to move on.'

'How far behind you?'

Joe shrugged. 'Who knows? A day, two days, a week maybe.'

'That's bad. I'm sorry to hear that. How'd they find you?'

Joe glanced towards him and laughed gently.

'Yeah, I guess I already know,' Jackson said. 'There are spies everywhere. It was some pretty powerful people you rattled. If they want to find you, I expect they will. What about your wife and kids?'

'They're protected. My father in law's a pretty influential guy. He's scary too, in a quiet, diplomatic sort of way. He works for the Government.'

'What if his power wanes?'

'Then I'll go home and fight it out and probably get killed - anything as long as my family are safe.'

The car pulled up at the kerbside outside a small terraced house. The curtain flickered and then the door opened.

'Here.' Jackson held out a card. 'Take this. Consider it a Get Out of Jail Free card. Ring me if you need help anywhere in the zone.'

Joe laughed. 'I've got one of those from someone else, someone rather different from you, Jackson, an imam I met at the trial. I'm supposed to save it for one of those rainy days when I'm in danger of drowning.' He slipped Jackson's card in his wallet. 'Thanks.'

'Let's hope you never need either of them.'

'Let's hope.'

Joe opened the door and stepped out onto the uneven pavement. Jival came towards him and held out a hand.

'Joe?' Jackson lowered his window. 'There are more friends out there than enemies. Remember that. The country is changing. It just needs a little push.'

Joe nodded. 'My problem is sorting the good guys from the bad.'

Jackson revved the engine gently and the car moved slowly away. The window closed and he was hidden behind its protective glass.

'Come in,' Jival said, 'meet my wife and children. Let's get you a change of T-shirt. That one looks like a nightdress.'

Turbulence

The door closed behind them.

Chapter 8

That night when Haasita and the children had retired to bed, Joe and Jival sat in the small living room and talked into the early hours of the morning.

'Two white guards took a lot of interest in you.'

'Two? I only saw Jackson. He was my driver tonight.'

'The other was a few years younger. I didn't like him. He sneered a lot; looked as if he'd just wiped me off his shoe.'

Joe tried his best not to look concerned. 'What was he asking?'

'Where you came from, where you were going, where you were staying, how long. I said to him, 'Ask about me; I can tell you about me. Him I hardly know. We shared a bus attack together, that's all.' In the old days, he would have hit me. Not now. I think he misses the old days.' He looked carefully at his companion. 'Are you worried about something, Joe? Some trouble, maybe?'

Joe shook his head, but not convincingly. He was worried about home, his wife and the girls; he was worried about the men following him; he was worried about a white police officer asking too many questions. He was worried about his journey north. He was worried whether he would find a job and somewhere to escape to and for how long and whether he would ever see his family again. You can only live on hope for so long.

'Is someone after you, Joe? I couldn't help noticing you didn't want to hang around after the ambush. Is it the terrorists, maybe?'

'No, not them; it's not that simple.' He paused momentarily before he spoke. Trust didn't come easily anymore. He looked at Jival. An open, friendly face looked back. It was a face he thought he could trust. 'A couple of truly unpleasant white militants think they owe me some payback. It's a long story.'

'It's a long night. We've got a while if you want to talk.'

Joe told him the story. It was a relief to tell someone else what had happened. It was pretty much as Jackson had described. He encountered a couple of white thugs beating up an Asian guy and his girlfriend. He weighed in – rather foolishly he now thought – using their discarded weapons against them. He waited for the police and ambulance to arrive and watched the two men arrested and taken away. Her listened to their threats but paid little regard to them – not then at least. Now, too late, he took them seriously.

'I'd like to think I'd do the same,' Jival said, 'but I'm not sure I would.'

'They tried to make out it was heroic but it wasn't.'

'You just got angry?'

There was a subtle glint of irony, small enough to ignore.

'Walking past would have been harder. Brave people make choices. I had no choice.'

'What about the trial?'

Joe smiled ruefully. 'I stayed at the scene until the police arrived and I made a statement. That was my big mistake. I should have got out of there, remained mysterious, like a weedy Batman. Anyway, I testified against them and the whole story hit the headlines and caught what they described as 'the popular imagination.' The Government latched on to it. It was good timing for them, and my father-in-law was involved in secret negotiations, so he was pretty keen to make the best of the opportunity. I got railroaded onto the TV and radio news.'

'It must've been a lot of pressure.'

'I could've lived without it - all the press and the cameras – it wasn't for me. I like a quiet life. I thought about backing out, running away from it all but then...' He waved a hand helplessly, disinclined to continue.

'Then what?'

'Then I got a visit from a smart-looking man in an expensive suit. He said he was speaking on behalf of some important people, top Government people, even politicians. He wouldn't name names, of course. They wanted me to 'soften' my account, 'tone it down' or make light of it as if it was some common every day event, not that serious. He explained it was in my interest to do as he asked. It sounded like a threat, like they'd send a couple of thugs to speak to me nicely.' He laughed softly. 'It irritated me. In the end I just said what I saw, nothing else. No wasted words. They tried to make out I was trying to be some big man, some hero type. I had to tell them I was five ten and eleven stone and I wasn't going to get any bigger and if it was all right with them, I'd just as soon go home if they could get on with it and stop asking stupid questions.'

'I remember some of it in the papers and on the news. It made a difference, I think.'

'I was about as scared as I've ever been. I just had no choice – the attack, the trial – no choice whatsoever. Once I stepped on that moving pavement I couldn't get off. And don't think I haven't regretted it sometimes, especially after the trial. For a few weeks I had to be someone else – a different me. I thought it would settle down eventually. It didn't; it got worse.'

'What happened?'

'Pretty soon after – maybe a couple of weeks – the police called and told me if I wanted to see my children reach their next birthday, I should enter the witness protection programme. There didn't seem a lot of choice. There were some pretty unpleasant people who wouldn't let things rest, especially when they learned my ethnicity, and saw it waved like a badge of honour across the newspapers. There was one in particular who seemed to have a lot of influence and a particular grudge – he's called Caine, Nathan Caine. I was to disappear for a while and then my family would join me.'

'I assume it didn't work out like that.'

'No, I never managed to shake them off. We even tried killing me off in a fake accident but that didn't work either. I'm still ahead of them – just – but there've been a number of close calls.'

'What about your family?'

'They're safe. It's me they want.'

'You're sure they won't get at you through your family?'

'They wouldn't dare. We have bodyguards. My father-in-law works for a pretty important guy – in the Government.' Even to Jival he wouldn't say the name. Everybody knew Sebastian Steele; everyone had an opinion; Sebastian Steele – architect of the ceasefire, negotiator of a lasting peace.

Joe turned away and glanced across the room; framed photographs stood on a dresser - family snaps, smiling faces, celebrations and birthdays, Haasita and the children, dark eyes excited, smiling for the camera. A wave of nostalgia flowed through him. He had pictures like that, back home.

'So, what do you do next?'

'I keep running.'

'You can't run forever.'

'I hope I won't have to. For now, it's the only thing I can do.'

Run to Alan's, he thought, lie low, make plans, maybe get a job on a cruise ship or go back on the rigs, make a new, temporary future and wait until, one day, he could go home to his family, and knowing all the time that Meg and Jessica were getting older, growing up without him, that Hannah was bringing them up alone, that the years they should have spent together were passing relentlessly.

'I can't trust anyone – even the police. The people following me must get their information from somewhere.'

'But the police know where you are now.'

'Yes.' Joe's voice betrayed his anxiety. 'I'll move early tomorrow and get clear by mid-morning. I won't tell you where I'm going, so you'll not need to lie.'

'You think they'll come here?'

'I hope not, but I don't like the sound of that white guy you described.'

Jival's dark eyes had a shadow; he was thinking hard, about Haasita and the girls, fear and anger mixed, but mostly fear. He knew the best place to live, even now, was somewhere off the radar. Suddenly there they were - his family - four tiny lights on the edge of the screen, one almost synchronous bleep.

'I hope I don't bring you any trouble,' Joe murmured. 'I wouldn't have come here if I'd known.'

'I'll get my brother to stay a day or two. He's got some influence in the community. No-one will trouble us while he's about.'

'You're sure?'

'Positive. When he starts speaking, people start listening. They wouldn't want that. He has connections.'

'Ok, as long as you're sure.'

The next morning, he left early, just as two dark-eyed, bright-faced children ran down the stairs to catch a glimpse of their strange visitor. They stood shyly in the doorway and watched as Haasita handed him some food she had packed and Jival held him like a wayward brother. Joe thought of Hannah and Meg and Jessica and waves of guilt and pain and nostalgia drove through him.

'When you're safe, you let us know,' Jival said. 'You hear me?'

'I hear you.'

The children peered from behind their mother and smiled mischievously. When the door closed, Jival picked up the phone and called his brother.

Less than an hour passed before the doorbell rang.

'That'll be Dinesh.' He looked at Haasita and his smile showed relief. 'We'll be okay now.'

As he turned the latch, the door was pushed open and two men stepped past him into the hallway. They walked straight into the living room. He heard one of the girls cry out.

'Where is he?' a harsh voice demanded.

Jival recognised the first man and his uniform. The white guard he had seen at the station, the sneering one, flashed a card and a piece of paper.

'A warrant,' he snapped.

The girls ran to the sofa and clung close to Haasita who held them tight, her legs curled beneath her, her arms closed around them and her eyes dark and dangerous. Come near my children; you come near my children; you just dare.

The second man didn't speak. He didn't need to. He was six five and pale, very pale, with short, blond hair cropped so tight to his head it looked like blemished skin. A livid scar on his cheek was the only colour on that pale, white face. He looked around the room and a momentary squall of disgust, contempt and hatred spread from him. He spat on the carpet.

He looked official – but not police and not local. Jival couldn't look at him without a tremor of fear. He had ice-blue eyes so cold they turned him, if not to stone, at least to something without strength to resist. It drew courage from him like blood in a transfusion. He slumped down beside Haasita.

'Where's the Jew?'

'Gone.'

'When?'

'I don't know. He was gone when we got up.'

Nathan Caine picked up a framed photograph of the family. He held it between two fingers and dropped it casually on the floor. He ground the glass and the picture beneath his heel and the wooden frame splintered and broke.

'When did he go?'

'I told you. I don't know exactly. It must have been about five, I suppose. I'm telling you the truth. I don't know any more.'

'Where's he going? – And before you say anything, be careful about the words you choose. The words, "I don't know" won't do. The words "I don't know," carry a penalty.'

'But I don't – I really don't.'

Caine took two steps across the room. Before anyone had time to move, he was behind Haasita and he dragged her head back by the hair. He had a knife at her throat. A small ruby of blood formed and then broke and trickled. The children screamed and cowered down but even now she would not release them.

The sneering one looked anxious. This was more than he expected.

'Tell him what you know and we'll be out of here.'

'He wouldn't tell us where he was going. He said it was better we didn't know, that it was safer that way. Let her go, please let her go,' he almost screamed. 'I don't know any more.'

Caine looked at him closely and then released his grip. His fingers held the sofa back either side of her head very close to her throat. Then he raised his hands and wiped them on his shirt as if they were contaminated by the contact.

'See what you've made me do.'

The door opened and a middle-aged Indian with immaculate, greying hair and an expensive suit stood there.

'What's going on?' His voice was peremptory and the look he gave, through stylish, steel-rimmed glasses, was authoritative and resolute. 'I said, what's going on?'

Nathan Caine looked at him with undisguised hatred. He flashed a card in front of him contemptuously. 'Show him.'

The police officer handed him the warrant with jittery fingers.

'You recognise me?' Dinesh asked imperiously. 'You know me? I am councillor for this ward. I am on many committees. I know many people.'

The agent nodded.

'Have you finished?'

'Yes.'

'Then I suggest you leave.'

Caine looked at him for a moment as if weighing a response. Then he brushed past Dinesh without speaking and stood by the outside door.

'Check the upstairs rooms,' he said to the officer.

'And who are you?' Dinesh demanded.

Caine didn't answer. He opened the door and stood on the pavement outside, lighting a cigarette. A small group of neighbours, disturbed by the shouts and cries, stood in the road, staring and muttering. A black car with darkened windows stood beside them, the engine running. Caine looked from side to side and then stared directly at them, each in his turn. His look was contemptuous and sneering. He turned and spat. One young man stepped forward but before he could reach Caine the door of the black car swung silently open and another man stepped out. He was no taller than the young man but the broad frame and bull neck and the cold, black, snake eyes stopped the young man in his tracks.

'Bull' to his friends – of whom there weren't many - stepped to Caine's side and they exchanged a few words. They stared contemptuously at the crowd until the officer emerged.

'He's not there.'

'Where do you think he's gone?' Bull asked, his voice low, his eyes firmly fixed on the small, muttering crowd.

'He'll be heading north,' said Caine. 'Let's try the railway station.'

Caine threw his cigarette end on the road then they got in the car and drove away.

Jival spoke quickly to reassure the group on the pavement. 'We're okay. It's all over now. My brother-in-law is here. Dinesh will settle matters. Please, go home. We're alright. We're all fine. Thank you. Thank you.'

They gradually dispersed and he walked back into his house. As the door closed behind him, Jival leaned against it and sighed with relief. He was off the radar again, back where he wanted to be, back where he was safe.

Chapter 9

Joe bought a phone in the city centre and found a small botanical garden where he could sit to call Hannah. The scent of early flowers and cut grass stirred him like a memory.

'It's so good to hear from you, Joe. I've missed you so much. Where are you?'

'How are the girls?'

'They miss you, Meg especially. She's moping around the place a lot. Jessica hides it better but she's unhappy too. Are you okay?'

'Have you had any problems?'

'It's quiet here. Nobody bothers us. We've got that guard at the gate too. He must be bored out there. The girls take him sandwiches and coffee and soup but he must wonder what he did wrong to get this job.'

'It won't be the same guy all the time.'

'It's hard to tell. They all have that same look.'

'Are you at your sister's?'

'Yes.'

'Are you staying there long?'

'Lisa wants us to stop for a few weeks but I've said no. We'll go home in a few days. The girls need their routine and their school. I miss you, Joe.'

'I'll find somewhere safe and call you. Maybe I'll find somewhere safe for us to live. We could move again.'

'Not again, Joe. The girls are at school now. They've got friends. It's not fair to keep moving them.'

'You're right, I know. I'll think of something.'

'Perhaps they'll get tired and leave us alone. They've got to give up sometime, haven't they? They can't hunt you forever.'

'I suppose so.'

'You want to speak to the girls?'

'Not this time. I need to keep moving. I'll phone again in a few days. Try not to worry.'

'Is everything ok, Joe? You sound tired, tired.'

'I'm fine. I'll call in a couple of days. Tell the girls I love them. Big kiss.'

'I love you, Joe.'

'I love you.'

Hannah closed the phone and sat back. Sunlight slanted through the window, brightening the flowers in a vase on the table and casting a warm glow across the walls. It was peaceful and quiet, the sort of spring day Hannah loved. But there was little peace for her today and the quiet of the house contrasted painfully with the tumult of her thoughts.

The door opened and Lisa walked in.

'Was that Joe?'

Hannah nodded. She couldn't trust to words. Her lips trembled.

'I hope he knows what his selfishness has caused. He's got a lot to answer for.'

'Don't start, Lisa, please; not now.'

Lisa sat down beside Hannah. It was hard to see them as sisters. Lisa had dark hair and dark eyes and was built to a larger scale than her slender, blue-eyed sibling.

'I can imagine what Mum would've made of it. It was always family first for her.'

'Dad likes Joe.'

'Mum's looks and Dad's temperament,' she said, 'that's you. I got Dad's looks and Mum's scepticism. You got the best deal in looks but you picked up Dad's stubbornness and you trust people, just like him. He was never a good judge - still isn't.'

'Whereas you?'

'I know when a man is so right, he's wrong. Joe has responsibilities. He should put you and the girls first. He should know what he is and where his priorities lie.'

'He's always cared for me and the girls, you know that. He'd do anything for us.'

'Then why are you in this situation?'

'Because he couldn't walk by.' Hannah's voice conveyed pride and her eyes the stubbornness her sister spoke of.

'A better man would've walked by. A better man would've thought of the danger to his family. He's a family man. He had no right playing the hero.'

Hannah's eyes were dangerous. 'There is no better man, not to me,' she said, 'and he wasn't playing.'

Lisa knew better than to speak, but she snorted disagreement. She picked up a magazine and pretended to read.

'Where is he?'

'He wouldn't tell me, not on the phone. He says it's better that I don't know.'

'When's he coming back?'

'He'll come back as soon as he can, you know that. Where are Jessica and Meg?'

'They've just taken some coffee out to the guard on the afternoon shift. My two are with them. Do you want to collect them all and go for a walk? It's too nice a day to sit around in here moping.'

Hannah nodded. 'That sounds like a good idea.'

The lane was quiet, the hedgerow bright with early hawthorn and wild cherry and the trees in fresh leaf, all newly dressed in spring clothing, light, airy, full of colour. The breeze was warm and the air hazy with insects. Behind them the children were laughing and calling, playing some game, newly invented. They stopped and looked at a butterfly on fragrant, white blossom.

'Everybody's life should be like this,' Hannah murmured, 'then maybe people wouldn't be so hateful.'

Lisa put her arm round her shoulder. 'Perhaps one day.'

'I mean,' said Hannah, standing still, 'why would anyone want to hurt other people? Why would anyone hate someone so much they'd like to hurt them, even kill them? I don't understand. Look at the children back there. We made them; we brought them into the world. They have this one chance, just this one shot at life – and then oblivion. I just want everyone to have the chance to be as happy as them.'

'You sound like Joe.'

'I suppose I do,' Hannah laughed softly. 'I caught atheism off him. It's my tragedy.'

'Maybe that's where Joe and I differ,' Lisa said. 'I want to put a ring round my children and protect them. I've got no room for anyone else. Joe tries to make room for everyone.'

'Like Father?'

'Pretty much; they both have a price to pay. But so do you, Hannah, and so did Mum and that's not right. Joe didn't give you a choice any more than Dad asked Mum what she wanted. I think worrying about him killed her in the end.'

'That's not fair, Lisa. Dad worshipped her. They were happy.'

'Maybe,' Lisa said, 'maybe; but she's still dead and she worried every day.'

'He just wants to make the world better.'

'I know; all I'm saying is maybe he should have made her life better and thought about her first. You've got to decide who you are and what matters most.'

'There are people out there who would snuff the life out of children like these,' Hannah was following her own thoughts. 'And why? Because they're black, white, Hindu, Muslim, Sikh, Jew? Who gives a shit what they are? They're tiny specks of life, brought into the world and playing in the sun. Haven't they got the right to a chance of happiness?'

'Of course, they have.'

'That's what Dad fights for – and Joe too. Unfairness and injustice make them angry.'

'That's a fight for an army of people, not two men with families. The price they have to pay is too high.'

They walked along the path to where a group of trees and bushes cast a flickering sunlit shade over a wide pond. Tall grasses grew at its edges and small, yellow flowers wound through them. Hannah knelt down beside it.

'Come and look at the pond,' she called back to the children.

Meg stood still on the path watching a butterfly. The others were hidden somewhere off the edge among the trees.

'Come and see the pond.'

Slowly one then two then three more faces appeared, flushed and excited. Jessica took her cousins' hands and ran towards her mother.

'It's a lovely pond,' cried Meg. 'Look, there are little silver creatures swimming in circles on its surface.'

'Whirligigs,' her mother told her. 'Tiny beetles.'

The others ran to the far side of the pond, still intent on their game.

'Careful!' Lisa called. 'Alec, stop showing off to your cousins. You'll end up in the water. Jade, come away from the edge.' She laughed. 'I wish my two were like Meg. Look at her, sitting there quietly watching the pond creatures.'

'I worry about her. She misses Joe.'

'She's a sensitive little soul, always has been.'

'Yes.'

Meg was kneeling at the pond's edge now. She was looking deep into the water.

'There's a newt, mum, on a flat stone. You can see its legs and its little eyes. Come and look.'

The two women knelt by the water and looked down.

'It looks all pinky underneath,' Meg whispered. 'Look, it's going. It doesn't like us staring at it.'

'Are there any toads or frogs?' Hannah asked.

'I'm going to look further round.'

'Be careful.'

Meg jumped to her feet and walked carefully to a corner where the water was shallow and green shoots emerged above the surface.

The two women sat back, momentarily free.

'What happens to you and the children if they find Joe?'

'I don't know. I don't like to think about it. So far we've been lucky.'

'Luck doesn't last. What would you do?'

Hannah shrugged.

'Let's hope.'

Across the pond, Jade and Alec were searching for Jessica among the trees.

'Keep away from the water now,' Lisa called. 'Jessica, will you look after your cousins?'

Meg was sitting quietly among the sedges. Jessica was nowhere to be seen.

'Where's Jessica?' Hannah stood up. Her face was flushed and she looked scared. 'Where is she?'

'I think she's hiding,' Jade called. 'We'll look for her.'

'No, come back here where you're safe. The water's deep. Go and play with Meg.'

'Jessica! Jessica!' Hannah looked round. 'I can't see her, Lisa. Where's she gone? Jessica?'

Lisa stood beside her sister and laid a hand on her arm. 'Hey, what's this? They've been playing hide and seek, Hannah, that's all. She's okay. Don't worry.' Her eyes followed the edge of the pond round to the furthest corner. 'Look, there she is.'

They saw at once that something was wrong. Jessica was emerging slowly and backing step by step towards them. She was moving uncertainly, her eyes fixed on the bushes. After a few steps, she turned and ran around the pond edge towards the two women.

'What's the matter, Jessica? What's happened?'

Jessica held Hannah's arm tight and from the safety of a close embrace she looked back and pointed.

'There's a man,' she said softly. She didn't want him to hear. 'He scared me.'

'Meg, come here! Jade, Alec, come here now!'

'Where was he? What was he doing?' Hannah knelt beside Jessica and held her. 'Tell me, Jess.'

Jessica pointed again. 'He was over there, by the field edge, near the fence. He saw me and he just stared. Then he stepped towards me.'

'It was probably the farmer or someone out for a walk,' Lisa said.

'No. He wasn't a farmer. He was watching me. When he saw me, he came towards me; look, he's there now.'

A figure appeared from between the trees and bushes at the corner of the pond. He was short and wiry, his dark hair cut short, forty maybe, wearing jeans and a check shirt. He stood watching them.

'What do you want?' Hannah shouted.

Lisa gathered the children like a sheepdog gathers a flock. They stood behind her, watching around her legs.

'What do you want?'

'Can we go home, Mum, I'm scared.' It was Alec. 'I don't like it.'

Jade whimpered and held close. Meg hid her face. Only Jessica stared at the man, the same defiant expression her mother wore.

Hannah shouted a third time. 'What do you want?'

'Go away!' Jessica yelled.

Still the man didn't move. He stood beside the trees and now an unpleasant smile passed briefly across his face.

There was a sudden movement behind them. The women turned to see the bodyguard, hired by their father, approaching from the path.

'I heard you shout. What is it?'

Hannah pointed, but the man had stepped away and disappeared through the trees.

'A man, there, at the corner of the pond, he was watching us.'

'Wait here. I'll search. Don't move.'

The bodyguard unfastened his gun. He stepped carefully along the pond bank, moving branches from his view, half crouched, ready.

'No,' Hannah shouted. 'Let him go. Take us back to the house. I want the children safe in the house right now.'

The guard stepped back. He kept his eyes focussed on the place the man had been as they backed towards the path. He ushered them towards the house, turning every few steps to look back. When they were safe in the house he stood in the garden and looked to left and right. He opened a phone.

'Get a car to watch the lane,' he said. 'We may have trouble here.'

Chapter 10

Joe decided to walk to the railway station. He'd had enough of buses and he didn't trust taxis. You could be traced through a taxi ride. If he was being followed, and he felt sure he was, it was better to avoid obvious traps. Besides, the morning was reasonably fine and the Station from which trains led north was no more than an hour's walk and the route relatively simple. A few cars passed and a few pedestrians. He turned for a short distance onto a wider road. There were more people about, people from an Asian or Middle Eastern background - Indians, Pakistanis, Syrians, Iraqis, a few Afghans, maybe some refugees fleeing crises in their own countries. There were a number of white Europeans too.

Joe listened to the babble of familiar and unfamiliar tongues. Sometimes he recognised accents as local to the area but he could make out very little of what they were saying. Then local voices rose and fell, replaced sometimes by something Eastern European, sometimes Urdu, Guajarati. Sometimes he just couldn't tell.

He had time to linger and enjoy the diversity. He paused and listened and looked around. The shops were as varied as the accents and announced themselves with a discordant variety of colours and odours. There was something exhilarating about it but something unnerving too, like visiting somewhere new on holiday. Joe felt momentarily elated as if something ugly and monochrome had been brushed aside and replaced with colour.

He opened the door of a small convenience store to buy a couple of items to eat on his journey. The Asian shopkeeper spoke in an impeccable, local dialect.

'Best pastries for miles around,' he said as Joe looked at the display to make his choice. He turned and spoke a few words in an unfamiliar language to another customer. Then he added for clarity, 'You tell him. Go on. Tell him about my pastries.'

'Best for miles around,' the customer laughed. 'If you believe what he says, it's the best shop too. If you can't buy it here, you can't buy it anywhere.'

'See?' The shopkeeper beamed. 'Best shop too. Tell your friends. Try this.' He cut a piece of spiced, cooked meat and held it out on a knife for to Joe to take. 'Don't ask how I give it such flavour. I could tell you but I'd have to kill you. It's the spices you see; my own recipe.'

Joe nodded. 'Good,' he said, wiping his fingers, 'better than good.'

He glanced around. After the war his great grandfather had a corner shop like this. Always ambitious, he had worked hard throughout the forties and fifties and earned enough to buy a second and then a third shop. Later, when Joe's grandfather moved out to start a family of his own and he had time on his hands, he became a local councillor. As a child, long after his great grandfather had died, Joe visited those streets with Alan and his father and grandfather but the shops had gone and the streets were alien and unfamiliar. He could remember the disappointment on his grandfather's face and the silence that gradually grew around them as they walked. When they got home, they talked long into the evening recalling those long-ago days, the dull clatter of the till, the bell above the door, the stacked shelves and the smell of polished wood.

'Always he was moving, my father, always he was busy, all day from early morning until late evening when the shop closed. Then he sank in that old leather chair of his and fell asleep by the fire. "Work hard," he told me, "and you will control your own future and you will rely on no-one. And if you can help others on your way, well, all the better." It was good advice, Joseph and Alan, good advice.'

Two more customers entered and moved along the narrow aisle, disturbing his reverie. One looked Eastern European, maybe Romanian.

'Bloody foreigners,' the shopkeeper called out.

The Romanian looked up and gestured. 'Cheeky bastard,' he called.

It had the familiar sound of well-rehearsed repartee.

The shopkeeper and the customer at the till laughed.

'He only knows about twenty words of English and you just heard two of them,' the shopkeeper said, loud enough to be heard. 'Go back where you came from,' he called.

'Fuck off, Paki.'

Again, the laughter.

'That's another three.' The shopkeeper turned back to Joe. 'You're not local. I know everyone round here. Just passing through?'

Not local, no, he thought, but part of this. Carried by a wave of nostalgia he recognised the burden of something lost and of something owed.

'I'm on my way to the station, heading north, to family.'

'Getting out?' The second customer, a wiry, mean-faced man stood beside him. 'Don't blame you. I'd go myself if I could. I'll have my cigarettes and paper.' He turned to the shopkeeper briefly and then back to Joe. 'The place is full of bloody foreigners. You can travel for miles without seeing a white face.'

The shopkeeper was unsympathetic. 'If they all look like yours, I'd think myself lucky. Most of the faces I see know how to smile. There you go.' The shopkeeper handed him the cigarettes and newspaper and took the money he was offered.

'What have I got to smile about? I'm a foreigner in my own country.'

'You always were a bloody foreigner.'

'Even the bloody newspapers are foreign.' He turned and walked towards the door. 'Now they're going to rule the bloody place. I don't know why I stay here.'

'You love the repartee, that's why.' The shopkeeper grinned and winked at Joe. 'And you can 't be arsed to leave. On your way to work, are you?'

'Fuck off. There is no work. All you fucking foreigners have taken the jobs.'

He walked out and shut the door heavily behind him.

'Do you get much of that?'

'If someone offered him a job, he'd have a seizure. No, we get on well around here, pretty much so, anyway. It's live and let live and have a joke along the way. It's not so good a few blocks east. I'd try and avoid it if I were you. It's religion, see, fear, ignorance, poverty and bloody religion – especially bloody religion.'

'I don't think God believes in religion,' Joe said. 'He's got more sense.'

'Bloody right, but take the main road to the station. Keep out of the side streets if you can. It's still angry and resentful round there.'

'Thanks, I'll do that.'

By some act of malignant fate Joe, who had every intention of heeding the advice he was given, took a left where he should have gone straight on and corrected himself by going straight on when he should have turned right. He became aware of his mistake as the narrow streets closed in and cultural diversity gave way to something mono-cultural and alien. Bright colours turned back to monochrome. He no longer dared smile at the few people he passed. They looked at him suspiciously, as if he were an enemy. He didn't belong on these streets. Why was he here? What did he want? The hostility he felt was only matched by the fear in each passing face. The devolution proposal had reached the very edge of this tiny, shrinking enclave. It had beaten at the door and invited those within to step out and draw down the barriers, but there had been no answer. From behind their closed windows, stubborn faces looked out and waited until the visitor at the gate withdrew.

Joe passed a group of bearded youths on a street corner, uniformly dressed in pale collarless shirts and dark trousers. They stood talking beside a rusting iron fence which surrounded an old, closed-down primary school. It had been turned into a community centre at some time in the past but was now deserted and the paint on the information board beside the fence had flaked and fallen away. The group eyed him suspiciously and fell silent. He felt their eyes follow him as he increased his pace. Their cold, resentful stare reminded him of the men who had attacked the bus and the police.

He sensed they were about to confront him but someone was approaching them along the footpath and they paused. The newcomer was similarly dressed and was bearded like them. He looked little different to any other tidily dressed young man of his faith walking down a city road but there was a certainty about his step and something in his upright posture that suggested a successful, highly educated young man, maybe a university graduate. The only incongruity was his presence on those mean streets among the young men he approached. He glanced towards Joe and then paused and looked more closely.

Joe recognised him at once, feeling suddenly cold. The last time he saw him he was supervising a scene of murder and brutality. He had raised a handgun towards Joe and mimed shooting, an action that could, on another day, have resulted in the end of life. Joe remembered how he had walked towards each wrecked police car, how he had leaned forward and how he fired into them, once, twice. He killed the police officers as coldly and as casually as if he were treading on ants. The police called him Akmal. Joe increased his pace. It was time to get out of here.

The group of young men grew silent and parted as if to allow Akmal his natural place at their very heart. Even at a distance, Joe could see how he stood above them not only by virtue of his height but by some strange authority. The group gathered and he spoke briefly and then they parted again and allowed him to pass. They closed in behind and followed him to walk along the street.

'Shit,' Joe swore. They were heading directly towards him. He turned to cross the road but at that moment a car approached and he was forced to wait. The group gathered around him and dark, emotionless eyes captured him in an unblinking stare.

'Hi, how're you doing?' He tried to act casual, to ignore the obvious menace, to elicit some friendliness, one young man speaking to others.

'What are you doing here?' A wiry youth with mean eyes and a small scar on his forehead spoke. 'These streets aren't for you. You're not welcome.'

'Just heading to the railway station; I'm going north to visit family.' He tried the friendly smile again. He searched for something to say, some words that would deflect them from their menacing purpose and engage them, even momentarily. 'I think I took a wrong turn. Which is the quickest way to the railway station?'

'I can show you how to get to the hospital.'

Joe joined in their laughter but with undisguised anxiety. 'If I don't get the train my aunt will probably...' He hesitated for just a moment and his voice betrayed him, '...kill me.' His laughter was very hollow.

The leader, Akmal, was watching him closely.

'I know you.'

'I doubt it. I'm new in town. I'm just passing through.'

'No, I definitely know you.'

'Maybe I just look like someone.'

'No, I've seen you before, and recently too.'

Joe saw recognition dawn in his eyes but he also saw a small opening in the group around him and he took immediate advantage of it. He crossed the road and headed down a side street. The main road was only fifty yards away and he could see cars passing and people crossing. It might as well have been fifty miles. He had a few yards advantage but it was not enough and the youths gathered around him again.

'I think we need a long talk, you and I.' Akmal turned to the wiry youth. 'Take him, Salim.'

'Where to?'

'The warehouse.'

Joe's arms were pinned painfully behind his back and his neck was held in a lock which made breathing difficult and walking almost impossible. He was dragged, stumbling at the centre of the group, as if caught in a rip tide from which there was no escape. They crossed the street and retraced their route past the community centre. Then they turned down a side street.

Once off the road, his head was covered in a musty hessian bag. They pushed him forwards, through a creaking metal gate, across a stretch of what felt like broken tarmac to a heavy steel door. He heard them fumble to unfasten a padlock. The door opened smoothly and then it closed behind him with a solid thud. Bolts were slammed shut and he was enclosed and imprisoned within. He was dragged across an open space which echoed strangely around him, and up to another door. It opened and he was flung from the darkness of the hessian sack into the deeper darkness of a cell. He scurried back into a corner like some wounded animal in search of safety and lay there, breathing heavily.

'Where am I?' he shouted.

'What do you want?' he shouted again.

No-one answered and the silence closed around him like a rope round his throat.

Chapter 11

'There's no reason to believe they're looking for you or have any desire to hurt you.'

The police inspector spoke patiently, repeating reassuring phrases over and over. He looked tired. His eyes were bloodshot and he was grey and unshaven. Inside a shabby coat, a shabby body loitered. Lisa recoiled from him.

'Have you slept in that coat?'

'Yes,' he said sourly, 'in these clothes and in the back of a car; so be polite, eh?'

'I'll be polite when you start to take this seriously.'

'It's hard not to be serious when you've only had three hours' sleep in forty-eight hours. It's also hard to be patient. Now, let's go over the details, shall we?' He looked at her sharply. 'Where are the children? Are they safe?'

Hannah was sitting on a chair by the window. She paid little attention to the conversation. She was thinking about Joe, about the children, about their home and especially about the man by the pond.

'They're upstairs. There's a policewoman with them,' Lisa said.

'There's no reason to believe they don't know where we are,' Hannah said without looking at them. Her gaze took in the garden, the birches and the flowers, the blue sky lined with filaments of drifting cirrus cloud, the sun dropping slowly. 'They're always there, just behind us. We never seem to escape them. Perhaps he followed us here.'

D.I. Stone shook his head. He frowned as the ache in his head grew in intensity.

'No-one suspicious has been hanging around your house or the school. We know that. No-one has been watching you here. Have you got any paracetamol? I think my head's going to burst.'

Lisa rose irritably to her feet and went through to the kitchen.

'She's not a very tolerant person, your sister, not very sympathetic.'

'She doesn't suffer fools gladly – present company excluded, of course.'

'Of course; now tell me about the man again.'

Hannah sighed and raised her hand to her brow.

'I've told you everything I can.'

'Tell me why you were so certain he was a danger to you. I mean – excuse me for being blunt – he could have just been someone out for a walk who suddenly stumbles upon an unexpected game of hide and seek; there he is, a man standing in front of a frightened little girl and then, even worse, her family. Families can be pretty defensive; he probably took a minute or so to think about it and then took off rather than waiting to explain. Right now, he's probably sitting in a cottage somewhere, telling his wife what happened and bewailing the fear and distrust that has taken over his world. Who could blame him? I saw a sign in a playground the other day. It said, "No children without an adult and no adults without children." What sort of a message does that send?'

Lisa came back in and handed him a glass of water and some tablets.

'Thanks. I'll be able to think more clearly when I've shifted this headache.'

'I've just checked the children. They're fine. They think it was just one big adventure. Jessica is telling the policewoman what she would have done if the man had come any closer. From the sound of it, he was lucky he backed off when he did.'

'It was the way he looked at us,' Hannah said quietly, 'sort of triumphant. He had a sneering smile. He knew who we were. It was obvious he knew.'

'It's not easy to read a face that far away. Maybe you just saw what you expected to see, what you feared most?'

'We saw what we saw. We're not imagining things,' Lisa snapped.

'No, I'm sure you're not. But the evidence, the actual evidence of what you saw and what you heard – and I'm sorry to say this - is flimsy. I have to ask these things. We can't send the local constabulary scouring the woods to look for a man who's doing nothing more sinister than going for a walk. Are you sure he wasn't local?'

Lisa shook her head. 'I know everyone within two miles of here.'

'There's not much to go on.'

'I'm not sure why you bothered coming if that's all the help you can give.'

'I came because your father insisted. He asked for the best. He got me. He's an influential man, your father, in a quiet sort of way. He had my superiors hopping round. I was on a stakeout. I'd been there for forty-eight hours. "Leave the stakeout to your sergeant," they said. "This is more important. Get yourself down there straight away." So here I am.'

'What are you going to do now you're here?'

'I think Hannah and the children should go home, where we have better security in place. We'll make sure no-one is following. My guess is that this man – if he was what you think he was – comes from the town here. I don't think he'll have been doing anything more than a bit of casual snooping. He probably knows who you are, Lisa, and comes up here every now and then, in case Joe or his family turn up. Joe is the prize, after all, not you or Hannah. Excuse me being blunt but you're not even a consolation prize; it's Joe they want. They're only interested in you because you might lead them to him. We'll add a couple of extra guards for a day or two to make sure no-one's watching but I don't think there's much to worry about.'

'What will you do about the man?'

He shrugged. Lisa bristled irritably. Hannah's gaze had returned to the garden.

'We can do a photo-fit and circulate it, but we won't find him.'

'Is that all?'

'What did you expect, dogs and an armed response unit?'

'Yes.'

Stone sighed and shook his head. 'We've had more cutbacks than a hairdresser's shop. You're lucky to get me. We'll get a WPC to drive your car,' he told Hannah. 'You and the girls can come with me in my car. We'll have a couple of cars on the lookout to make sure we're not followed and to act as decoys if necessary.'

'How very reassuring that is.'

Lisa folded her arms and turned away. Stone looked at her. His sharp, dark eyes took everything in, despite the uninspiring evidence of his appearance.

'This headache's getting worse.' He picked up the sheet of tablets. 'Mind if I take these? I think this is going to be a nine-pill day.' He turned to Hannah. 'I'll come back for you in a couple of hours. There are police officers on all the footpaths and roads. There really is nothing to worry about.'

'I know.'

'It's more than my job's worth to put you at risk.'

'Yes,' she agreed.

'Your father works with Sebastian Steele, doesn't he? He worked on the ceasefire and now he's working on the devolution agreement?'

'Yes.'

Stone rubbed his head with one hand then turned and left the room.

'I'm going to phone Dad.' Lisa strode towards the telephone.

'Don't do that, please. He's done everything he can,' Hannah said.

'They aren't taking us seriously. He asked for their best detective and we get Stone. Does he look like the best to you?'

'He seemed quite... professional.'

'You always see the best in people,' Lisa fumed. 'As for this nonsense about going home, I simply won't hear of it. You can stay here where I can keep an eye on you all. The children love having their cousins here. Jessica and Meg spoil them. Adam will be home soon. He'll say the same.'

Hannah shook her head. 'Stone's right; I must go home. We have security in place. It was silly of me to come here. I could have put you all at risk. Besides, being away from school isn't good for the girls. They need their friends and their routine, especially with Joe away.'

Lisa sighed. 'Let me speak to Father at least.'

'I'll call him once I'm home. Honestly, there's no need to worry. What D.I. Stone said is true. They won't bother us. They never have done. There's no reason why they'd start now.'

'And will you tell Joe?'

'He'll phone in a few days. I'll tell him then if I think it's necessary.'

Lisa looked at her. 'I can always tell when you're lying to me,' she said. 'You were always a poor liar - completely transparent.'

'He's got enough to think about. If I tell him, he'll come back and that's just what they want.'

'He should be with you.'

'I wish he was; so do the girls. But he can't be, not yet.'

'You should tell him to get back here now and look after his family. It isn't all about him. He's got responsibilities.'

Hannah shook her head firmly.

'He'll come back when it's safe for all of us, especially me and Jessica and Meg.'

That night as she lay in bed at home and darkness settled around her, she felt less secure. She stared at the ceiling and watched the moonlight as it slipped through a gap in the curtains, which moved softly as if trapped in a restless breeze. She felt the refreshing air brush her cheeks. It took only that brief moment to realise the implications of what she saw and felt.

'My God, the window's open.'

She threw back the duvet and stumbled across the room. The sash window lay open; not by much, just sufficient to allow the passage of the cold, night air, but open nonetheless. She swore silently and looked around.

'The girls,' she cried.

She slipped across to the door and crept along the corridor to the room the girls shared. They lay in undisturbed slumber. Meg, foetus-like, lay curled under the covers, her face scarcely visible, her tiny body moving softly as she breathed. Jessica lay on her back, the duvet hanging on the floor. Her hair spread across the pillow like a strange halo. Her mouth lay half open as she too breathed softly.

Hannah drew the duvet over her and stroked her cheek. Behind her, Meg moved gently and murmured some indistinguishable words, her dream momentarily breaking like a wave on the shore. Hannah turned from them and slipped back to her own room.

The phone at her bedside rang.

'I saw the lights. Are you alright?'

It was the bodyguard Stone had posted outside the house.

'Yes; I left a window open. It gave me a fright. I'm okay now.'

'I'll walk the perimeter. You get to sleep. Don't worry; no-one can get through.'

'I know. Thanks.'

Nonetheless, the incident worried her. She saw now how fragile her security and that of her children really was. As she drifted into an uneasy, dream-filled sleep, she felt herself rise above the tiny house high into the dark sky. Below her, the house lay warm and safe, hugged close by the surrounding trees and fields, changing only as the seasons rose and fell. A tiny light flickered in the window and she knew that within that room her children lay and she lay with them. It was such a tiny, fragile light.

As she rose higher, she sensed she was not alone. There were others out there too and they were heading silently towards the light. They formed into monstrous shapes and grew solid as they dropped down and settled on the tiny rooftop. Then they crawled with icy relentlessness towards the window, open once again, and slipped like shadows into the room.

The children! Meg! Jessica!'

'Joe!'

She cried out and sat up in bed, her heart racing, her breathing rapid and painful in her chest. Unconcerned by the hour, she reached for her phone. It was a moment before anyone answered.

'Dad? Dad, I'm so scared. I'm so very scared.'

Her tears flowed and she sobbed.

Chapter 12

In an obscure corner of the capital city, in a dreary garret room in a Nineteenth Century terrace, a group of self-styled Independent Nationalists met each Friday at eight o'clock. From seven thirty they could be seen approaching the house, carefully obscured from cameras and enquiring eyes by hoods and scarves. They slipped unnoticed through the door of number 247 Victory Road and clambered up the narrow, creaking staircase. A mumbled password gave them access to the meeting place where they gathered around the bare table. To either side of them the ceiling dropped gloomily towards a deeply curtained, dormer window which stood sentinel over the darkening streets. They sat in the centre of the room below the high part of the ceiling, a single bare light hanging above them, casting a pale glow which gave up hope and faded into shadows as it reached the walls and windows. It had the look of a macabre chapel. For two hours they made plans, plotted conspiracies, and discussed politics.

Membership of the group had declined over the years. Plans came to nothing. They did little but talk and complain and make idle threats. The central committee to which they were affiliated made few demands – the occasional smashed window, an arson attack, a beating. Occasionally, bored, they would emerge from number 247 to walk the streets in search of a victim of their own to attack before retiring to the pub to celebrate. Once, spurred into unusual activity by the discontent of their declining membership, they tried to fire a mosque, but their ineptitude led to capture, court cases and incarceration. Members walked away and joined other, more successful groups and they were reduced now to a hardened core.

Then one day, about six weeks previously, two strangers appeared with orders, they said, from the central committee and the group was called upon to act.

Bull sat at the table head now, his broad arms resting like logs on the wooden surface. Beer cans and a couple of newspapers lay in front of him and the air was thick with smoke. Polystyrene food containers were strewn about. He had been speaking for some time and it had evidently been a strain. He fell silent, looking round morosely. At last, to break the awkward silence he raised a can.

'To our success, and to a better future,' he said and drank.

'The future,' came the response.

'And no fucking mistakes.'

One final swig emptied the can. He crushed it flat with one hand and cast it on the floor.

No mistakes - that had been the bulk of his little lecture, that there could be no mistakes, not now, not after all the planning and six weeks of preparation. His small, dark eyes scanned the gathered group. He didn't seem impressed. He drummed his fingers irritably, broad, thick fingers on gnarled, knotted hands, fists as worn as driftwood. Muscles flexed on his shoulder and neck.

Two thin, mean-looking regulars faced each other across the table. They reached out and clashed cans in an ugly salute and laughed, wide-mouthed.

'It's up to us now, Jake,' one of them cried. He was a sallow, jaundiced figure, eaten to such a degree by malice and envy there was little left. 'It's time to take back what's ours.'

The second wiped a hand across his short-cropped hair and a short burst of laughter erupted, like gunfire, from his lips. His eyes flickered towards Bull and the fourth figure at the table.

'They won't know what fucking hit them, Terry. Here's to us!'

Terry raised a hand in mock salute. 'Fuck 'em all,' he said.

The third of the conspirators leaned back and watched them. His lips moved in the semblance of a smile. 'It'll be the biggest thing to hit the capital in years,' he said. 'There'll be one shit storm when it's over. We'll be heroes.'

Vasey shared the group identity, the cropped hair and the tattoos. 'Hate' was tattooed across the knuckles of one hand. It was repeated on the other. His small, rat eyes looked from Terry to Jake and then to Bull. He hated the people around the table as much as he hated the Jews and the blacks and the Muslims, and he hated in particular the tall, pale figure standing silently against the wall beside the door.

Vasey had been the leader until six weeks ago then they sent this new man for a special mission and he brought Bull with him as private muscle – as if he needed it. Vasey was just like the others now – a fucking soldier, nothing more. His eyes moved slowly and sought out their new leader leaning casually, his foot raised on a chair. Caine's white face took on a ghastly pallor in the artificial light. Vasey's eyes flickered and moved away as a cold stare settled on him and fixed him with an icy, unblinking look.

Caine was scary alright, with that scar and the white face and short cropped, blond hair. Every time he spoke it made Vasey want to shudder. He was well connected; he had links in the city and knew a few politicians on the right. He was educated in one of those posh independent schools, not Tatton Road like the rest of them. He looked down his nose at them – especially at Vasey.

'There'll be no celebrations when this is over.' Caine said. He looked at them with that cold, superior look of his. 'We want outrage – outrage, anger, fear and impotence. Then we can act and show people they don't need to be scared. Everything's in place. We're ready. We'll have hundreds on the streets within a day, maybe thousands. The protests will turn violent; there'll be deaths.'

'And then?' Vasey asked.

Caine ignored him and continued.

'We target mosques, temples, synagogues. We attack the Muslims, the Jews, the Sikhs, the Hindus, the whole fucking lot of them, especially the Muslims. There'll be retaliation of course and more riots. We'll attack again and again. It'll descend into anarchy. Then the politicians and the police will take over. We have enough top men to turn things our way.'

'How do we know that?' Vasey asked.

'I told you. I work for them.'

Vasey eyed him suspiciously. What did that mean, he worked for them?

'And us? Is everything in place to get us out?' Vasey asked. 'I don't want to be sitting there with a smoking gun in my hand surrounded by troops.'

'That would serve no-one's purpose.' Caine yawned idly but his eyes fixed Vasey like nails. 'Everything is ready. If you stick to the plan, you've nothing to fear. You know what you have to do. Do it just as I've told you and you'll have time to get far away. The police will be very slow to respond when the reports come in.'

'How can you be sure?'

'I'm sure.' Caine had the look of a man who would tolerate no more questions. 'Then you disappear for a few months,' he said.

'And you?'

Caine smiled again. White, shark teeth flashed in a white, shark jaw. 'Then my people begin the serious work and things change forever. The government will fall. There'll be new leaders and new politics, no more of this weak democracy where everyone talks and no-one acts. And there'll be time to settle some personal grudges,' he said. 'Time for some payback,' It was clear he was thinking of someone in particular. 'You'd enjoy a bit of payback, wouldn't you?' he said, looking around the table.

It was clear from their eyes that they would.

Bull glanced at towards Caine but those pale eyes had not shifted from the figures before him.

'Get some rest,' Bull said, 'and keep a low profile until Friday. Don't do anything stupid and don't draw attention to yourselves. You understand me?'

'And check the weapons one more time,' Caine said. His eyes still hadn't moved. His cheek pulsed as if the scar had a life of its own.

Within a minute, the room emptied and everything fell silent. Caine walked to the window and looked out into the street.

'You'll be revenged within a month, little brother,' he murmured, 'and Joe Savage will be dead.'

'Do we know where he is?' Bull asked.

'He's heading north. His brother lives south of Triente. I guess he'll hole up with him for a while. Maybe we should arrange a visit.'

He looked out of the window down the empty street.

'Nothing can save you now, Joe. This week or next you'll be dead, and so will your wife and kids.'

Chapter 13

Joe felt himself pushed down on an upright chair. Salim tied his legs and arms so tightly the plastic cable ties bit into his flesh. Then the hessian bag was removed from his head and he blinked in the glare of the single paraffin lamp swinging on a chain from a low ceiling. He was in a bare room. Paint flaked off the walls and here and there, in corners, there were patches of damp. Only one small window set high in the wall vainly offered an illusion of daylight and the air was musty and stale.

Beyond the door he could hear footsteps. They sounded hollow as if in a huge and empty arena. He imagined a high roof and a bare, concrete floor, broken windows and the rusting remains of a dead industrial past. The footsteps slowly disappeared into some strange distant place. A solitary voice called out momentarily, a distant door slammed shut and then everything was still.

Salim turned and left. There was only one other person in the room with him now. He stood behind the door and stared at Joe for a moment before he turned a chair round and sat down, legs astride and his arms resting on its wooden back. Joe recognised the tall, bearded figure at once even without the black handgun which he swung casually from one finger. He lifted it so it hung in front of Joe's face.

'You've seen this before?'

He spoke slowly and quietly. His tone was measured and calm.

Joe stared back. He didn't speak.

The man reached behind him where Joe's possessions lay scattered across the floor. The canvas rucksack lay discarded beside them. He picked Joe's wallet and fingered idly though the contents.

'Are you worth anything to me, Joe? Would anyone pay for your safe return?'

'I'm not worth paper money, if that's what you mean. You can measure my value in loose change.' He looked around the room as coolly as he dared. 'Is that all you are, common kidnappers?'

The figure turned the hand gun towards Joe. He pointed it carefully at his head. He mimed shooting and then laughed slowly, as if the air he expelled carried a price and should not be wasted.

'You're very brave for someone tied to a chair.'

'Then untie me.'

'Perhaps...in time.'

He continued to look at the contents of Joe's wallet. He picked out a card and looked at it with particular care.

'D.S. Jackson,' he read. He turned it over and read the scribbled message on the back. 'Why do you keep this in your wallet?'

'Jackson gave it to me.'

"Contact me at once if the holder of this card requests your help.' It's an abrupt message, straight to the point. I would expect no less of D.S. Jackson. What did you do to deserve this privilege, I wonder?'

He looked up sharply and locked Joe with an inquisitive stare. Joe refused to flinch.

'I got caught up in a terrorist attack. I guess he thought I needed a break.'

'Is that what you think I am - a terrorist?'

'It seems an appropriate word. How would you describe yourself?'

'I wouldn't be so dismissive as to classify me with a single word. Mine is a complex world. Only my religion holds its shifting plates in place.'

'You kill indiscriminately and you terrorise people who can do you no harm. Not exactly the modern view of religion, is it? Very Fourteenth Century.'

'History is littered with the corpses of those who did no harm. If the dead victims of your government policy in the Middle East were stacked together, they would form a sizeable mountain – Palestine, Syria, Lebanon, Afghanistan, Libya, Iraq, Iran. You people got rich selling arms to both sides and stole land from everyone. Your policies were exploitative and hypocritical.'

'They were disgusting and immoral and make me ashamed, but it doesn't make what you do any better.'

'We're fighting back. You've spent a hundred years treating the countries of the Middle East like colonies. Under the pretext of destroying tyrants, you kill children and women. You sell the ingredients for chemical weapons and cry out in horror at their use. Your country makes me sick.'

'It makes me sick too. It makes any decent person sick. It still doesn't justify what you do. But it's not just my country – it's your country too.'

'It's not my country. I don't believe in your laws and your government. Governments don't make our laws – only God.'

'And I don't believe a hundred deaths justify a hundred more.'

'If it's the will of God...'

'It's not God's will, it's yours – just yours – the rest is an excuse, an illegitimate self-justification.'

'When we are finally victorious, we'll live by God's law.'

'Who will decide guilt or innocence? God? Or you?'

The man stood up suddenly. His manner became cold and his eyes deadened. He flicked through the few remaining items in Joe's wallet – a debit card, a couple of club membership cards from home, a small photograph of Hannah and the girls.

'Don't damage that,' Joe said. 'It's important.'

'Your family?'

Joe nodded. He couldn't take his eyes from the photograph which the gunman turned slowly between long, dark fingers.

'Don't you have a family?' he asked.

'I have no family, just my faith and my comrades.'

'Does your mother see things in the same light? Perhaps she just feels betrayed and deserted by her son?'

The man stared defiantly and for a moment, his eyes flashed dangerously.

'We must all make sacrifices.'

'Most of your sacrifices seem to be made by other people.'

He deserved the blow which flung him sideways on the floor, he knew that. He deserved the bloodied mouth and the cut lip. He had earned the bruised arm, still tied behind his back. He stifled a cry as his head hit the concrete and breathed heavily through clenched teeth. For a moment he feared what might follow.

'You have a big mouth for someone whose life hangs by a thread.'

The man turned to leave the room, taking Joe's wallet with him.

'You haven't told me your name,' Joe gasped. He spat blood onto the floor.

The man stopped for a moment.

'Call me Akmal.'

Joe heard his footsteps fade and a distant door close. He lay still and groaned heavily. He couldn't move from where he had fallen and his arm throbbed. He shuffled to ease the discomfort but it made little difference. Eventually he lay still, held tight by the chair.

What if I were to die in this place? He thought. He tried to brush the thought away but it was too late. It lingered like the aftertaste from bad food. He thought of Hannah, Jessica and Meg and of his home. He thought of the events which had brought him to where he now lay.

I had no choice, he told himself but it rang hollow. Of course, he had a choice. He made a choice. He chose to act in the way he did despite his family, not because of them. He made his choice because to do otherwise would have been a betrayal. But the only person he would have betrayed would have been himself. Instead, he told himself harshly, he had betrayed others. He had betrayed those closest to him.

He lay on his side, numbed by the thought that he might never see them again. Perhaps, had he known then that he would be facing death in so short a time, he would have acted differently. Two years ago, he could have walked by, called the police, refused to testify. Yesterday, he could have hidden himself behind the crumbling wall and watched as Alex, the driver, was shot and killed. But he knew that were the same situations to arise tomorrow he would act no differently.

He tugged at the cable ties which held his wrists and ankles. It did little good, the plastic just stretched and then dug deeply into his flesh. It would cut through to the bone before those ties would break. He lay still and allowed a strange calm to drift over him. He could do nothing but wait.

An hour passed, and then another. Gradually he lost all sense of time. The door opened once and an unfamiliar, bearded face looked in. Then the door slammed shut. Finally, it opened and two men came in and dragged the chair upright. They cut the ties which held his hands and feet. Someone else emerged from the darkness outside the door and flung a thin mattress on the ground. He disappeared for a moment then returned and placed a bucket in the corner.

'Why won't you let me go?' Joe cried. 'What do you want?'

No-one spoke. One of them unhooked the paraffin lamp then they turned and left the room and the door slammed shut. He heard bolts slide and a key turn. He sat on the mattress alone in the darkness with thoughts he could not shut out. No light broke through the high window now. It was night. Eventually, exhausted by his thoughts, he fell into a restless sleep. Every few hours a door opened and someone stepped into the room and he awoke to see a figure in the shadows watching him. Once, as the slender filament of light stirred the darkness, indicating dawn, a younger man entered with a bowl of water and a towel. He removed the bucket and left. A moment later he returned to replace it.

Eventually the door opened again and Akmal walked in. Two others, heavily bearded, entered behind him. Joe recognised the narrow face of Salim, the wiry one, the joker. Akmal indicated the chair and Joe stumbled to it and sat down.

'Are you hungry?'

Joe nodded.

'Thirsty?'

'Yes.'

Akmal nodded and Salim left the room.

'Anything else you need?'

'Freedom?'

Akmal smiled.

The door opened and a metal bowl of watery soup was handed to him. He winced as the hot liquid moistened his dry lips and the cuts in his mouth. A cup of water was placed on the floor.

'Let's begin again,' Akmal spoke calmly. 'I want to know what you are worth to me, Joe.' He turned the chair and sat down as before. Salim and a short, stocky figure Joe didn't recognise stood by the door and watched. 'My friends are inclined to kill you. They think you're of no financial value to us but that your death would serve as good propaganda. Civilian deaths always have a capacity to shock and terrify. Savage deaths such as you face show people that we're implacable, that we have no better nature to which they can appeal and that we are relentless and unstoppable. It's some time since we last demonstrated our power. Some would say it's long overdue. So, Joe, don't underestimate the importance of this moment. You have one opportunity to tell me why they shouldn't have their way.'

Joe was thinking quickly. 'Check my wallet. You missed something. There's a small tear in the leather. It's inside that.'

Akmal drew the wallet from his own pocket and handed it to Salim who studied it closely then drew out a piece of paper, neatly folded twice. He opened it and spread in flat between his hands.

'Read it.'

'I can't. It's in Arabic.'

Akmal looked at him with contempt. 'Pass it to me.' He held out a fine fingered hand, like the hand of an artist. It looked like a hand which would be more at ease holding a pen or a paintbrush or a musical instrument than a gun. Somehow it made him even more frightening.

Akmal read the paper closely. He looked at Joe and their eyes met for a moment. He turned to his colleagues at the door.

'It seems we've captured a hero,' he said. He turned back to Joe and waved the paper towards him. 'I remember this. It was a good action. But what followed was not. My recollection is not good. I don't read the newspapers or watch your television propaganda but I do recall you became a tool of Government propaganda. You were the future, they said, because you placed justice and fairness before race and religion.'

Joe laughed dryly. 'That wasn't my idea.'

'You went along with it though.'

'If it helped...'

He stopped. It didn't help Akmal and his followers.

'I didn't want to be used as propaganda. Things spiralled out of my control. But I don't regret what I did. I'd do it again.'

Akmal studied him closely. His dark eyes seemed to cut a path through him but Joe refused to flinch. There was no going back now. Akmal stood up suddenly and left the room, clutching the paper from Joe's wallet. Joe could hear him outside. He was speaking quickly and urgently, probably on a phone. A moment later, he returned.

He paced across the room and then back again. He stared at the paper and then paced again. Finally, he stopped in front of Joe.

'Watch me,' he said.

He took the paper and, without taking his eyes off Joe, he tore it across the centre. Then he tore each piece in half again and then again. He let the pieces fall through his fingers like confetti.

'I think Joe needs some company,' he said, 'to help him see things more clearly.'

The two men seemed to understand. They lifted Joe by his arms and led him out of the door and along the side of the vast empty factory floor. There were some metal stairs at the end, leading down to basements. At the bottom, a long corridor led between other rooms. They stopped outside one and unbolted and unlocked a door, then pushed him inside and slammed the door shut. He lay on the damp ground in the darkness, breathing heavily.

It took some minutes for his eyes to become accustomed to the darkness. The only hint of light slipped through a grille at the top of a wall. It touched the dark room like pity. A cold draft sighed sympathetically.

It was a moment before the light penetrated the darkest corner where a hunched figure lay watching him. Slowly it rose to its feet and groaned with the effort of movement.

'Who are you?' Joe's voice was hushed and sank without hope in the damp air.

The figure drew back into the corner as if he wanted to vanish into darkness.

'Why are you here?' Joe asked.

The figure suddenly slumped down again on the cold floor. In the darkness Joe could hear him crying silently. Nothing moved. It was a ghastly, terrible sound.

'I'm Joe.' His voice was a whisper. 'Where are we?'

A dry, cracked voice spoke. It seemed to be possessed by no earthly body. It rose from the silence like the voice of someone long dead. 'Tell them I've done nothing. You tell them.'

'Who are you?'

'You tell them. Do you hear me? I'll not be tricked. I'll tell you nothing. You tell them. I've done nothing.'

'I don't know what you mean. I'm not a spy.'

'You tell them.'

'I'm not one of them. I'm a prisoner here too. Joe, I'm called Joe.'

The figure suddenly lurched forward. Joe saw now that he was restrained by chains which held him to the wall.

'Don't you think I've told them everything? I'd say anything. Look at me. Look at me.'

Joe saw him clearly now for the first time.

'My God,' he cried, 'Oh God.'

He could hardly distinguish the man's face for blood and bruises. His eyes were swollen shut. He crouched forward no longer capable even of sitting upright. He shook two hands towards Joe.

'Look,' he said. 'Look what they did to me.'

Joe could see the bleeding stumps where two fingers had been removed above the joint.

'Tell them I've nothing more to say. I've said everything.'

He drew back into the corner. He could barely cry through his broken teeth and cracked lips. The sound was horribly alien, like a sound from the depths of a Mediaeval Hell.

Joe was tempted to slip away into a different corner as far away as he could from the ghastly figure. He was repelled by the obscenity of his wounds and the stench which came off him and filled the room.

For a few minutes, repulsion and pity struggled for dominance. Then Joe crawled across the room to the young man's side. He reached an arm around his shoulders and held him. The young man slumped against him.

'Mikhal,' he mumbled through his tears. 'My name is Mikhal.'

Chapter 14

The day passed slowly then the long, cold night and the next day. Once, someone opened the door to remove the bucket they were forced to share. Then the door closed and they were alone. Mikhal slumped back against the wall and said little so Joe was left to face the nightmare of his own thoughts. The hopes he always expressed – to Hannah, to the girls, to Lisa and Adam, to Martin and Alan – that one day they would be allowed to live the modest life they had always imagined theirs by right, fell away and he was left to face the awful truth. Maybe life would always be like this. Maybe the only satisfactory conclusion would be his death. At least then, after a period of grief, his family would escape the purgatory in which they dwelt and slowly move on. In the silence, all his schemes and plans were just delusions. He would spend his remaining days running away until eventually they caught up with him. Then he would die. That was all. He was simply postponing the inevitable.

He tried to brush away these dark thoughts and think of other things but everything drew him back.

It was a relief when, just after midday as close as he could estimate, the door opened and Akmal stepped in. He looked at the two men crouched together in the corner of the room and spat contemptuously.

'Get away from him,' he snapped at Joe. 'Have you no dignity?'

Joe didn't move.

'He stinks and now you stink. You wear his blood and shit. You are beneath contempt. You,' he said to Mikhal. 'Get on your feet.'

Mikhal pulled away from Joe's restraining hand and staggered to his feet. He leaned against the wall and coughed painfully and held his chained arms across his ribs.

'Apostate!' Akmal yelled. 'Traitor!' With the back of his hand he dealt a crushing blow. Mikhal fell to his knees. 'Get up!'

Mikhal staggered to his feet and fell again as another blow stunned him. Fresh blood oozed from his nose and lips.

'Look at him,' he shouted at Joe. 'He's an animal. He's less than human. You should be ashamed to be near him.'

A wave of fury and fear drove through Joe but he struggled forward and knelt between the two men. His hand rested on Mikhal's shoulder.

'Leave him alone.'

Akmal laughed. 'You have no bargaining power. Your own life hangs by a thread. His is forfeit.'

Joe refused to allow his eyes to flinch.

'I would rather stand at his side than yours.'

The kick that sent him sprawling backwards numbed his senses. For a moment he couldn't move, he couldn't think. He breathed heavily and felt the blood drip down his face and onto his shirt.

'You have no principle,' Akmal shouted. 'You have no self-respect.'

Joe crept forward and resumed his place at Mikhal's side. His eyes met Akmal's. For a moment they were locked.

'Why do you do this? You can't save him. You can only die.'

'I don't care.'

He was lying, he knew that. Of course, he cared. He didn't want to die. He didn't want to leave Hannah and Jessica and Meg. There was so much he wanted to say to them, so much they still had to share. They stood before him as clearly as if they were in the same room. He could reach out and touch them. But that was no help to him now. He drove their image away.

'I don't care,' he repeated.

Akmal stared at him and his eyes flickered with uncertainty. He turned away and left the room. The two captives slumped back into the corner. For a few minutes only the rasping of their breathing broke painfully through the silence. Mikhal rested his head back against the rough stone.

'Why?' he asked. 'You don't know me.'

Joe had no answer.

'Because...just because.'

'I don't deserve your kindness. I was one of them.'

'I don't care. It doesn't matter.'

'You can't save me. They're going to kill me. I knew that the moment I walked away from them. There was never any other outcome.'

'But you still walked.'

'It was easier than staying.'

He closed his eyes and slumped against Joe. The darkness seemed to gather even more closely. What feeble light the grille permitted through made little headway. No-one came near them now. Hunger and thirst began to gnaw at Joe. He could think of little else. His mouth felt dry and his lips cracked and rough. Eventually, despite the pain and discomfort, he slept. He awoke once. There was no light penetrating the grille. There was no sound. For a moment he thought Mikhal must be dead but then he heard the steady rhythmic rasping of his painful breathing. He slept again and only awoke when weak bars of light patterned the rough wall.

Eventually the door opened and Akmal appeared, once again flanked by two others. He nodded and the two men stepped forward and hauled Joe to his feet.

'You're a lucky man, Joe. I will honour the promise made by the Imam in your letter. You are free to go.' Once again, those dark eyes, now confident and assured, locked Joe in a cold stare. 'Go. You're free.'

Joe looked at the open door. Never had he felt such a desire to stumble forward, to grasp the freedom he was offered, to run and never to turn. But something he could barely comprehend prevented him from moving. He shook his head. He crouched down and took Mikhal by the arm. He dragged him to his feet. 'Unfasten him. He's coming with me.'

Akmal laughed and looked at his two colleagues. They laughed uncertainly.

'You're a brave man, Joe, but you're a fool. Why would we let him go free?'

'You've done enough,' Joe said. 'Killing him won't make any difference. Let him go now and everyone who sees him will know the extent of your power. He'll be a living reminder of what happens to people who cross you.'

'Killing him will be a better warning.'

'And what would killing me do?'

'We don't plan to kill you. We respect the word of our Imam and we'll honour his promise to you.'

'Then you must free him too. I won't leave without him.'

'I don't understand you, Joe. Do you want to die?'

'You can have no idea how little I want to die, but I won't leave without him.'

For a moment there was a look of admiration in Akmal's eyes. He turned to his two colleagues.

'It seems we are faced by a man of principle. I admire principle, even when it is wasted on scum like this.' He levelled another kick at Mikhal who slumped, groaning, on the floor. He drew a pistol from his waistband and levelled it.

'Forget me, Joe,' Mikhal gasped. 'Save yourself. It's too late for me. I'm ready to die.'

Akmal looked from one to the other. 'Two men of principle,' he sneered.

He lowered the gun towards Mikhal's leg and fired a single shot. Mikhal screamed with pain and crumpled, writing on the floor. Akmal turned to Joe. He raised the gun and pointed it at his head.

'If we meet again, I shall kill you. You may have principles but you have no self-respect, no dignity. You are my enemy.'

He allowed the hand holding the gun to fall to his side. He spoke in a whisper to the others and then left the room. Joe didn't see him again. The two men lifted him roughly and covered his head once more in a hessian bag. They dragged him, stumbling, out of the cell. They crossed a vast space and then a second door opened and Joe was aware of daylight filtering through the hessian and a chill breeze penetrating his clothing. They stopped and opened a sliding door, probably a van, and he was bundled inside and flung down on musty sacking. His rucksack was flung in after him and the door was slammed shut. A few minutes later it opened again and Joe felt something heavy thrown beside him before the door shut once more, the engine started and the van pulled slowly out onto the street. Soon he could hear other traffic. They must have turned onto a busy road.

After half an hour the van pulled up and stopped. The door slid open and the hood was pulled from his head.

'Akmal says you're to see this. He says he too is a man of principle.'

Through the door he saw the vast city hospital. He knew now that the weight beside him was Mikhal. The two men rolled out the motionless body and dropped it heavily on the ground. Joe heard a faint, muffled groan then the door shut and the van accelerated away. Twenty minutes later it stopped again. The door opened and Joe was bustled out onto the pavement. One of his captors nodded towards the railway station about a hundred metres away.

'Go now and don't come back. Akmal said to give you this and to tell you we have taken nothing. We are not thieves. He leaves you a little warning.'

He handed him his wallet and with it a single bullet. It was to remind him of the bullet Akmal had chosen not to fire, Joe knew that. The message was clear. There would be no further chances.

The van pulled away and Joe was left alone. He walked unsteadily towards the railway station and the security of a thin, afternoon crowd of travellers. He scanned the departure board. There was a train heading north in an hour. He bought a ticket and then walked across to the newsagent's stand. He picked up a newspaper and glanced at it. Within its pages the inconsequential clashed with the tragic like alien cultures - millions were dying in an African state after another failed harvest, a soap star had left a series after fifteen years, a model was wearing a provocative dress and dying children crouched, helpless, in a refugee camp. Joe shuddered in the chill air which meandered through the concourse. He replaced the paper and drifted unsteadily down the platform to wait for his train. It was running late.

When it arrived at last, half an hour later, he settled himself in the carriage, leaned his head back and closed his eyes. A middle-aged woman with a small, leather suitcase came to sit opposite him but she saw the bruises and dried blood on his face and on his clothes and thought better of it. She moved further along the carriage and sat down. She opened the window beside her and mumbled something to someone he couldn't see, no doubt drawing their attention to his appearance and the stench from his clothes which filled the carriage. He was left alone for the rest of the journey. Few people got on the train and those that did avoided him. It was evening when he reached Triente and changed from the train to a local bus and almost dark by the time he reached the village where Alan lived. Even then he had to walk for half an hour to reach the narrow lane which led to the cottage. He paused outside the lounge window. A light glowed behind the closed curtains and he could make out voices on the radio. He could picture Alan sitting there, his eyes half closed. Something stirred in him like the ache of nostalgia.

He tapped at the window gently. A face appeared. A moment later, the door opened.

Chapter 15

'Jesus, Joe, you look like you've been hit by a tram.'

Alan was four years older than Joe, with dark eyes in a round, nervous face. He was slightly stooped and round-shouldered as if he had been born ready-formed to sit behind an office desk. He sported a newly grown short, dark beard of soft hair. He hurried Joe through to the living room, where a splash of colour and light engulfed him. Joe was aware how clean and warm everything was and how cold and sordid he must look.

'Where's your phone. I need to phone Hannah. I lost mine in the city.'

'Not yet. We'll get you cleaned up first and find you some clothes. Where have you been sleeping? In a swamp? You stink.'

'Thanks for the observation. But yes, a shower would be welcome.'

'What the hell has happened to you? I was expecting you a couple of days ago. I'd just about given up.' He held up a hand. 'Never mind, don't try and tell me, not yet. First things first, have you eaten?'

'Not for a while.'

'How long?'

'Maybe yesterday, maybe the day before, I can't remember.'

'Get a shower while I get some food on. I can see we have a lot to talk about. Jesus, Joe, what's happened to you?'

'But Hannah...'

'Shower and food first, I think, or she'll be able to smell you down the phone line.'

Alan was right, of course; it would do no good to speak to Hannah yet. So much had happened and he had to think what to share and what to retain. His role now was to reassure. The truth could wait.

'Have you heard from her? Is she alright? She'll be worried.'

'You can speak to her in half an hour. Now shower. I'm not sitting here with someone who smells like a sewer.'

Joe allowed the hot water to soak down from his hair to his face and body and slowly he washed away the blood and the grime. The stench that had accompanied him was replaced by the fragrance of shower gel and he felt his body glow warm and clean. But there was no gel, no deodorant and no soap strong enough to wash away the images that fouled his mind. They would need a different sort of cleansing.

Alan opened the door and threw in some clothes and a black, plastic bin bag.

'Put everything you're wearing in the bag. It can go straight in the bin. Those are some clothes of mine. As for food, I've got some new potatoes and salmon. Will that do?'

'I could eat the bin bag.'

'Coffee's on.'

'I'll be down in ten minutes. I haven't enjoyed anything as much as this shower in a long, long time.'

As he dressed in the warm, clean clothing and then sat down to a meal in the spotless kitchen, he felt the ugliness of the past few days slip away. While he was showering, Alan had been working. The windows had been open and air freshener applied. Everything was clean again, as if the pollution he had brought with him had never been.

The meal finished, Joe took his coffee into the hallway and called Hannah. A man's voice answered but Hannah grabbed the phone before he had time to speak.

'Joe? Is that you, Joe?'

'Who was that?'

'Detective Inspector Stone - he's in charge of security. My dad arranged it. Where are you, Joe? Are you at Alan's?'

'I just arrived.'

'Why were you so late? I've been worried.'

'I got held up,' he laughed gently, 'literally.'

He described the attack on the bus and his subsequent interview with the police and the evening spent with Jival. That much he felt he could tell her. He played down the savagery and the danger, and spoke at length about Jival's kindness and the similarity between their families.

'They have two girls, like us, only younger, about four or five.'

He didn't mention Akmal or his captivity in the deserted warehouse. There was no point in worrying her. It was over; he was safe.

'What about you? How are the girls? I miss you. Every day I miss you.'

He recalled those moments in the warehouse cell when he thought he wouldn't see them again. He shuddered and tears, long restrained, pricked his eyes.

'Are you alright? You sound strange,' Hannah said.

'I'm just tired. It's been a long day.'

As long as a lifetime, he thought. Could anything ever be the same? He told her about D.S. Jackson. There were good people out there, he reminded himself. It was easy to forget, easy to sink into the dark mire and see nothing but the creatures that lurked there. They were like monsters from a child's dream, only real and unforgiving. Only the recollection of moments of kindness and compassion could drive them away, like a mother's comforting words.

'The girls are back at school. It's better for them. It was a mistake running away.'

'Like me, you mean?'

Too sensitive, he thought, too touchy. She'd caught a nerve. He passed it off as a joke and laughed.

Hannah spoke quickly. She was used to defending Joe from accusations like that. 'That's different; you could be killed. No-one will bother us, not really. D.I. Stone is very thorough.'

'I don't understand. Why is he there with you? Has something happened?'

'Nothing important,' she said.

'Is that nothing important or nothing at all?' Joe asked, aware of his own deception.

'Nothing, it's just dad being over protective. You know what he's like. Stone's reviewing our security. How's Alan?' she asked and their conversation turned to the mundane and the routine.

'Fine – more than fine, he's thriving up here.'

'How long will you stay with him?'

'A few days - I need time to think.'

She knew what that meant. One morning he would wake and know it was time to move on. Something – perhaps a solitary figure on the lane, perhaps a car, perhaps nothing more than a momentary alarm caused by the brushing of a branch against the window or a strange sound in the night – something would resurrect those familiar fears. He would be concerned for Alan. Anyone who helped him was putting themselves in danger. It was too much to ask of anyone for long. He would leave.

'Where will you go?'

'I don't know. I'll try and get a job. If not, I'll move on perhaps north again. Do you remember our holidays in the Mountains?' Another wave of nostalgia, another memory, passing over him like sunlight. 'Perhaps we'll go again one day soon. I love it there. I feel free in the mountains. I feel safe.'

'When will it end, Joe? I don't know how much more I can take. It's been two years now.'

'Soon,' he said, 'I promise.'

He felt the weight of that promise like a stone round his neck.

'The girls are asleep. They'll be disappointed they missed you.'

'I'll call tomorrow after they come home from school.'

'I miss you.'

'I miss you too.'

He put the phone down.

'Can you find a number for me, Alan?' he called through to the lounge. 'The General Hospital in the Zone – Midway Primary Care Trust, I think it's called.'

Alan turned to the computer and brought up the number. Joe rang it and reached a switchboard.

'Someone I know was admitted yesterday. He was left outside the hospital. He'd been badly beaten. I want to know how he is. He's called Mikhal. That's all I know.'

'Just a moment; I'll put you through.'

Another voice answered, a deep voice like a chain smoker. Joe repeated his request.

'Are you a relative?'

'No, I'm just...just a friend.' It seemed a strange word under the circumstances.

'Were you the friend who dumped him at the roadside and left him there, nearly dead?'

'No,' he said hotly.

'Could you tell me your name?'

'I just want to know he's alright, that's all. You don't need my name.'

There was a moment's silence.

'He'll live. No thanks to the thugs who beat him. Another day would have killed him. He's got a fractured eye socket, a broken pelvis, severed fingers, internal bleeding, several missing teeth, broken ribs, not to mention the gunshot wound – shall I go on?'

'But he's okay. He'll live?'

'Yes, he'll live.'

'Tell him...just tell him Joe phoned. He'll understand.'

He replaced the phone. Alan was standing in the doorway behind him.

'I need to get a new mobile' Joe said.

'You can use the landline.'

'You never know who's listening,' Joe said. 'I've learnt to be cautious. I get a new sim every few days. I'm not even sure it does any good. I saw it on a film somewhere. It seemed like a sensible precaution.'

Alan leaned back and laughed. 'I doubt they've bugged my phone and if they'd bugged your mobile, they'd know your location in a matter of seconds. That's technology for you.'

'I daren't trust anything, Alan. Nothing feels safe, not anymore.'

'That sounds horribly like paranoia, Joe.'

Joe shook his head. 'It's not. It's real. They have people everywhere and sooner or later, if no-one stops them...'

'Come on,' Alan said. 'Sit back and put your feet up. You need to rest. We'll talk later.'

During the riots and the subsequent discontent, Alan had moved from his work in a city law firm and set up a private practice further north. He had settled into rural life, grown a tidy beard and was sometimes seen to wear a shirt without a tie. His cottage, while surrounded by fields and hills, was sufficiently close to a main road to allow him ready access to his practice but isolated enough to provide him with the security and the sense of peace he craved.

Joe looked at him now.

'All you're missing is carpet slippers, a pipe and a dog at your feet,' he complained. 'I envy you.'

Alan smiled. 'If you can't beat them, run away.'

He noticed the change in Joe's expression.

'Sorry, I didn't mean that how it sounded.'

'I know.'

'I just want to live my life without thinking about people who want to destroy it.'

'It's what most people want - just a little peace and space to live their lives. That's what makes the fundamentalists and the terrorists so frightening. They defy all our efforts at comprehension. It's as if we belong to different worlds. How can you talk to people you can't begin to understand?'

'"The best lack all conviction, while the worst are full of passionate intensity." W.B. Yeats: The Second Coming.'

'Why is everything such a mess, Alan? I don't understand. I don't know where these people come from or what they really want. I was on a bus attacked by terrorists, you know. They were just killing, killing as if it had no meaning. Then I was kidnapped by the same group. How's that for bad luck?'

He told Alan about Akmal and his group. 'It's a strange thing to say, I know, but he wasn't without an integrity of sorts; deluded and misguided, of course, savage and cruel undoubtedly, but not without a perverse sort of honour. I can't help feeling we're responsible, you know, for creating these monsters. Our policies in the Middle East have been little short of evil. How many families have been destroyed as a result of what we did?'

Alan shook his head. 'You've given him more consideration than he warrants. I have no such difficulty. A monster is a monster – whatever its colour, race or religion.'

'Even monsters come from somewhere. That's what really scares me. I keep trying to imagine the trajectory that brings them to this point. It was as if everything that he ever was, all that human complexity, had been compressed and suppressed until all that remained was defined by one thing – an all-consuming and terrifying belief. It appalled me.'

'They'll only ever be a minority.'

'I used to think that but economic decline, unemployment and crap jobs, the places they're herded into, the lack of hope...it's a breeding ground. When they think they've got nothing left, someone comes along and gives them God or a cause. Unscrupulous people, clever, well educated people, give them leadership and before you know it things fall apart. That's why the settlement has to work. Otherwise...' He fell silent.

'You think too much. The politicians will sort it all out.'

'Maybe, if they're given time. But...'

'What?'

'I don't know – bad feelings.'

'Were you scared?'

'I thought I was going to die. I thought I'd never see Hannah or Jessica or Meg again. It was almost unbearable.'

'I haven't got a wife or children, but I can imagine it.'

Joe laughed softly. 'It took everything I had to mask my fear. I didn't take my eyes off him. I never flinched. I wonder if he knew I was a gibbering wreck below the surface.'

'Maybe that saved you.'

Joe smiled. 'No. I was saved by a simple piece of paper given me by an Imam after the trial. His was the mosque where the couple I protected went to worship. It saved me once; it won't save me again, Akmal made that clear.' He remembered the bullet Akmal had given him. 'I won't get a second chance. If we meet again, he'll kill me.'

He paused for a moment.

'That wasn't the worst of it, though.'

He explained how he met Mikhal and what happened.

'You could have been killed.'

'Perhaps, but I wasn't.'

'Anyway, you're here now and you've got time to arrange your next job. You stay here as long as you like.'

Joe shook his head. 'I'll only stay a few days. They'll find me; they always do.'

Alan stared in front of him. 'I won't let them rule my life. You must stay.'

Joe smiled. 'Thanks, Alan, but a few days rest will be good enough.'

'And then?'

'Find a job, move on, keep going.'

'It's not much of a plan, is it?'

'No, no plan at all. I'm tired, Alan, tired of running, tired of hiding and tired of being afraid. Sometimes I just want to stop and wait for them to find me.'

'They'd kill you.'

'I know, but at least Hannah and the girls could start a new life.'

'They don't want a new life; they want the old life back again.'

Joe drew Akmal's bullet from his pocket and stared at it.

'I know.'

Chapter 16

For the next few days, Joe recuperated. He spoke to Hannah more frequently, often from the village, and he spoke twice to Jessica and Meg. The questions were always the same.

'When are you coming home, Dad?' It was Meg, anxious as usual, Daddy's girl.

'Soon, very soon.'

'Tomorrow?'

'Maybe not tomorrow but soon.'

'The day after?'

'Soon.'

'Will you come back before my birthday?' That was Jessica, always pragmatic.

'Yes. It's a few weeks yet.'

'Will you bring me a present?'

'Of course I will.'

'We miss you. Meg sometimes cries in bed at night.'

He heard Meg protest in the background and Jessica respond.

('No, I don't!'

'Yes, you do, I heard you.')

'I miss you too,' he told them both, his heart beating louder. 'I'll be back soon.'

It was another promise and another burden, another link in the heavy chain of responsibility. He closed the phone, tired and depressed.

Alan was working late that night, so Joe walked to the village and had a meal at the hotel. It was after nine when he made his way back to the cottage. He could see the trees beside the gable silhouetted against the sky. Stars peered through the branches, small eyes watching. Alan was back, his car parked in the drive, but the house was in darkness. Joe knew at once there was something wrong.

The moon was nearly full and its light caught the outline of a second car, half hidden beneath the trees on the road side, just beyond the driveway to the cottage. The driver smoked a cigarette, his elbow resting casually on the open window. Joe could see the smoke escape into the air, the dull glow of the tip, the broad, dark shape of a man's face. He drew back into to the cover of trees and slipped over the wall which surrounded the garden. He waited for a moment, his back pressed against the rough stone, breathing heavily. There was no sound from the car. Keeping low, he crept across the lawn towards the cottage door. As he dropped down beside it, the car's engine started. Joe ducked to one side behind some shrubbery and sank low on the ground as a headlight beam passed across the cottage, illuminating the dark windows and walls. It drew away, passing the gate and disappearing down the lane.

The front door lay open but Joe crept towards the lounge window. He stood beside it, his back pressed against the roughcast wall, and glanced in through the glass. There was no-one there, nothing to see, just darkness and shadows. Without a sound, he stepped over the level flagstones round the side of the house towards the kitchen. Crouching there, he heard the car return. Its lights brightened the trees along the lane. It stopped and the car door opened and the driver walked along the path towards the open door.

Joe could hear voices in the kitchen and there was a small light now as if from a cigarette lighter. He crouched below the stone sill and raised his head to look inside. He reeled back and pressed himself close against the stone. He waited. No-one moved. Nothing changed. A low hum of conversation escaped from within. He inched forward again and eased his head above the sill.

Joe recognised the man who had just entered. Tall, thin and pale in the moonlight, a livid scar across his cheek, he looked down at a prostrate body on the ground. He levelled a kick at the head and the figure on the ground groaned, turning a bruised and bloodied face towards the window. Alan lay hunched on the kitchen floor, curled foetus-like to protect himself from further blows. Even in the light of the moon, Joe could see his bruised eyes, his torn mouth, the blood and phlegm. Caine looked down at him and spat.

'Jew,' he snarled.

A second figure emerged from the shadows.

'What do we do now?' Bull wiped a bloody fist on a towel.

'Now we wait.'

'And him?'

He indicated the body on the floor.

'Later,' Caine said. 'No loose ends.'

Joe reached in his pocket. This was no time for foolish or precipitate action. He called the police and whispered a detailed message with a patience he didn't feel. Then he inched closer to the window again to hear the conversation within.

'We should be in Zarten.' Bull sat down at the table. 'I don't trust them...They're fools... What if it goes wrong?'

'Nothing will go wrong. Everything's in place. Even those idiots couldn't get this wrong. Besides, it's nothing to do with us.' Caine smiled icily. 'We were miles away. Witnesses at the hotel can testify.'

Bull laughed and then swore coarsely.

'I've hurt my fucking hand,' he snapped. He kicked the prostrate body half-heartedly. Alan flopped over and moaned.

Joe knew they were waiting for him. He looked round for something, anything with which he could help Alan. Then he stopped and waited, breathing slowly. To race in with a weapon would help neither of them. They'd be dead in minutes. He had to wait for the police. He looked at his watch.

They'll be here any minute now, he told himself.

He listened for sirens approaching along the lane from the village, for an ambulance, for cars. Minutes passed. Five minutes came and went, then ten, then fifteen; still nothing. Where were they? What was keeping them? He eased himself carefully forward and looked in from the darkness. Alan was lying still now. Bull and Caine were sitting back on kitchen chairs. Caine lit a cigarette and held it casually between long fingers. Nobody spoke. Caine flicked ash casually towards Alan.

Joe reached for his phone and rang again.

'Where are they?' he hissed. 'It's a fucking emergency.'

He was put directly through to a police officer.

'Where exactly are you, sir?' the officer asked, 'in relation to the intruders?' His voice was calm, controlled. Joe explained he was beside the kitchen window from where he could see the people inside.

'Stay right where you are,' the officer advised. 'Don't move. A car will be there in a few minutes. It's already on the way.'

A few minutes passed. No car approached, but inside the cottage a mobile phone rang. Joe saw Caine take it from his pocket but he didn't wait to hear what was said. He knew what it meant. He sped quickly and silently into the shadows cast by bushes and trees, where he crept into the undergrowth and flung himself on the ground, breathing hard.

He could imagine how Caine reacted to the voice on the phone, how he span round towards the window, how he snapped instructions at Bull as they sprang towards the door and flung it open.

Now he could hear him.

'He was here; he was outside the fucking window.' He looked around and swore. 'Check the drive and the lane. I'll check the garden and the outbuildings.'

From where he lay, Joe saw Bull in the light cast from the door. He had no torch and peered into the darkness either side of the drive. He passed close and Joe pressed his face down into the soft grass beneath the tree. He breathed slowly and waited. After a moment, he raised his head. Bull was in the lane. Joe could hear him walking alongside the boundary wall. It was time to move.

He rose, but crouched low, looking towards the still open doorway. He sped across the grass and rested with his back to the wall just outside.

Alan, he thought. *I've got to get Alan.*

There were no sounds inside the house but he knew Bull would soon return from the lane and in the meantime, where was Caine? He took a deep breath and turned but, as he did so, he heard a sound from beside the house. Someone had tripped over the hosepipe left coiled beside an outside tap. He heard Caine swear. It was too late; he couldn't get into the house. Caine would round the corner and see him. He turned away and ran around to where the back garden adjoined a field.

Across the field he could see the lights of a farmhouse and a couple of small houses. He had only a moment to make a decision. Behind him, Caine shouted.

'Bull! I heard him. Get around the back. Quickly!'

Bull's heavy feet sounded on the gravel.

Joe ducked low and fled across the open field. He was lucky. The moon had slipped behind clouds at the first appearance of the two men and it remained there as if ashamed to share the night with them. Joe stumbled and fell and ran on again, certain they were following close behind him. At times he was sure he could hear their harsh breathing and he scrambled even faster over pasture rutted with the hoof prints of cattle and littered with dried clods of earth. His lungs burned, and the sweat ran off him, cooling as it met the night air. Eventually, he reached a gate into the farmyard and climbed over it, breathing heavily. He ran through mud to the farmhouse door, where the outside light caught him in a sudden beam. Bent over, he beat heavily on the wooden panels and shouted. The door was flung back and light flooded out.

'Alan needs help,' he gasped. He pointed back over the field. 'My brother...he's been attacked...two men. They're still there.'

The farmer was a burly young man in his late thirties. He was wearing shorts and a tee-shirt and had obviously been disturbed from sleep. He brushed a hand through dishevelled hair and rubbed his eyes. Another figure appeared behind him, an older man, probably in his sixties.

'What's going on? Who's bloody shouting at this time of night?' He saw Joe. 'Who the hell are you? What do you want?'

His son interrupted him. 'Phone the police, Dad. Someone's burgling Alan's place.' He turned to Joe. 'Alan's been hurt, you say?'

'He's lying in the kitchen. I saw him through the window. He's taken a beating.'

'Police!' The young man turned peremptorily to his father.

Joe shook his head. 'There's no time. I called the police. They won't come.'

The two men looked at him incredulously.

'I can't explain now. The men were looking for me. It's complicated and there's no time. Please? If we wait for the police, we'll wait forever. It'll be too late.'

'Wait there.'

The door closed. A minute later the two men emerged in gun boots, heavy outdoor coats flung hastily over their nightwear. The old man had a shotgun.

'My wife's calling a couple of the farm workers,' the old man said. He stopped at the field gate and levelled the shotgun towards the distant cottage. He fired a shot above the trees and then another. It echoed in the darkness like thunder. A flock of pigeons rose from the trees and fled, escaping from one darkness into another. 'Just to let them know we're coming. That should give them pause for thought.'

'Let's hope so.' His son clambered over the gate and set off into the darkness. The older man reloaded the shotgun and followed him. By the time they reached the cottage, two other lights were approaching from the farm workers' houses along the lane. They arrived at the door in time to see the headlights of a car swerving and vanishing down the lane. Caine and Bull had gone – for now.

'I knew the shotgun would see them off.' The old man winked. 'Now, let's see to Alan.'

They found him in the kitchen. He had struggled to his feet and was heading to the sink. He splashed water over his face.

'Do you need an ambulance, Alan?'

Alan shook his head. He sat back on the sofa and held a warm cloth to his eye and lips. 'It's not as bad as it looks. It's just a few bruises.' He turned to his brother. 'Sorry, Joe, I tried to hold out.'

'Forget it; I'd have done the same.'

The young farmer arrived from the kitchen carrying a tray of drinks.

'I found a bottle of brandy. I didn't think you'd mind, under the circumstances.'

Alan took a glass. He grimaced as he raised it to his lips.

'I was helpless. I wanted to fight but I barely raised a fist before they floored me. It was pathetic.'

'No, it wasn't,' the old man said. 'You can't beat people like that with your fists. They'll always win. With respect,

Alan, you're not a fighter. I've seen bigger muscles on a crane fly. You use the law. In the long run, the law will win.'

'You think so? I wonder? I've never seen anyone like that before. I've never been that *scared* before. They would've killed me without a second thought. What does the law matter to people like that?'

'They've gone; they'll not come back,' Joe said.

The old man turned to Joe. 'Now, Joe, I think it's time for that explanation you promised us. Fill us up, David.' He raised an empty glass towards his son. 'Why were they looking for you? What have you done?'

Joe did his best to explain the events which had led to their current situation.

'And you think someone here tipped them off?'

'Yes, I'm sure of it. The emergency call wasn't answered. Someone intercepted it.'

'Well, we'll sort that out later,' the old man said. 'We'll get to the bottom of it. We don't like that sort of thing around here, no matter what the reason. I know there's a lot of ill feeling out there but it's no excuse for things like this. I've never held with all these immigrants settling here, myself. I hardly recognise the place anymore and I don't like it. I remember the country when it was rare to see a foreigner. I used to point them out to David when he was a little boy. "Look, David, there's a black man over there." If you heard a foreign voice on the streets, you turned around to look; even an American accent caught your attention. Now they're everywhere. And the country's cut in pieces like a bloody jigsaw. It doesn't seem right.'

'It doesn't mean the place is any the worse for it, Dad,' David said. 'I think we're shaping up into something really good. It's a bit fragile yet, that's all, a bit vulnerable. If we can get a few years without trouble and if the economy picks up, who knows, we might have a chance.'

The old man sighed. 'Nothing stands still. Look at how farming's changed. Even the animals have bloody passports

- which is more than a lot of the immigrants have.' He laughed. 'And everything's computerised. You can't fart in a farmyard without filling in a form.' He leaned back and sipped his brandy. 'I've got no time for these Nationalists and Fundamentalists. Our country has always got on pretty well in its own tolerant sort of way. People moved here and in time they became part of the fabric – like your people, Alan. It was the numbers, see, and the speed it happened, and then the country deciding to sail off into its own sunset and the economy going through yet another bad spell...And it was religion. You can't have your country ruled by religion. It's not democratic.'

Joe thought of Akmal. He thought of Mikhal.

The old man bristled with annoyance. 'My father - David's grandpa - was in the war fighting Fascism. He was lucky. We won and he survived. He always said we didn't see off the Fascists in order to have some other bastards tell us what to do and what to think. You've got to think for yourself and look forward. It's the future where you'll sort these things out, not in the past. You can't go back. The past isn't there anymore.'

David's face broke in a wide smile.

'He's a philosopher, my dad,' he said.

'He's a philosopher with an empty glass. Fill me up.'

They left ten minutes later and Joe and Alan were left alone.

'I'm sorry, Alan. I brought this on you.'

'You've nothing to be sorry for. What'll you do now?'

'I'm going to leave tomorrow.'

'I told them you had a friend on the Coast and that you planned to go there in a few days. I don't know if they believed me.'

'Thanks. That might give me a bit of time.'

'You can't keep running, Joe. You only just escaped this time. Sooner or later, they're going to catch you. They're getting closer all the time.'

'I know.'

'What'll you do?'

'Like I told you, maybe I should turn and fight.'

'That'd play into their hands. You'd lose. You can't beat them like that.'

'Then I'll have to beat them another way.'

'Yes, but how?'

'I don't know, Alan. I just don't know, but I've got to do it. I can't just lie down.'

'Have another brandy. Let's put our heads together, do a bit of plotting like in the old days, see what we can come up with.'

Chapter 17

Sebastian Steele had been charged with many complex negotiations during his diplomatic career. He had lived and worked in many places across the world and had engaged with many governmental heads, both benign and malignant. Nothing, however, had given him greater personal satisfaction than the leading role he played in the political settlement which ended the civil unrest and the insurrection in the cities and towns of what was now generally referred to as the Devolved Zone. It was Sebastian Steele who had devised, negotiated and overseen the implementation of the agreements which led to the ceasefire. It was his plan which would lead to the formation of a devolved administration which would control the cities and towns of the zone.

Normally a reticent man who preferred to live in the diplomatic shadows, he had been exposed unwillingly to the full glare of political scrutiny, particularly as the elections approached when the administration would be inaugurated. Few people imagined such an outcome was possible after the violence which had erupted across the area. They wanted to know more about the man whose dogged persistence had made it possible.

He was interviewed on The News Channel by Denise Swann, a most experienced correspondent. Initially the questions had been factual, reminding the audience of the progress of the settlement. As the interview progressed, Sebastian Steele was invited to express more personal views.

'Were you surprised that the insurrection started within predominantly white militias?'

'I always viewed them as disillusioned and underprivileged, rather than merely white.'

'Nonetheless, most commentators anticipated the first outbreaks would be caused by minority elements of the immigrant community.'

'Both communities, white and immigrant, were maligned by association with minorities over whom they could exercise little control. Most people are fundamentally peaceful and united. Economic factors fostered a general discontent which minority groups were able to exploit.'

Interviewing Sebastian Steele was like sucking water from a stone. Ms. Swann tried again.

'What part do you think religious extremism played in the insurrection?'

'The devolution agreement provides for a secular assembly. Education is based upon a secular model, but it is underpinned by the shared and agreed values of religious communities and of the nation as a whole. The churches, mosques and synagogues have the capacity to provide more detailed religious instruction which adheres to those values. This was all agreed. An atmosphere of religious tolerance has played its part in the peace.'

'Nonetheless, there are minorities who remain alienated by the settlement.'

There was a silence.

'Have you no response to my question?'

'It wasn't a question. It was a statement. I don't agree with the premise so I cannot comment. There are people and small communities who remain underprivileged and in need of our support in order to feel truly involved. There are proposals within the settlement agreement to help such groups and individuals. They aren't alienated by the settlement per se but by the on-going, adverse conditions of their lives.'

It was time for Denise to glance at the clock and change tack with what dignity she could. Perhaps more personal questions might pay off.

'You achieved an outcome that few people imagined was possible. What personal qualities do you think helped in that process?'

Sebastian impatiently brushed an invisible speck from the trousers of his dark suit. A dark suit, a pink shirt and a plain tie – those were his trademark, nothing ostentatious, nothing to make him stand out from the crowd. He was of medium height and silver haired, created by God, he explained patiently, to live in the background. He still didn't understand what had projected him forward.

'A fear of failure,' he said, 'and colleagues far more able than I.'

The interviewer laughed.

'Other people have referred to your patience, your optimism, your dogged determination and your attention to detail. Would you agree that those are your strengths?'

'Others might call me stubborn, implacable, relentless and bloody-minded.'

'They also say you understand the points of view of very different groups.'

'It's very kind of people to say so.'

'Do you see that as a particular strength of your character?'

'I would be a poor negotiator if I failed to listen to the different parties.'

'It has also been said that you struck up a strong personal relationship with key protagonists.'

'It would be fair to say I am loved and loathed in equal measure.'

The correspondent saw the end of the interview in sight and felt an overwhelming sense of relief.

'What's next for Sebastian Steele, a seat in the government, perhaps?'

'At the moment I long for nothing more than a seat at my own fireside, a glass of expensive wine and my family and friends around me.'

'It must have been a difficult time for your family.'

He nodded. It had indeed. It still was. He had barely seen them for several months.

'Thank you, Sebastian Steele.'

He was expected that day to report to a Parliamentary Committee on the staged devolution of more complex policy areas. He was due at Greyminster, the national administrative centre and seat of government, at one. It was a fine morning and the sun was shining. In the past he would have walked, despite the distance, or maybe taken the tube to Greyminster. Unfortunately, his recent high profile now warranted a car and an armed guard. He resented the curtailing of his personal freedom but it was a price he was condemned to pay. His life, he knew, would never be quite the same again. He emerged from The National Television Centre with a friend and colleague of many years at his side.

'This is most depressing, Martin,' he muttered, 'and most unwelcomed.'

He nodded now to the first of the anonymous bodyguards who awaited him at the door. His official car, a black limousine, pulled up outside. Two bodyguards stood to left and right as he crossed the concourse and the narrow pavement. They didn't even glance towards him. Their task was to monitor the street, nothing else. Their hands rested on holstered pistols. It took a matter of seconds for him to disappear inside the car, for Martin and the guards to join him and for the doors to slam shut.

The limousine, its darkened windows hiding the occupants from inquisitive eyes, had covered less than half the distance to Greyminster when the gunfire began. Two hooded figures armed with Kalashnikov AK47s were standing on the busy roadside, one firing towards the car, the other randomly towards pedestrians, vehicles, windows. People fled along the pavements then stumbled and fell. Some were screaming. Others ducked down side streets and ran away. A mother and child lay on the road, puddles of blood widening around them in a silent circle. And still the gunmen fired.

The driver of the limousine floored the accelerator and the tyres screeched. It was time to get his passengers out of there, away from danger. A people carrier suddenly emerged at speed from a side road and drove into the front wing, diverting the car sharply across the pavement and into the front of an office. Masonry crumbled and fell. Shattered glass cascaded like a hideous fountain.

The two gunmen continued their rapid fire. An elderly man, unable to flee, slouched back against a shop front and looked at his bleeding stomach with incredulity. Cars, their windscreens smashed with bullets, careered to a halt, drivers slouching over steering wheels or tumbling like grotesque mannequins onto the tarmac. And still people fell and still they screamed and shouted. A bus turned the corner and was caught in the fire; more people bled and died. In the distance, police sirens wailed.

The passengers in the limousine hadn't moved. The driver lay slumped forward over the steering wheel. The agent beside him was trapped, his door firmly embedded in the fallen masonry. He struggled for his gun and tried in vain to reach the door. The rear door creaked opened momentarily and an arm hung down, but a blast of gunfire drove the passenger back to crouch behind the protective glass and bulletproof steel.

A hooded figure ran towards the limousine. He fumbled underneath the vehicle beside the door and then retreated. He pressed the horn of the people carrier once, twice, and suddenly the firing ceased. From a side street, three motorcycles appeared. The gunmen threw down their weapons, clambered on the pillions and the bikes sped away.

It was only a matter of seconds before an explosion ripped open the limousine. The occupants were helpless. No-one could survive the blast. Thirty-seven people were killed in the attack. Sebastian Steele and his colleague,

Martin, died in the limousine with the bodyguards and the driver. The other victims were civilians, whose indiscriminate deaths added to the chaos and horror. Countless others lay injured on the city street.

The attack had lasted less than five minutes but it was eight minutes before the police arrived on the scene. The nearest armed response teams had been busy elsewhere, a false alarm as it turned out. Caine's hidden allies had done their work well.

Ten minutes later, several miles away, the motorcycles disappeared inside an old warehouse. Two minutes after that, a couple of nondescript vans emerged and turned in different directions. The occupants looked like young, white workmen on their way to work. They bore no resemblance to the hooded terrorists who had ambushed the limousine and wrought such havoc. The witnesses, and there were many, were clear on that point. The attackers were of Middle Eastern origin. They wore dark masks and they shouted in Arabic, over and over, 'God is Greatest! God is Greatest!'

It was what everyone had dreaded. It was what everyone had expected. It was another terror attack on the streets of the capital.

There were three other victims that day. Their passing appeared in no newspapers and was subject to no investigation. Their weighted bodies sank without notice into the deep ocean. No-one would mourn them. No one would grieve. Terry and Jake - the two gunmen - and Vasey, who planted the bomb which destroyed the limousine, deserted their white vans and ran to where another nondescript vehicle was waiting for them. The driver would take them to a harbour where a small fishing boat was waiting. It would take them to a place where they could disappear into the shadows. Other people, members of other groups to which they were linked, would provide them with new identities and new homes.

The driver didn't speak. They barely noticed him even as he shepherded them into the rear seats of the car, its darkened windows obscuring them from sight. They tried to engage him in their raucous, adrenalin-fuelled celebration, but he didn't turn and he didn't respond. He listened impassively as they bragged of their achievement and laughed and swore. His eyes betrayed no emotion and his face was expressionless. They paid him no more attention.

He drove them to the quayside and led them to the small, inshore fishing vessel.

'Get below and stay quiet,' he said. Those were the only words they heard him speak.

'Is there anything to drink? We want to celebrate.'

He closed the hatch behind them. He heard them open the cupboards and there was a cry of elation as they found the bottle of whisky and glasses. He started the engine and steered the vessel out of the harbour and along the coast.

When he opened the hatch again, he held a silenced pistol. Three shots immobilised them. He concluded his work with three more shots to their heads. An hour later, the boat slipped silently back into the harbour and drew up by the pontoon. Only one figure emerged. He walked along the quayside to where a car was parked behind the harbourmaster's office. He drove away towards the south along the coast road. No-one noticed.

Caine left no loose ends.

One notable victim that day was Sebastian's colleague, Martin. He died at his side. It was a tragic death for a man who had served his friend and colleague throughout their days together in the diplomatic service. His silent contribution to the settlement made him, in Sebastian Steele's mind, indispensable in the outcome.

He was Martin Savage, Hannah's father.

Turbulence

Chapter 18

Joe was watching the television in the kitchen of Alan's cottage when the news started to trickle through. His rucksack lay beside him, ready for his departure when Alan got back from the doctor.

'We're receiving unconfirmed reports of an explosion and a gun attack in the centre of Zarten. There are no further details yet but we believe there are several casualties. We will keep you informed as further information reaches us.'

A few minutes later the news reader was back.

'We can now speak to our correspondent at the scene, Tom Vincent. Tom, what can you tell us?'

Tom was on his phone and spoke breathlessly.

'I was walking towards Greyminster when I heard the explosion, Karen. I came straight down here. It's no more than five minutes from the parliament buidings. It's a scene of devastation, with shop windows blown out and masonry lying on the road. There are bodies strewn on the ground. I can see a young woman lying in a pool of blood and a child lying dead beside her. Across from her, medics are trying to help an elderly man. The police and ambulances are everywhere, taking care of the wounded. A bus has crashed into a wall and the windows are riddled with bullet holes. On the other side of the road a car bomb has ripped through a black limousine lying beside a blue people carrier, under the rubble of an adjacent building. The roads have been sealed off and armed police officers are guarding the perimeter. It's a scene of utter carnage.'

'Do we have any information about casualties?'

'No details yet, but it's obvious there are several fatalities and many, many wounded.'

'Do we know who was in the black limousine, Tom or why they were targeted?'

'We have no confirmed information yet but the fact that it is a black limousine of the sort used by senior Government officials would

suggest it is someone of importance. Ministry officials are being tight lipped but there are already rumours circulating that it is Sebastian Steele who, we know, had just concluded an interview with our own Denise Swann and was heading to a meeting in Greyminster.'

Within minutes a camera crew was on the scene and Tom now faced the camera from beyond the cordon which had been thrown around the scene. He repeated the same information in the same shocked and breathless manner.

'Do we know who was responsible, Tom?' Karen asked from the studio.

'It's too early to speculate, Karen. It has all the hallmarks of a terrorist attack but no-one has yet claimed responsibility.'

Thirty minutes later there was another news bulletin. Karen spoke in the sombre tone of a consummate professional.

'The identity of the victim of the car bombing in the centre of the capital has been confirmed as Sebastian Steele, the architect of the devolution agreement and the man widely credited with bringing peace back to the streets and unity to the Nation. He was travelling from the Independent Television Centre, where he had just concluded an interview, to Greyminster, where he was due to report on progress.'

They broke for a moment to show a photograph of Sebastian Steele and to run some footage of him entering and leaving a number of buildings and shaking hands with a number of people. She spoke again to Tom Whalley, at the scene.

'What news do we have about the other casualties?'

Joe leaned forward and listened more closely.

'There are twenty people confirmed dead and many more injured. The number of fatalities is likely to grow. Ambulances have been taking casualties to hospitals around the city depending on the severity of their injuries.'

Within an hour, Tom was able to report in a less breathless and more subdued tone that *'the city is in a state of shock, people are numb and the scene is something you would expect to see in a war zone, not in the centre of a major city.'*

A tourist who was nearby when the attack took place was able to describe how he heard the explosion and the gunfire and saw a plume of smoke rising from the scene. A woman on her way to work sobbed into a handkerchief as she described how she rounded a corner to see two men firing at the cars and people on the street. She watched with horror as one man emerged from a four-wheeled drive vehicle and put something under the black limousine. A moment later, motorcycles came out of the side street and the three gunmen were driven away, she said. The car exploded and flames gushed from it.

'What did they look like?' Tom was sombre again but unable to hide a tinge of excitement.

'They were Islamic terrorists, just like you see on the television.'

It was the perfect place to conclude.

'Karen, it's back to you in the studio.'

Joe turned off the television. He stared blankly at the screen. A car pulled up outside with a screech of brakes. Alan burst through the door.

'Have you heard?'

He nodded numbly.

'My God, Joe, Sebastian is dead.'

He nodded again. He couldn't speak.

'The shit'll hit the fan now.'

'Hannah.' Joe reached for his phone to call home. 'God knows what she must be thinking. Steele was her Godfather.'

It was D.I. Stone who answered.

'Where are you, Joe?' he asked.

'I want to speak to Hannah.'

'She's asleep. The doctor gave her some medication. The news has hit her hard, especially without you.'

It felt like an accusation.

'Sebastian Steele was her Godfather.'

'I know...but her father...Haven't you heard? He was in the car with Steele. He's dead.'

Joe reeled as if from a blow to the chest. 'Tell her I'm coming home. Tell her I'll be there as soon as I can.'

'It won't be easy to get through, Joe. There are already people out on the street. By this evening there'll be riots.'

'I don't care. Tell her I'm coming.'

'Joe, listen to me. Things are chaotic right now but Hannah and the children are safe. I promise you. I promised Martin Savage I would look after his family and I intend to do so. Don't ask me how I know, but it's my guess that trains will be cancelled within a day and only essential traffic will be allowed along the main arteries. The AS6, the AS1 and AS5 will be closed to anything else. You'll not get through.'

'I need to be with my family. They need me now.'

'Okay, okay, I can see I won't persuade you to wait, but be careful. You're no use to anyone dead. Hannah has her sister with her. She's here now. Do you want to speak...?'

The phone had been snatched peremptorily from his hand.

'Do you see what you've done? Do you see?'

'I'm coming home, Lisa. You were right, you've been right all along. How's Hannah?'

'It's rather late to be worrying about Hannah. What do you think will happen once the guards are removed? They won't be here for long now that Sebastian Steele is dead. It was only his influence that made it possible in the first place.'

'Stone says...'

'Stone!' She spat the name. 'Where are you, Joe?'

'At Alan's.'

'Are you safe?'

'I think so.' He didn't mention the events of the previous evening. There was no point now. There were other priorities.

'You should be here with Hannah.'

'I know. You can't make me feel any worse than I do.'

More calmly, Lisa told him 'Stone is right, though; it won't be easy to get back. Everything's a mess. No-one seems to know what's going to happen. It feels like we're sitting on a powder keg in a ring of fire.'

'What can I do?'

'*Do*? There's nothing you can *do*. It's far too late for you to *do* anything. Father was just the same, always wanting to *do* something, always trying to change the world. And what good did it do? Now he's dead and we're alone.' Her voice broke and she sobbed.

'I'm sorry.'

Lisa fought back her tears. 'I know. I know. He could no more help himself than you can. You're both infuriating. But you've got to understand, Joe. Now he's gone and Sebastian Steele has gone, everything has changed. We're not safe anymore.'

'Tell Hannah I called. Tell her I'll phone this evening. And tell Stone I'll phone back. I've got this idea...but I need to think.'

'How will you get back?' Alan asked when Joe put down the phone. 'You could go around the conurbation, I suppose, avoid the main city centres.'

Joe shook his head. 'It'd take too long. I'll head straight through the zone. When I get through it's only fifty miles.'

'The whole place is in chaos.'

'Yes, but...'

'What about the guys who are after you? They'll expect you to go home. They'll be waiting.'

'I know. It's time to stop running, I guess. You've seen High Noon – Gary Cooper and all that?' He laughed half-heartedly.

'You need a plan.'

'I may have one.'

'You'll need a better one.'

Joe telephoned Stone towards lunchtime.

'Don't patronise me, Stone, and don't lie to me. How long have I got before they take away the bodyguards?'

Stone sighed. 'I got a call. They want me to withdraw from here by the end of tomorrow. I won't leave, of course. I made a promise and I intend to keep it, but I won't be able to stall them forever. There'll be a couple of part time guards for maybe three or four days. I'll take some leave and stay on a bit longer myself because don't like being manipulated and I feel as if someone is tugging on my strings.'

'Is my family in danger?'

There was a silence.

'It's difficult to say at the moment.'

'Is Lisa there? Is that why you can't speak?'

'Yes.'

'Just yes or no, then.'

'In which case, I think yes.'

'They know I'll come home?'

'Yes.'

'They won't stop until I'm dead or I stop them.'

'I believe that's the case. Things have changed for all of us.'

'Just one more thing, Inspector, do you believe that Islamic terrorists were behind the assassination?'

The silence was even longer.

'The evidence certainly points in that direction. Some people are very keen that they should be blamed.'

'That's not what I asked. Do you personally believe they were behind it?'

'Generally, I believe what I'm told. However, in moments of independence I'm inclined to make certain observations which many of my colleagues share. It seems to me that Piers Goodwin and other political figures on the far right were remarkably well positioned to take advantage of this event. Their actions were rapid and well co-ordinated. They're using social media already to call out their forces. It looks like they were primed. Goodwin, in particular, was very quickly on the front foot. I suspect a number of less salubrious newspapers will be preparing to stir things up. By contrast the Islamist groups seemed genuinely surprised at the assassination, although I doubt they will shed many tears.'

'Is someone steering enquiries?'

'Goodwin has a lot of followers in influential positions.'

'Who can I trust?'

'Trust? I'd avoid the word, if I were you.'

'Tell Hannah I'll phone this evening. Look after them for me, Stone.'

He was about to put the phone down when he heard Hannah's tired voice in the background. The door had opened and closed with its familiar sound. She grabbed the phone from Stone. Joe heard him murmur, 'I'll leave you to talk,' and the door closed.

'Joe? Oh, I'm so pleased to hear your voice. It's awful, Joe.' She broke down and sobbed. 'Where are you?' she asked at last. 'Are you with Alan? Are you safe?'

'Yes. Don't worry. I'm fine. I've seen the news on the television.'

'Are you coming home? Stone says you should wait but I want you here. I need you.'

'I'm coming home,' Joe said firmly. 'It may take a few days, but I'm coming home. I'm not running any more. I'm sick of it. We'll be together.'

'Things are a real mess, Joe. Stone thinks we're on the edge of something really bad. There are riots breaking out all over.'

'I'll get through, even if I have to walk all the way.'

'You've got to go through the zone, where the troubles are worst, Joe. Stone says parts of it'll be cut off within a day or two.'

'Stone seems to know an awful lot for a simple detective inspector.'

'He's been very good to us. Don't listen to what Lisa says. You know how she can be when she's worried about anything. She hits out at whoever's nearest.'

'I doubt that Inspector Stone is quite what he appears. He probably works for the Security Services.'

'Should I trust him?'

'We have to trust him. There's no-one else now.'

'The girls ask about you every day. They know something's wrong. I haven't told them about Father yet. I don't know how to start.'

'Your father was one of the finest men I ever met.'

Hannah laughed sadly. 'He liked you. You could never aspire to the heights of Sebastian Steele in his esteem, but you ranked very highly.'

'I'm not sure I deserved it. A better man would be by your side, not at the other end of the country but you'll be safe while Stone's there. It's still me they want, not you.'

'I'm scared, Joe. I'm really scared. What about the children? What about Jessica and Meg? What have they ever done?'

It was another blow, another silent accusation. She was right. They'd done nothing to deserve this. But had he? He went over it, time and time again. Why would anyone continue week after week, month after month, seeking revenge for what he'd done? One of the thugs was Caine's brother – so what? People got over worse things? Was it because he was Jewish then or did Caine and Goodwin think people still looked up to him as some sort of figurehead for tolerance and the new future? If so, they were seriously deluded. People would have forgotten far more important things than Joe Savage during those two years.

Maybe there was something else. He had insulted Piers Goodwin at the trial, and in the full glare of the media. Goodwin, a megalomaniac, a vain narcissist and a self-publicist with the sense of humour of a lava flow, had been a laughing stock for days. He tried to brush it aside with a few witticisms and snide remarks but the image clung to him like a bad smell. Goodwin wouldn't have forgotten that. Maybe he was needling away in the background, goading Caine, looking for a victim so he could show how dangerous it was to cross his people, how it was impossible to hide from their retribution.

Enemies in high places, he thought, *that was just what he needed.*

'Listen to me, Hannah. Nothing is going to happen to you or the girls. I promise you. I promise. I'm coming home and I won't leave again, not ever.'

'Yes, but how can you stop them, especially now my father...' She sobbed again.

'I don't know. I'll think of something. There'll be no more hiding, Hannah, no more running away. It's over.'

'Shall I tell Stone?'

'He knows. Tell him I'll phone when I get the chance. I need to think. I've got this idea but....'

'What if you're caught or killed?'

'No-one is going to kill me. I've got too much to live for. Besides, I've promised. I always keep my promises, don't I?'

It was as if he were speaking to a child. You made promises like that to the very young, reassuring them, comforting them, telling them that bad things could never happen. But children knew better, didn't they? It was adults who lied to themselves.

'Will you be alright, Hannah?'

'I've got the children. They keep my mind off things. And Lisa is here. A neighbour has taken her two in the daytime and Adam is with them at night. Half the time she drives me to distraction, but we help each other through.'

'When's the funeral?'

'I don't know yet; Stone says next week probably, if they release the body. There'll be a lot of people. I don't think I could cope alone.'

'I'll be there.'

'I love you.'

'I love you too.'

He closed the phone and sat back. 'I've got to go, Alan.'

'And your plan?'

'I've got to think it through. It's risky and I'll need a lot of help. I don't know... I'll phone you.'

Chapter 19

Akmal too had been watching the news. Now he hurried purposefully along a narrow alleyway behind a terraced row of brick houses towards one in particular. His followers had already gathered together in the kitchen at the rear. He heard their laughter as he opened the door from the walled yard and walked in. They were in celebratory mood. They pulled up chairs around the kitchen table, still talking excitedly.

He looked at them contemptuously and frowned.

'It's a masterstroke,' Salim was saying. 'There'll be riots on the streets.'

Akmal was silent. He looked at them angrily, his eyes dark and brooding.

'What?' he asked menacingly. 'What are you talking about?' His voice was restrained like a coiled spring. His companions didn't seem to notice.

'Sebastian Steele is dead,' Salim cried. His narrow face creased in callous laughter, as narrow and drawn as his wiry frame, 'It's all over the news.'

The group were jubilant. They laughed and shouted. Akmal watched them impassively until slowly they became aware of the menacing look in his eyes and fell silent.

'I want to know who's responsible,' he said, the syllables of his fury precise and crisp.

'Who cares? It's a victory.' Salim's voice was hesitant, almost apologetic.

'I want to know who did it,' he repeated. 'Did you hear me or shall I repeat it?' He leaned towards the speaker. His eyes were unflinching and threatening.

'It doesn't matter who did it. He's dead. He's fucking dead.'

Akmal landed a blow across his face. Salim fell back and reached a hand to his bleeding mouth. He looked angrily at Akmal, his fists clenched. For a moment they faced each other, then Salim turned away and sat down on a wooden chair. 'I was just saying, that's all; what's the matter with you?' The others fell silent.

'Can't you see there's something wrong?' Akmal yelled. 'Ask yourselves, why didn't we know about it? Why weren't we told to prepare?'

'There are other cells in Zarten. It must've been one of them.'

'No.' Akmal hit the table heavily with his fist. 'That was the mistake we made during the riots. We had no unifying structure. It was agreed we would never make that mistake again. We have to find out who did it. If it's one of ours, I need to know. Two of you get on phones and computers and find out. The rest of you get out on the street and make sure our people are ready to fight. Quickly, before it's too late. Now get out. Get out! I need to think.'

The group dispersed. Only when they were outside did they speak.

'He's lost it; he's fucking lost it.' Salim held a handkerchief to his bleeding mouth. 'It doesn't matter who did it.'

'Are you going to tell him that?' someone asked from the back of the group. 'No, I thought not, so let's get on with what we need to do, shall we?'

They disappeared quickly in different directions.

Akmal sat at the table for a moment, deep in thought. He walked through to the small, sparsely furnished lounge. A laptop sat on a table by the window. He switched it on and waited. The television, mounted on the wall behind him, was giving the latest news. There were nationalist protestors out on the streets already. A mosque had been attacked, an Asian shop fire-bombed. It looked like they'd already got the upper hand.

'They were waiting,' Akmal muttered. 'They were ready.'

The reassuring face of a prominent, well-manicured politician stared seriously out of the screen. He spoke firmly as he reassured viewers that there would be no descent into anarchy. The police and the army were ready to intervene. Unrepresentative groups who performed such despicable acts, he said, would never be allowed to destroy the way of life the people of the country cherished. The Government, of which he was a Minister, would do all it could to ensure the devolution settlement would succeed. They owed it, he said, to Sebastian Steele and Martin Savage.

Akmal glared with distaste at the face on the television.

'What does that complacent fool know?' he muttered. Didn't he realise the white nationalists were already mustering their political forces? Didn't he understand that newspapers would soon be fanning the flames of racial hatred? Soon that arrogant fool wouldn't have a job at all. There'd be a new party in Government.

'We weren't ready,' Akmal muttered. 'We weren't ready and they knew it.'

He turned to the computer. If he was going to stop them, he had to act quickly. He had to draw out all the forces at his disposal and concentrate them in key areas of the city. They had to wrench the initiative now or it would be too late.

'This time it's civil war,' he murmured. A momentary exhilaration stirred him and drove away his fears. 'Civil war,' he repeated.

He didn't intend to lose.

Chapter 20

Joe took a local bus to Triente that afternoon. It was early evening before he caught the train towards the Devolved Zone. Nobody disturbed him, nobody spoke. At each successive stop a few people got off and fewer clambered aboard. At town after town the stations were deserted. People were staying at home, waiting to see what happened. They would close their doors and watch the news and the same questions would be asked over and over again. Who was responsible for this outrage? Why did they do it? What did they hope to gain? But what would concern them most was another, deeper question. It would be whispered quietly when the children had gone to bed. *What happens now?*

A young couple had been sitting opposite him but now they moved to empty seats where they could be alone. They cast a couple of glossy magazines on the seats beside them and spoke in soft voices. A hush of conversation drifted from further down the carriage. A guard passed once to check tickets, and once a trolley was wheeled past offering coffee and biscuits. That was all. Everyone was subdued and anxious. Stop by stop more people left and the carriage grew quieter. No-one was heading towards the cities unless they had to. Tomorrow, offices and factories would be empty and silent. Everyone knew the next few days would be unpredictable.

He gazed out of the carriage window. They'd passed the northern towns now, mercifully without trouble, and had sunk once again into the darkness of countryside and scattered villages. Everything outside was hunched under glowering, overwhelming clouds. Rain was falling and the stream of water created crazy patterns down the glass through which he glimpsed the lights of houses, roads and cars. Crazy patterns to match his crazy thought, he told himself. As the minutes passed, the lights became fewer and the gaps between clusters wider. The train passed rising banks of fields and low hills where the rain intensified and a dark mist gathered. Night time was arriving early.

It was eleven o'clock before the lights of towns began to emerge from the darkness. Twenty minutes later, the train pulled to an unexpected halt several miles short of the first, major conurbation. The lights went off and the passengers sat in an eerie darkness. For several minutes, nothing happened. Then the train began to move again, but now it was retreating, moving slowly back towards the darkness from which it had emerged. The guard entered the carriage.

'We'll be going no further tonight. The line is blocked ahead of us. There are riots everywhere.'

There was a silence. People glanced at each other across the dark carriage, sharing a fear they couldn't express. Suddenly, an elderly woman gasped. Her cry broke upon them like a shockwave. She pointed through the window. Outside, a number of figures were moving like ghosts in the darkness. They were passing the train and heading onwards into the city, like scavengers heading towards a kill.

'What do these people want?' she cried. 'I don't understand. Why can't they leave us alone?'

The train passed briefly beside a main road and street lights cast a dull glow. Joe watched figures pass in twos and threes, their faces caught momentarily in the subdued light. Some carried baseball bats or clubs but most were unarmed. An occasional figure wore a rifle strapped across his back. Only once did one of them stop. He turned towards the train and picked up a stone. The glass of Joe's window cracked but did not shatter.

'Where are they all going?' the elderly woman cried.

'They're going to where the fighting is.' the young man said. He looked up from his phone where he was watching the latest news. 'Mosques and churches are burning, shops have been looted, businesses destroyed. There are barricades in the streets. Everything is falling apart.'

The train lurched to a standstill in darkness once more.

Another stone cracked against the window. Joe looked around. The woman, the young couple, two middle aged men and him – they were the only people left. The carriage lights flickered on.

'Turn the lights off,' Joe called. 'We might as well be on television.'

The guard spoke into a handset and the lights went out.

'What do we do now?' Joe asked.

'Stay here. It's safer than out there.'

'We can't just sit here. Sooner or later they'll turn on us.'

The guard spoke urgently on the handset. He turned back to Joe. 'We're going to try to ease back towards the last village. There's a stop there which we don't use on this service. There's not much there, a shop, a hotel and a few houses but it'll be enough – and better than here.'

'Call the hotel, tell them we're coming.'

He nodded.

The train slowly edged backwards, metre by metre, as if trying to avoid attention. It slipped into the darkness, moving slowly, invisibly away. Behind it the wave of silent ghostly figures parted to allow it passage. Their attention was elsewhere, focussed on the conflict towards which they were moving, to the battle waiting for them. Soon they disappeared altogether as the railway line turned away from the roads. Eventually the few lights of the tiny junction flickered into fragile life behind them.

'There's the hotel.'

They pulled slowly towards the stop. The lounge lights in the hotel shone dull red behind closed curtain. A door opened and a beam of light shone like a searchlight. It seemed to lock onto them, creating a wide, bright pathway. The carriage doors opened with a hiss.

'Quickly now,' the guard said.

He stood by the door as the young couple and the two men jumped down and ran to the hotel porch. Welcoming arms drew them inside. Joe saw half a dozen other figures emerge from different carriages and run or stumble indoors. With the guard, he helped the elderly woman from the train and walked her across the grass and the road to the open door. The driver hurried in behind them. The door closed, the lock was turned and bolts slid to. Coffee and sandwiches were set out on tables and the landlord busied himself resurrecting the warmth of a log fire from dying embers. A television on the wall repeated the sombre news over and over and each repetition added to the fear and gloom.

There were just fourteen of them in the lounge bar - the driver and guard, Joe, the old lady, the two men and the young couple and six people from other compartments, mainly older people trying to get back home before the trouble intensified. They murmured quietly to each other and watched the scenes on the television in mesmerised disbelief. They were part of that now, playing a walk-on part in the drama, the shocked onlookers at the scene of a tragedy.

Chapter 21

It had all happened so quickly. At first the news had been optimistic. Within hours of the assassination, groups of people of every ethnic background had gathered together on the streets. It was an expression of faith, an expression of belief in a cause for which victims had died. There was an outpouring of shock and grief. Silent vigils were held as evening darkness gathered and people got together to pay tribute to the men who had brought them peace and hope.

For a few hours, the nation held its breath. It looked as if things might be alright. If they could get through just one night without violence, perhaps things would settle down and the process of reconciliation and rebuilding could begin again. Public figures began to emerge from all quarters, calling for calm, offering reassurance, gathering communities together within a protective wall of what they repeated over and over again were universal values.

There were sporadic outbursts of violence of course, but it looked initially as if the response across Zarten, the Devolved Zone, and the rest of the country would be the same. Shock and grief would reinforce the common values which now bound people into one diverse but unified nation.

Stone and his colleagues knew better. They heard different sounds rumbling from the bleak recesses of the night. There was a rush of activity on social media and the dark web. Encrypted messages flew like silent darts. Something was happening. The sounds were sombre and menacing. They called for revenge, for retribution and for rebellion. Creatures deep in the troubled darkness were emerging and preparing for the moment they had long awaited.

Stone, sitting with Hannah and Lisa as events unfolded, saw his worst fears realised. He saw hoards emerging. Militant nationalists were calling out their forces. He saw quite clearly now that the events which followed the assassination were as carefully planned as the murder itself and they were directed to one end – insurrection and the destruction of the accord.

On television news, one question was repeated over and over again. Who was behind the assassination? There were rumours and there was a great deal of speculation but no satisfactory conclusions. There was insufficient evidence. On social media there was no such uncertainty. The attack had all the features of the trademark savagery of Middle Eastern groups. It was an act of brutality comparable to anything that had happened before, in this and other capitals across the western world. Who else could it be?

The group at the bar slowly dispersed to the rooms the hotel owner had placed at their disposal. Joe shared a room with the guard and the train driver. They had little left to say to each other. Exhausted by the events of the evening and calmed to somnolence by the combined effect of food, warm drinks and brandy, they soon slept. Perhaps the morning would bring better news.

Joe fell asleep thinking of Hannah, of Jessica and Meg. Thank goodness, he thought, they're far away from scenes of rioting. At least they were safe from that.

When he awoke the next morning, he'd made up his mind what to do. He would continue his journey home, regardless of conditions in the city. He would find a way through the huge central conurbations of the Devolved Zone, even if it had to be on foot. Hannah and Jessica and Meg were waiting for him, fifty miles further south and they were connected to him not by a meandering, circuitous thread but by a straight, broad line. He would follow that line and go home.

He dressed quickly and went down to the lounge, his rucksack already packed and ready. The hotel owner emerged from the kitchen where he'd been preparing breakfast.

'You're early. Did you sleep well?'

'Very; can we switch on the television? I want to catch up on what's happening before I leave.'

Together, they watched the early morning headlines. It was just after seven o'clock.

The news was worse. Mosques and synagogues in different cities had been targeted in co-ordinated attacks. Individuals had been targeted and beaten; shops had been ransacked. There had been several deaths. Prominent politicians called for calm; but others softly fanned the flames of hatred. There were riots and counter-riots on the streets. Roads from North to South past the Devolved Zone were impassable. Rail services were suspended. All flights from Central International Airport were postponed. Only essential traffic and convoys of heavily armed vehicles moved along the major roads.

From a room in Greyminster, the chancellor addressed the nation. She sat behind a polished desk, her hands clasped in front of her, and spoke directly to camera as she called for calm and restraint. She expressed again her grief and horror at the death of Sebastian Steele and the other victims. She mentioned Martin Savage in generous terms and noted his great contribution to the peace. She described how the members of the Government had met overnight and had decided, for the safety and security of the general public and the state, to call upon the armed forces to restore calm to the streets and informed the audience in the most sombre terms that it was necessary and correct to put in place a curfew in those areas where the violence had been most extreme, particularly in the conurbations of the newly established Devolved Zone. She called upon everyone to comply with the curfew and to stay indoors after eight o'clock that evening. She refused to lay the blame at any door and asked people to wait for the outcome of the investigation.

Her broadcast was followed by interviews with the leaders of the two main opposition parties and local politicians. The message was the same. Stay calm, stay indoors and let the police and the armed forces do their work.

The hotel owner stood up and turned back towards the kitchen.

'They're not very convincing, are they?' he murmured. 'I think they're terrified of what's about to happen.'

'Do you think a curfew will hold?' Joe wondered.

The hotel owner glanced back. 'Do you?' he said. The door closed behind him.

He returned a moment later and left plates and dishes on a table. Then he brought cutlery and a jug of milk. Cereal and cups and saucers followed.

'Right, that's it for now, until the others come down. What are your plans?'

'I've got to get home,' Joe said.

'Where's home?'

'Near Dowlheim,' Joe told him.

'But that's beyond the Devolved Zone. You've seen the news. You'll never get through.'

'I have to. I promised.'

'Promises won't make it happen,' the landlord said doubtfully.

'It'll be quiet now for a few hours. Even those bastards have to sleep, don't they?'

'If you reach the Zone before curfew you'll still need somewhere to stay. Do you know anyone?'

Joe nodded. 'Maybe,' he said. 'There's someone I met on the way up here.'

'Can't you wait a day or two and see what happens? Maybe the troops will settle things down again?'

'No, I've got to go. My family need me. My wife's father has died, just recently. There's the funeral and everything...'

'I'm sorry. Jesus, what a mess,' the landlord murmured. He turned back to the screen where a picture of Sebastian Steele had appeared. 'I had a lot of respect for Steele,' he said. 'I couldn't say that for many politicians. He was a good man. I sometimes wonder if there are enough people like him left.'

Joe turned sharply. 'There are; there have to be. Otherwise, what's left for us? What future is there for our children?' He looked at the clock on the wall. 'How far is it to city?'

'The way things are at the moment it'll take you several hours. You start to reach the built-up areas after about twelve miles or so, but from then on, it's just going to get harder and harder. Can't you find an easier route?'

Joe shook his head. 'I'll follow the main roads and the railway line.'

'You're going to walk?'

'I don't think I've much choice, do you? Maybe I'll hitch a lift here and there but I don't think many people will be driving that way. Have you got a map?'

The landlord brought a local map from a small bookcase which housed tourist information and leaflets.

'Take it. It won't be any use here for a while. We'll have a lot more refugees before we have tourists.' He smiled grimly. 'Still, at least we aren't in the firing line, like the poor souls where you're headed.'

'There'll be a lot of firing lines and a lot of gaps between. Maybe I'll get lucky.'

'I hope so.'

Some of the other guests made their way into the lounge. The young couple and the old woman were followed by the guard and the driver. They nodded a greeting, then sat and watched the news.

'Toast, jam, tea, coffee, cornflakes and a full, healthy breakfast,' the landlord told them. 'Anyone arguing with that?'

He retired, smiling in adversity, to the kitchen.

Joe sat by a table and checked his route. He could follow a road which ran alongside the railway line for several miles. He might be lucky and get a lift. If the road was bad, he could slip down onto the tracks and follow the railway into the city. There'd be no trains. If he could avoid the gangs, if the daylight brought some respite, if...if...

He frowned. The city - that was where his real difficulties would begin. How would he pass through that huge conurbation before the curfew? The dangers of being caught there after dark were many. The police and the army were one thing; but the white militias and Akmal's terrorist forces were quite another. He brushed the thought aside. Better to reach the city and worry about the future when he got there. At least it was in a direct line to his home.

Shortly after breakfast he donned his pack, bid a farewell to his fellow travellers and set off on his journey.

The landlord and the guard watched him from the window.

'Do you know him?' the landlord asked.

The guard shook his head.

'I didn't recognise him at first. He was that Jewish guy who testified against white thugs who attacked an Asian couple. He was on TV a bit, a couple of years back. Funny, I thought he was dead.'

'Yeah, I remember,' the guard said. 'Well, he won't find many friends where he's going.'

Chapter 22

Akmal paced the room. The other members of his group were assembled around the table. The tone was sombre and subdued. Salim licked his swollen lip, and watched Akmal closely.

'You discovered nothing – nothing.'

'No-one knew anything about it.' Salim was the only one to speak. The others glanced at each other and averted their eyes when Akmal caught them in a fiery stare. In the background, a television repeated the news over and over. He barely heard it.

'It was the white militias,' he said. 'We've been outmanoeuvred.'

'Does it matter? It serves our purpose well enough.' Salim stared at him sullenly.

Akmal looked at him with contempt.

'Why don't we just claim responsibility?' Salim continued. 'It's not too late.'

Akmal leapt forward and held Salim by the shoulders.

'Don't you understand yet? Listen to the news. Armed, white militias have surrounded the devolved parliament building. They've captured key installations. They control City Hall, the railway stations, news outlets. They're manning barricades on all the major roads. What possible use will it be to claim that we planned the Zarten attack?' He pushed Salim away. 'They want people to think it was us. What's the point in confirming precisely what they want people to believe? You're a fool, Salim. Don't you get it, even now? They want to bring the settlement to an end. They want to see riots on the streets. They want to reopen the conflict and this time they plan to win, and they have the advantage because they were prepared.'

He paced the room. 'Get me the map,' he snapped. 'We've got a lot of people out there now but we need them in the right places.' He pored over it and indicated key positions, streets, squares, housing estates.

'First we defend our own,' he said. 'We establish barricades here, here and here.' He pointed quickly at different locations. 'We consolidate what's ours and then begin to fight back. The troops and police will be paying more attention to the white militias for a while. We need to use that time and use it well.'

Akmal looked up at the television where a politician, grey-haired and well-dressed, was speaking in a confident and assured tone about the threat from minority factions such as his. It was Piers Goodwin.

'This was clever, very clever,' Akmal said. 'Everyone is convinced it was us. Now the politicians who have secretly supported the white nationalists for years are speaking out. They feel confident. Look at the papers too.' He picked one from the table and jabbed at the headline with a finger. 'They say these white thugs are defending democracy.'

'Nobody will believe them,' Salim said.

Akmal looked from Salim to the others with anger and contempt. 'Plenty of people will believe them. It's what they want to hear and it's their excuse. People are stupid.'

'So, we fight.'

He nodded. 'It wasn't our choice to begin now but we have no alternative. We're at war.'

Another face appeared on the television screen. It was a still photograph from some years previously. Akmal recognised it at once. It was Joe. He turned and watched.

The reporter recounted Joe's story and then explained that one of the victims of the assassination, the man who had died in the car beside Sebastian Steele, was Joe's father-in-law. Akmal heard his name with incredulity. Martin Savage was co-architect of the despised settlement, a formulator of policy, and one of the men responsible for the planning of the newly devolved administration. Akmal brought his fist down so heavily the edge of the wooden table fractured and broke away.

He turned and left the room. The door slammed heavily behind him.

Chapter 23

Stone was standing at the end of the garden. He was talking to Casey, the agent he'd brought to the house to act as bodyguard to Hannah and the children - one of his own people, he told them, completely reliable.

The children liked Casey.

'He's funny. He tells us stories about when he was a little boy,' Meg said.

'Sometimes he has sweets in his pocket,' Jessica said.

'So long as he does his job,' Lisa muttered, 'I don't care how nice he is.'

Hannah stared out from the kitchen window and watched the two men. Meg pulled up a chair and climbed beside her.

'Where's Jessica?' Hannah asked.

'She's in the lounge with Aunty Lisa. She's getting ready for school.'

'Why aren't you getting ready?'

'I'm going to stay at home today and look after you. You look sad.'

Hannah smiled and hugged her. 'That's very sweet but I'd rather you were at school. If I need looking after, I'm sure Lisa will manage. Now go and get ready.'

'Are you unhappy because of grandad?'

'Yes.'

'Jessica was crying last night but I looked after her.' She nodded seriously.

'I wondered why you were in the same bed this morning.'

'I'm good at looking after people.'

'Then you must go to school with Jessica and look after her there. See she doesn't get upset.'

'I'll tell her teacher to send for me if she's upset.'

'I've written a note for your class teachers and the head teacher. Will you take it for me?'

Meg nodded and clambered down.

She paused for a moment. 'I was upset too,' she said, 'so we were upset together.'

She ran through to the lounge.

Hannah turned back to the garden where Stone and Casey were still talking. She could tell by their posture and by the way they continually glanced round the garden and along the lane that they were worried.

A car drove past and they fell silent and watched it. The guard's arms hung by his side and Hannah knew from the way his hand moved towards his belt that he had a gun at his waist. She recognised the car. It was owned by a neighbour on his way to work in Dowlheim. He glanced towards the house as he passed. Hannah could imagine what he was thinking when he saw the two men. The car disappeared along the lane and Stone and the guard relaxed again.

Stone glanced back towards the house. He saw her and waved. It was a falsely reassuring wave, just as anxious as the smile that accompanied it. It was the sort of smile you presented to a crash victim. 'You'll be alright. Everything is okay. The ambulance will be here soon.' And all the time you feared the ambulance wouldn't arrive in time.

The kitchen door opened and the children ran through. She turned and smiled. Her smile carried the same false reassurance as Stone's. Everything will be alright. There's nothing to worry about. Grandad wouldn't want you to be upset.

Lisa came into the kitchen behind them.

'Now say goodbye to Mum,' she said, 'and go and stand with Inspector Stone and Mr. Casey until the car arrives.'

The children no longer went to school on the bus with the other children. They had a car and a driver. It was

Stone's idea. It was still a novelty and filled them with feelings of self-importance.

'It's because of Dad, isn't it?' Jessica had said, 'and now because of Grandad too. Inspector Stone is looking after us, isn't he?'

Hannah looked at Jessica and then at Meg. Her eyes were swollen and she looked tired. Poor Meg, she always seemed to carry the burden of the world's ills. She was so like her father and her grandfather.

'Can I stay at home?' Her lip trembled. 'I don't want to go to school today. Everyone will look at me.'

'No, they won't. Everyone will be really kind, won't they, Jessica?'

'You've got to come or I'll be on my own,' Jessica said. 'We'll stay together all day – at dinner time and playtime.'

'What if I get upset and cry in class?'

'Your teacher will understand and so will all your friends,' Hannah told her.

'Come on, Meg, let's go together.' Jessica held out a hand. Meg hesitated for a moment and then reached out her own tiny hand and the two girls walked down the path to the gate. Casey saw them approach and bent down to greet them. He said something and they laughed and then Jessica took his hand and Meg took Stone's and they stood at the gate.

'I like Inspector Stone,' Hannah said. 'And Casey is wonderful with the girls. He helps take their minds off Father.'

'Hm.' Lisa grunted. 'I suppose they're good for something then.'

'Oh Lisa, you're impossible. Well, I like them and the girls like them and, what's more, I trust them, so there.'

A car pulled up and a moment later they were gone.

'They'll be better at school,' Lisa said. 'It's no use them moping around the house all day.'

Hannah stared after them long after the car had disappeared from sight.

'It was good of you to come,' she said. 'But you have your own family to think of. You should go home.'

'You're my little sister. Where else would I be?'

'It's very kind of Adam to take time off work to look after Jade and Alec.'

'He sends his love. He wants to be here but...what's the point? The children are better at home. I'll stay till after the funeral.'

'We don't even know when the body will be released.'

They were silent for a moment, each with their own thoughts.

'Have you heard from Joe?' Lisa asked at last.

'No. I can't see how he'll ever get through now. Everything is so bad. It's been three days since he phoned and things seem to be getting worse rather than better.'

Stone came in through the door to the garden.

'Is there any tea? I've got a throat like a shingle beach.'

Lisa nodded towards the kettle.

'Anyone else?' he asked.

'No thanks.' Hannah sat down at the table beside the window. Lisa sat opposite.

'Is there any more news?' she asked, 'other than what we see on the television?'

'The violence is pretty much restricted to the Devolved Zone with just a few sporadic outbursts elsewhere. A couple of areas round the cities saw some trouble last night but they were pretty half hearted and quickly quelled. It looks like the curfew held in some places but not in others. That's the good news. Unfortunately, parts of the Devolved Zone are bad and getting worse and there are new riots breaking out in a number of Northern towns. It's fluid, hard to keep track. The troops are making a difference but there's still a lot of violence which they haven't contained. My information is that we should be tentatively confident - but these are early days.'

He glanced up at the television screen on the wall. It was turned low but, like televisions all across the country, it was rarely switched off. Things changed so quickly, outbreaks of violence erupted almost at random, like bush fires. You extinguished a fire in one place and another broke out somewhere else. No-one knew what would happen next and no-one wanted to miss the latest news. A smooth, silver-haired figure smiled benignly from the screen and spoke with assurance and reason.

'God, I hate that man,' Lisa muttered. 'He's poisonous.'

'He stirs hatred while giving all the appearance of being a benign, elderly grandfather. It's a gift.' Stone poured water into a teapot. 'Milk first then add the tea. The water should have gone off the boil before you add it to the pot, you know, for the best effect.'

'I doubt it will make much difference to a supermarket tea bag,' Lisa muttered.

'Like our friend there.' He indicated the smoothly polished face on the screen. 'No matter what he says or how he tries to market himself he's still just a cheap, supermarket tea bag - Piers Goodwin, mouthpiece of the far right. I met him once, you know. I was washing grease off my hands for days after.'

'He hated Sebastian Steele and my father,' Hannah said quietly. 'He probably hates us too.'

'The hatred of Piers Goodwin is a mark of honour.'

'Where did you meet him?'

'I had the dubious pleasure of hearing him speak. It wasn't a matter of choice. I was ordered to protect him from possible attack by a number of protestors, with whom I can now confess I had great sympathy. He has a wonderful knack of adding honey to poison and persuading his followers that the combination is not only harmless but positively beneficial. The audience was an eclectic mix of the frightened middle-aged and elderly middle classes, the discontented poor and a violent and unpleasant rabble. I marked out a couple of thugs in the audience – nasty types we'd had under surveillance off and on.' He grimaced. 'I see what you mean about these tea bags. I think I'll have coffee next time.'

'The coffee's no better. We haven't had much chance to shop recently.'

'The interviewer is having a go at Piers. Let's see how he handles it.'

Piers Goodwin smiled and pointed out to the interviewer where he was going wrong. He spoke for the majority, for those people who loved their country and their heritage, for those whose voices hadn't been heard by successive governments.

'Do you condemn the violence that is breaking out across the country?' he was asked again and again.

'I understand the anger and the outrage that has given rise to it. In our country we have vast numbers of people who do not share our values and who are bent on destroying our democracy. The very fabric of our society is being undermined. This recent assault is an example of the extent to which these people will go. The Government has completely failed to address the problem. It's hardly surprising that some of our citizens feel the need to act to save the country they love.'

'So, you condone the behaviour of right-wing nationalist groups in the zone controlled by the devolved administration and in other cities and towns across the country?'

Goodwin smiled a patronising smile and sighed. His words emerged slowly and reassuringly. 'I didn't say that. You are putting words in my mouth. I condemn the violence which made so many of our citizens believe they had no choice but to go out onto the streets to defend themselves. Even now our armed forces are being obliged, much against their will, to attack people who are doing nothing more than defend their homes and societies against the undemocratic forces who are attacking them.'

'What do you say to the people who suggest that the assassination of Sebastian Steele and the slaughter of all those innocent citizens were actually perpetrated by fringe elements on the right?'

'That's nonsense, absolute nonsense. It is fake news. Only one group had anything to gain from such an attack and it's more than clear who that is.'

The television screen went blank. Hannah threw the remote onto the table and looked out into the garden. 'Do you remember when Joe was on the television after the trial?' she said.

'Piers Goodwin called him a liberal opportunist who wanted nothing more than a moment of fame. Yes, I remember.' Lisa laughed. 'I also remember what Joe said. He never pulled any punches, did he?'

'Joe always said what he thought and believed, no matter what.'

'Like Father.'

'Yes.'

'*Piers Goodwin has raised himself on a pedestal,*' Stone quoted. '*Unfortunately, the foundation of that pedestal stands on a cess pit and one day soon he'll sink and become one with it, because beneath his polished veneer he's a shit and nothing more.*' Stone laughed. 'I remember it clearly. I doubt Goodwin has forgotten it either. The newspaper cartoonists had a field day. It's taken a long time for him to clamber back onto his perch.'

'Do you think he's behind the men who are persecuting Joe?'

'Yes, it's possible, maybe even likely. When I had to protect him, I stayed in the hall after the mindless hoard had disappeared, half of them full of self-righteous cant and the other half drooling blood from their jaws.'

'I thought you people were supposed to remain strictly neutral,' Lisa noted wryly. 'He's the leader of a political party, after all, and has a perfect right to air his foul views, provided he stays within the law.'

'Oh, Piers Goodwin always gives the appearance of being a model of political respectability. However, to answer your question, yes, I protect him when called upon but I also watch him carefully and I monitor every word he says and every person he meets. Goodwin is utterly ruthless, extremely cunning, a complete narcissist, and he never forgives people who show him up for what he really is.

'Anyway, at the end of the evening when the hall was almost empty and only a few sycophants were left, begging for autographs and the like, I noticed my two thugs standing at one side of the stage. After the last of the audience had gone, he walked across to them. He hadn't seen me. I was standing near the main entrance, checking security with a couple of officers. I was lost in the shadows.

'He was snapping orders at them and waving his arms about, all Hitler newsreel stuff. The shorter of the men was nodding and grovelling; looked like he was excusing himself. But not the second; no, he was quite different. He had the look of a wild animal, restrained but ferocious, you know?'

Hannah sat up and turned towards him.

'What were they like, these thugs?'

Stone looked at her and his eyes carried a message she clearly understood. 'The first looked like a nightclub bouncer, five eight or five ten maybe, neck like an ox, crew cut, ragged stubble, muscles and the tell-tale tattoos of the militant right - regulation right wing nutter. The second one, though, was distinctive. He was tall, maybe six foot five, maybe even an inch or two more. He was so pale he was almost white. Even his hair, cropped short as it was, was so blond it was almost indistinguishable from his head and face. He had a ghastly red scar across his cheek.'

Hannah had gone suddenly pale.

'Those are the men Joe warned me about, the men who are following him. The pale one's Nathan Caine.'

'When they finished talking, the two men walked down the hall towards me and I saw them close up. It wasn't a pleasant sight. The tall one had eyes like ice. I've seen some pretty unpleasant people in my line of work, but he was in a class of his own.'

'Did you know they were the men who were hunting for Joe?'

'Not then but soon after. I spoke to Sebastian Steele who, no doubt, spoke to your father. They chose not to burden you with information that might worry you and over which you had no control. Since then we've been investigating the connection between Goodwin and the movement these men represented but Goodwin is very, very careful.'

'You move in exalted circles for a mere Detective Inspector,' Lisa noted.

'Ah, I must apologise. It was a necessary subterfuge. There was no point making matters worse for you. My branch of law enforcement is rather more *specialised* than I led you to believe.'

'And when I phoned my father after our encounter by the pond...'

'He discussed his anxiety with Steele and it was agreed that I should appear on the scene for a while – just to be on the safe side.'

'And are we?' Hannah asked quietly.

'Are you what?'

'Safe,' Hannah said.

Stone ran his fingers through dark hair and grimaced.

'No,' he said finally. 'No, you're not safe at all. Of course, it's Joe they want, not you, but now that your protectors have gone, Goodwin can apply pressure of his own. He wants to force Joe to come back. If that means threatening you and the children then that's what he'll do.'

'He gets rid of the guards and Hannah gets left like a staked goat?'

'Yes.'

'Does Goodwin really have that much power?'

'Yes.'

'Can no-one stop him?' Lisa turned to him angrily.

'That's why I'm here. Wheels are turning. They're moving silently but they're moving nonetheless. One by one we're identifying those who share Goodwin's monstrous ideology.'

'And in the meantime?'

'In the meantime, Lisa, you need to go home. Your husband and your family need you and, to be completely frank, you're in the way here.'

Lisa howled a protest but Stone raised his hands and continued patiently. 'We'll have quite enough to do guarding Hannah and the children. I appreciate how much you want to be here with your sister, but you can help us more by moving back home.'

'I most certainly will not,' Lisa cried hotly. 'I've never heard of anything so absurd.'

'Please Lisa,' Hannah begged. 'Do as he asks; I'd rather you could stay, but Stone knows best.'

Lisa looked at Stone and then at Hannah.

'How do we know we can trust him? For all we know, he could be one of them. As soon as I'm gone, he'll send the guards away and you'll be in his power.'

Stone nodded. 'That is indeed a possibility thought not, if I may say so, a particularly logical one. We're I an enemy you can hardly suppose your presence here would cause me much concern – with all due respect, of course. I might even have the audacity to think you'd add to my bargaining power.'

'Joe said he was inclined to trust you,' Hannah said. 'I have to do the same.'

'Joe thinks the best of everyone; sometimes he can be a fool.'

'Please, Lisa. You'll be a phone call away and I'll speak to you every day, twice a day if you want.' She turned to Stone. 'Do you know yet when we can have the funeral?'

'Yes; the Government has expedited matters. Could I suggest early next week? That's five days? If Joe is going to get through, he should be here by then. The Government has plans for a memorial service for Steele, your father and the other victims the following week.'

'There seems to be an unseemly haste to get this done,' Lisa grumbled.

'I assume you want to use the ceremonies to galvanise opinion behind everything my father and Sebastian Steele represented?'

Stone nodded. 'It may make all the difference. We're on a knife edge.'

'You can't exploit a funeral like this,' Lisa cried. 'It's immoral.'

'It's what Father would have wanted, Lisa. You know that.'

Lisa glared at Stone. 'He wanted to be buried with our mother in the local churchyard. I assume we can respect his wishes.'

'Of course - I suggest you make arrangements.'

'And in the meantime?'

'In the meantime, you go home, Lisa, and stay with your family. I stay here and wait to hear from Joe. I hope to God he makes it in time.'

Chapter 24

They didn't hear from Joe the next day, or the next. Three more days and the funeral would take place. Stone was growing anxious. He tried to hide it from Hannah but he was beginning to believe that Joe wouldn't get through in time and that he'd been caught up in the violence in the city, maybe even hurt or killed. To add to his concerns, there were now only two bodyguards left, hardly enough to maintain the security of the family. Casey still patrolled the garden and the lane when he could, and another guard appeared twice a day to drive the children to and from school. Stone had persuaded two other colleagues to help him unofficially just until the funeral passed. Their covert presence offered a further degree of security. One was working with the janitor at the primary school Jessica and Meg attended. From there he could watch for any unwelcome visitors or intruders. The other monitored the approach roads for a couple of hours each day. For many hours of the day   and throughout the night, though, Stone was left alone with only Casey occasionally there to help him, when he could free himself from other duties.

Another day passed and still there was no word from Joe. Two days to the funeral. Anxiety turned to dread. Then, late that evening a call finally came through. The signal was bad and Joe's voice was indistinct. The call lasted only a matter of minutes.

'Where are you, Joe? What? What did you say? I can barely hear you?'

He listened closely.

'It's the day after tomorrow at two. Will you make it, Joe?' Joe's voice crackled indistinctly. 'What? Can you repeat that, Joe? You want me to contact who? Sheila Jones?

Who's she? Yes, yes, I understand. Yes, I will, I'll make sure she's here. Why is it important? Joe? Joe?'

The line had gone dead.

'What did he say? Is he safe?' Hannah was standing beside him.

'Yes, yes I think so. I couldn't make out much of what he said but yes, he's okay.'

'Where is he?'

'He didn't say. He wants me to find some journalist – Sheila Jones. Have you heard of her?'

'Yes.' Hannah's voice suggested a not-too-favourable opinion. 'I've met her.'

'What do you know about her?'

'She writes for one of the serious papers. She came here and spoke to us after the trial and then she wrote about Joe. I didn't like what she said. I didn't like her. She was very intelligent and very professional but her manner was artificial, like something she'd learnt from a book. She looked around our home as if she was weighing and valuing it. By the time she left I felt as if we'd been dissected on a laboratory table.'

For a moment she seemed disinclined to speak. Stone waited.

'She said Joe was being exploited by the Government for their own propaganda. She implied he was foolish and gullible to do as they asked. Her article wasn't always kind. When I read it, I felt as if we'd been betrayed. We'd allowed her into our house and this was what we got in return.'

'What did Joe think?'

'Joe respected her. He thought she was honest, that she didn't flatter and she didn't compromise and just wrote what she thought. Joe appreciated that sort of honesty even when it painted an unflattering picture of him. Typical Joe, isn't it?'

'Why does Joe want me to contact her, do you think?'

'He thinks he can trust her. I just hope he's right. What else did he say? Did you tell him about the funeral? Will he be here in time?'

'The line was bad. I couldn't hear much.'

'How did he sound?'

'Fine, he sounded fine – a bit tired, maybe.'

The door opened. Meg, in her pyjamas, crept in and clambered on the seat beside her mother. She snuggled close and yawned and rubbed tired eyes.

'Was that Daddy?'

'Yes.'

'Why didn't he speak to me?'

'It was a very bad signal, Meg. He could only speak for a minute. He didn't even have time to speak to me. He just spoke to Inspector Stone.'

'Is he coming home soon?'

'Very soon; now, come on, you should be in bed.'

'Five minutes?'

She curled in a warm ball close to her mother. Her eyes were already closing. Hannah held her close.

'Why would anyone...?' she began.

'Hush, better not to think about it.' Stone smiled.

'I think Joe has a plan,' Hannah said. 'Why else would he want to meet a journalist?'

Stone held the doors open as she carried Meg upstairs. He watched as Hannah lay the little girl's tousled head on the pillow and pulled the duvet over her, then knelt beside her and stroked her cheek. 'Daddy will be home soon,' she whispered. 'He promised.' Behind her, Jessica turned in her sleep and murmured incoherent sounds. Hannah bent forward and kissed her forehead.

From the doorway, Stone looked on and he too knew the burden Joe carried. That promise, and all the others that came before it, were like layers of rock pressing down on him, crushing him. Only hope sustained him against their relentless pressure.

Where are you, Joe? He thought. Where the bloody hell *are* you?

He didn't want to tell Hannah that behind Joe, quite distinctly even with that poor signal, he'd heard the unmistakable crack of repeated gunfire and the rumble of explosions.

Chapter 25

Behind the house where Hannah and the children lived, a field rose gradually towards a small copse of trees. As darkness drifted over the skyline, falling on field and trees like a black shroud, a solitary figure emerged and made his way towards the house. He moved slowly over the uneven ground pitted by the hooves of cattle. There was little to guide him. The moon was no more than a narrow crescent, a sickle blade in the darkness. It cast no light, even when it wasn't obscured by the clouds which crossed rapidly on a secret breeze which barely stirred the earth beneath. A more poetic nature might have visualised the clouds scurrying away from something they feared in the exposed sky and heading towards safety beyond the distant horizon. His, however, was a prosaic mind. He concentrated on each footstep and cursed the darkness so necessary to his task.

He bent low and crept towards the house. A light appeared in an upstairs window. He stopped and waited, resting one knee on the damp grass. A figure crossed the light, a child he thought. A moment later it crossed back - from bathroom to bedroom, he imagined. The light turned off as suddenly as it had appeared. He waited a moment then crept on, stumbling occasionally and swearing under his breath. Gradually, the silhouette of the house began to emerge from the background of trees, to stand darkly against the sky.

He moved to the right, away from the road where he knew a car was parked, its occupant sleeplessly watching the lane. He could approach the side of the house from here without fear of being seen. There was a stone wall to cross, some shrubs and trees to negotiate, then a garden shed and a pathway. He could picture the route clearly. He had been watching it from the copse for several hours. He left the binoculars beside a solitary holly tree growing just beyond the perimeter of the copse where he would collect them on his return.

His orders were clear. Caine had been very precise. He was to take no risks. He was to avoid being seen at all costs. He was to patrol the perimeter, check at each window and door for any weakness, search out vulnerable spots, ensure there were no traps laid, no men hidden there, waiting. He was to find a way of breaking into the house.

'You're a professional,' Caine said. 'That's why you're here. You're the best, or so they tell me. Case the place as if you were going to burgle it. Let me know how we can get in unseen.'

So here he was, applying his professional skills as he had so many times before. So why was he so fearful? He expected a certain tension, a certain anxiety – that was good; it kept him sharp. He knew the risks. If someone saw you, you could leg it, run as fast and as far as possible. If you were caught – well, that was a risk you took. The occasional spell in prison was something he expected. It formed an inevitable part of his CV. This was different, though. He knew he couldn't fail. He couldn't let himself be seen. He couldn't be caught. Caine had made that clear. He shuddered as he remembered how Caine had spoken. You didn't cross Caine, not ever. People who crossed him or failed him didn't live long.

Caine held him in that icy stare. The livid scar pulsed, like a warning.

'Don't disappoint me,' he said. 'I don't like disappointment. It makes me bitter and angry. I do things I regret. Do you understand me?'

He understood alright. It was impossible not to understand. A cold, hard intelligence shone from Caine like a laser.

He crossed a patch of soft ground just before the low wall which surrounded the side garden. Suddenly, from his feet, a snipe rose and disappeared into the darkness, twisting invisibly in the air and calling in alarm. He crouched down and listened but the only sound was his heart pounding in his chest. No lights appeared in the windows, no sound emerged from the house or the road. He waited.

He slipped over the wall and dropped down to creep through bushes towards the cover of the garden shed where he rested his back against its roughcast wall and breathed heavily, feeling the sweat down his back.

He looked towards the house and then slipped on soft feet towards the nearest window. The curtains were drawn. He drew a small torch from his pocket and checked the window lock, then crept slowly round the house. He wanted to finish the job quickly now, find what he needed and get back to the security of the copse. He moved round the house and checked each window methodically. They were all double glazed and securely locked. The doors were the same. Only one window offered hope of easy access, a small, rear window into a utility room which housed a washing machine and freezer. It was single glazed and a light catch fastened it to the wooden frame. He made a mental note and crept to the side of the house where the kitchen looked out over the garden. He had to be careful now; the car, if it was still there, was parked near the front of the house just beyond the trees.

The kitchen blinds were raised but there was no light within. He raised his head slowly above the sill, keeping his back to the trees so the slender beam from his torch could not be seen. He looked carefully within, peering into the empty darkness. He was not prepared for what he saw.

He gasped and fell back, then regained his feet and stumbled back again. The torch cracked against the paving and went out. He did not stop to think. In the darkness he turned and fled around the house. Within minutes, he was running and stumbling up the field towards the copse as if a host of devils were chasing him with whips and slings.

There was a deep pain in his chest and he struggled to breathe. He looked back again and again as if he expected to see all the demons of hell, but no-one was following him, no light had appeared in the windows and all was as silent and still as it had been before.

It was like something from a horror film. As he looked cautiously through that kitchen window the beam of his torch had picked out a silent figure. Someone was sitting on a chair at the far side of the room, someone staring directly at him as if they had been waiting for just that moment. The eyes caught his but they did not blink and they did not flinch. They simply stared. For a fraction of a second, which seemed like a minute, their eyes were locked. It was a horribly ghost-like apparition, grey and still. Its eyes never moved from his, never flinched. It was like staring into the grey, blank eyes of a corpse.

Even now, as he approached the copse and fell back against the tree where he had left his binoculars, he was haunted by that look. He hadn't believed in ghosts, not for years. Now he wasn't sure. Why else was he trembling and peering around him, wide-eyed, as if some creature of the dark was moving steadily across the sloping field towards him. The house was silent and still. Nothing moved; no-one raised the alarm. He shuddered.

Slowly, he grew calmer, the sweat on his face cooling, the pulsing in his head and chest and wrists subsiding. Slowly his breath came more regularly. He crept towards the back of the copse of trees and looked down, away from the cottage, towards a similar house by a winding lane; he breathed softly in the darkness. A solitary light shone from outside the front door of the cottage. Down there, lay safety of sorts. He scrambled over a fence and began the journey down to the road, to his car, hidden a mile away in a forestry car park. Soon he would unlock its doors, sink reassuringly into its plush seat and drive home.

Once home, he would be faced by a different dilemma; it was no less worrying and no less frightening. What was he to say to Caine? He made a quick, pragmatic decision. He would describe the utility room window and the means of access. He would say nothing else. If the house was haunted, let Caine find out for himself.

Back in the kitchen, Stone stood up and yawned.

'A good evening's work,' he murmured to himself. 'There'll be no more trouble tonight.'

He picked up a phone and spoke to Casey in the car on the lane.

'He's gone. I doubt this was anything more than a reconnaissance, but I think we can mark it up as a small victory. Get some sleep now. We'll be safe till after the funeral. And well done.'

He closed the phone, then stood for a moment and leaned on the kitchen table to look out of the window. The trees were darkly silhouetted, their branches moving slightly in the breeze as if incapable of rest. The lights of a car appeared on the lane as it turned towards the front of the house, and then faded to darkness.

He walked around the house once more and checked each door and window. He could no more sleep than the restless branches and the fretful clouds could cease their own movements. Like the slender moon, he kept a small watchful eye on the night. He returned to the lounge and lay on the sofa, staring at the ceiling.

'Where are you, Joe?' he murmured again, as he had so many times before. 'Where are you?'

Chapter 26

After leaving the hotel Joe walked for over an hour before a van passed and pulled up just ahead of him. There were few vehicles on the road and most of those were hurrying away from the city, not towards it. They were loaded with luggage on seats and roof racks - refugees fleeing violence. The few cars heading towards the city sped past quickly. No-one paused or glanced his way. Each face seemed tense and taut and preoccupied.

Joe ran forward. A man, grey-haired, about fifty and wearing white, paint-splattered overalls looked from the window of a work's van. It had 'W. Tyson and Son, Painters and Decorators' printed on the side panels and the rear doors. There was a telephone number and an email address.

'You look like you need a lift. Jump in.'

'Thanks.'

He clambered in beside the driver. A smell of paint and white spirit circled round him like a memory of childhood.

'Bill,' the man said, 'Bill Tyson.'

'Joe. Pleased to meet you, Bill.'

Bill held a cigarette in his right hand next to the window, which he opened a fraction to allow the acrid smoke out.

'Do you mind?' he asked, indicating the cigarette. 'Some people take exception.'

'There are plenty other things I could die of before that gets me.'

'Yes, times are bad. I thought we were past all that but it just goes to show. How far are you going?'

'Through the zone and fifty miles the other side,' Joe said ruefully.

Bill whistled. 'Is it a challenge or just an ordinary everyday act of madness?'

'How far can you take me?'

'Hollerein, it's not a long way but it's better than nothing, I guess.'

'Much better, I thought I'd have to walk all the way.'

Bill inhaled and blew a spume of smoke towards the window, holding the wheel casually with one hand. His face was grey and worn into deep wrinkles which seemed to have been chiselled from a substance more solid than mere flesh. A pair of bright eyes glanced out from beneath a furrowed brow.

'I'm collecting my daughter and her children from Hollerein. Where they live isn't safe now, especially at night. There are gangs of thugs roaming the streets, mostly heading to the cities. In some places, there've been running battles between the different factions. It's a madhouse. Her husband joined a local militia, just to protect their homes.'

'I guess it'll be quiet in the daytime. Even thugs and militants have to sleep.'

'Yes, I should get there and back before dark. I'll be a lot happier when I have them home. They'll be safe with us.'

'For now,' Joe murmured.

'How about you?' Bill asked. 'What's your plan?'

'I'll just keep walking till I have to stop.'

'It's not much of a plan.'

'It's the best I could come up with.'

'What's so urgent?'

'A death and a funeral; I want to be with my family.'

That, he thought, and an all too painful realisation that the hope he had clung to, that Caine and Bull would grow bored, that Goodwin would find a better outlet for his overweening vanity, were delusory. They wouldn't stop, not ever. There were new, deeper feelings of guilt too, brought into sharp relief by Martin's death. Hannah and Meg and Jessica deserved better - *better than him,* he thought. His stubbornness, his vanity, the whole self-righteous man of principle bit, now left a sour taste that he couldn't shift. Lisa was right all along.

There was something else too. Like his great grandfather and his grandfather before him, he was sick of running, sick of being the persecuted one, the victim. He couldn't live like that and he couldn't expect it of his family. It had to stop.

'There are things I've got to do,' he said. 'They won't wait.'

'Be careful; your family won't want two funerals.'

Fields and scattered villages slowly gave way to suburban housing. The roads, usually busy with traffic, were eerily quiet. Bill dropped him near a deserted railway station.

'Good luck,' he called.

'You too.'

Joe slung his pack over his shoulder and began to trudge along the road at the side of the railway line. At first, he made good progress and there were few signs of disturbance. A few shops had broken windows and a food store had been ransacked but most buildings were untouched. It was only as he reached the outskirts of the town in the mid-afternoon that his progress was slowed. A smashed and burnt-out car lay across the road and a group of youths gathered round its smouldering remains. He thought it wise to avoid a possible confrontation, so he clambered over a fence and down an embankment to the railway line. Half a mile further and another wrecked car, this time across the line, forced him to clamber back up and take to the road again. Then he encountered the first barricade. It had been hastily flung across the railway line and the street that ran beside it, no doubt to challenge the flow of enemy fighters heading towards the city centre.

The streets on either side looked increasingly like a war zone; windows smashed, brickwork riddled with bullet holes, stones and bottles scattered at random. Burnt-out cars and vans, some still smouldering, lay where they had died like casualties of a battle. The houses seemed empty at first but as Joe passed along the streets, he caught occasional glimpses of frightened faces behind the broken glass. Some children emerged from a side street. They stopped sharply and watched him pass, their eyes narrow and cunning. They had grown old quickly on those streets. A boy picked up a stone and threw it half-heartedly at him and they ran away into a dark alleyway with strange calls and cries; animals in their jungle.

It was on that street, beside a barricade, that he saw the first body. It lay curled on the ground in a pool of congealed blood. A gaping hole in the chest opened like a blank stare. The eyes stared upwards, the mouth half open, as if the dead man was still trying to work out what had happened or to cry last words to an empty sky.

Joe remembered stories his great-grandfather had told about the ghettos, the forced marches, the camps, stories his father had re-told to him. He would have encountered scenes like this, his grandfather too, as a small child. His great grandfather, Solomon Auer, had seen people die, shot in front of him and left in a roadside ditch like fallen stock. He had seen them stumble and fall, only to be left on the ground to die of starvation and exhaustion and he had walked on, unable to stop and help. It was that failure that hurt him most. Mostly, he reminisced about the helplessness they felt. They had no control, he explained, no power. They lived where they were told to live, dressed how they were told to dress and went wherever their enemies directed them. People in his family, he said, had been forced to live in ghettos and then marched from there to places far, far worse. They were butterflies in a hurricane.

When he escaped to his new homeland, and for the rest of his life, he told his stories to anyone who would listen. It was his way of empowering himself, taking control. 'You must never forget,' he told his son and his grandson, Joe's father. You must tell the stories. People must know.'

That's how Joe heard about his family.

Now he saw for himself things his great grandfather would have seen and he watched, as his great grandfather must have done, the people who took control and those it was taken from. He felt the powerlessness his great grandfather had described. He too had to walk past the fallen and yes, it felt like cowardice. He thought about his family and about the price they had paid.

Joe saw a lot more bodies that afternoon. They were spread out in grotesque patterns like some obscene art installation. Occasionally there were clusters, where particularly fierce encounters had taken place. From the colour of the bodies it was evident that the supporters of Piers Goodwin, political hero of the extreme right, had the better of the encounter. Theirs were the barricades, theirs the better vantage points, theirs the detailed preparation.

Before he reached the city centre, Joe had stopped looking at the dead bodies and they no longer shocked him.

Nothing, however, could prepare him for what he encountered as he reached the heart of the city. Heart? The city no longer had a heart; it had been ripped out and trampled underfoot. Armed troops stood on street corners and outside key buildings – the bus and rail stations, the Administrative Offices, the banks. The Nationalists had retreated to the barricades. Heavily armed troops patrolled the streets in pairs, checking each junction, each alleyway and each cellar. They watched the rooftops. Around them lay the remnants of a battle which had raged for three days. No building remained unscathed, no car un-burnt, no window unbroken. The detritus of days of violence and vandalism lay scattered around.

Joe walked cautiously through it. The road was littered with stones and broken bottles. Here and there, pools of blood curled round broken boxes and items wrenched from shops in an insane frenzy. The bodies from which the blood had leaked had been dragged away or collected in the morning by ambulances and troops but the blood remained, like an omen. Barricades lay half demolished at road ends.

Army vehicles were patiently flattening them and dragging the larger items aside.

There were very few people and no cars. It was horribly silent. Only the sound of barricades tumbling in a screech of dying metal broke the unnatural solitude. Those people who, by necessity or design, passed through the centre did so with their heads lowered as if to escape attention. No-one wanted to be on those streets longer than they needed. Occasionally a cry, like that of a wounded animal, emerged from a building, a home or a shop as an owner saw and understood the ruin that lay around them.

Joe stood and looked around. It was hard, almost impossible, to believe that people could have done this. Once again, he was appalled by the gulf that lay between these minds and those of the people he knew. It was incomprehensible that anyone could hate other people so much. He felt a surge of despair.

Two soldiers crossed the road towards him. One stepped forward; the second, his hands firmly gripping a machine pistol, stood back and watched for any unexpected movement.

'Let's see your papers,' the first demanded.

Joe rooted in his pocket and slowly produced his wallet, took out his identification card. The soldier looked from the card to him and back again. His wasn't a face which would smile easily, not until he finished his patrol and returned to barracks.

'What are you doing here, Joe? You're a long way from home.'

'I'm trying to get back.'

'You can't. You've got to turn back.'

'I can't; you don't understand.'

'The roads aren't safe. In a couple of hours, they won't be passable.'

'I've got to get back. There's a funeral.'

'There are a lot of funerals, Joe, too many to count. We still can't let you through.'

'I promised I'd be there.'

'You've got to turn back, Joe, no choices.'

'This funeral's special. It's Martin Savage. He's my father-in-law. I promised my wife I'd get back. I've got to keep going.'

The soldiers looked at each other and hesitated for a moment.

'Even if we let you pass, you won't get through in daylight and you don't want to be caught outside during the curfew.'

'Is the curfew holding?'

'It's holding in a few places, but the streets are dangerous. There are armed gangs, snipers, looters and local vigilantes. A lot of roads are still blocked. We knock down the barricades in the daytime and they get built back up at night. It's like a frontier town. There's not much law out there at night and the body count just gets higher.'

'How long will it be before you have control?'

The soldier hesitated. 'We're driving them back slowly,' he said cautiously. 'When's the funeral?'

'Three days.'

The soldier shook his head.

'I don't think you'll make it, Joe.'

From the distance there came a sound like thunder and a plume of smoke rose above the rooftops. There followed a distant rattle, like firecrackers. The soldier turned his eyes from Joe and scanned the rooftops and windows around the centre, looking jittery. His colleague turned his back and watched the other side of the square.

'You'll not find a room. The hotels that aren't closed and shuttered are crammed to capacity. Is there anywhere you can stay?'

Joe thought for a moment.

'Maybe,' he said. 'Someone I met a few days ago on my way north.'

'Then you'd better get there quickly. Where is it?'

Joe told him.

'That's a couple of miles east, close to a militant stronghold. Keep to the main roads and don't stop. We cleared barricades there this morning but they'll be up again soon. There are some nasty characters down that way and they're particularly dangerous at the moment – like cornered rats.'

'I know; I met them.'

'When?'

'On my way north; I was lucky to escape. I don't want to get caught twice. I wouldn't be so lucky a second time.'

He briefly described his encounter with Akmal. 'You know him?' he asked the soldiers.

'Yes, we know him. Most people who meet him don't have your good luck.'

Joe remembered Mikhal. He nodded.

'If it turns really bad,' the soldier said, 'head back to the army barracks; but don't say I said so. The compound was pretty full last night. It was like a refugee camp – men, women, children, even dogs and cats.'

'Thanks, but I'll keep moving. I'll try to reach Jival's house and see how things are tomorrow.'

'I hope you make it, Joe; your father-in-law was a hero as far as I'm concerned.'

'It's all fallen apart pretty quickly.'

'We'll build it up again. Most people, no matter what their origins, want it to work.'

'I hope you're right.'

Another explosion and a plume of grey, acrid smoke rose vertically and twirled in an ugly pirouette. It was closer this time, only two hundred metres away. The soldiers pulled away and ran back towards the roadside.

'Keep to the main roads and don't stop. First sign of trouble and you head back, hear me?'

'Yes, I hear you.'

He ran, crouching low, towards the relative safety of walls and shop-fronts. Then he turned and sped, as quickly as he could, down rubble-strewn side streets, along unrecognisable roads towards the small enclave where Jival lived. It took over an hour to reach the narrow row of terraces and Jival's small, tidy house. It was barely recognisable. The house was deserted. The front door had been kicked open and the windows smashed. All around lay the evidence of recent conflict.

'Hello?' he called from the door. No-one replied.

Jival's family possessions lay scattered across the carpet. Everything of value had gone; what remained had been torn from the walls or thrown down and trampled on the floor. Even food packets had been torn open and the contents scattered in a frenzy of hate. The dresser and cupboard lay on their sides, broken across the spine like wrecked ships. Someone had defecated on the carpet. Elsewhere, he caught the pungent smell of urine.

'Where are you, Jival? Are you safe?'

Perhaps the family had escaped before the trouble began. Perhaps his brother had found them somewhere to hide until it was over. He felt a sharp pain as he imagined Jival and Haasita and their children returning to that house. How would they ever recover from such a violation? He didn't want to stay in the house now, not like this. It felt like sacrilege. He turned away.

Outside, the street looked like the site of a battle; it was hard even to recognise it as the street he had visited, and difficult to distinguish it from all the other streets around. Nothing familiar remained. Even the lights had been shot out. He sat down by the outside wall to think.

As dusk settled, no lights appeared in the windows, no sounds emerged from within the silent shells. A solitary dog loped across the street and vanished down a cobbled alleyway between terraced rows. A wheelie bin lay on its side like a corpse, amid stones and bricks, bottles and discarded wooden clubs. Cartridge cases accumulated on one corner. Even the breeze had forsaken the area. The litter which had fallen from the empty bin lay motionless and undisturbed, as if it could lie there forever.

He heard gunshots again, only a street away, and voices calling. He looked around; a solitary, dark face appeared where a window had been, a woman's face. She saw him looking and disappeared at once. He imagined her scurrying into a safe corner, hiding from predators, her dull eyes anxious, her hands pressed against her ears to shut out what she dreaded to hear, hunched, terrified. Death lay out there. Perhaps its shadow would pass over her. Perhaps it would pass her door and continue along the street. She waited in the darkness, helpless to do anything else. At the end of the street, Joe heard it too. People were gathering. The barricades were rising.

From the other direction he heard a heavy vehicle approach. In a moment he would be trapped in its headlights like a frightened deer so he went back into Jival's house and closed the door. He fled up the stairs and into the bedroom and, crouching low by the windowsill, he looked out.

An army vehicle rounded the corner. It passed the house and stopped while heavily armed troops scrambled out of the rear and dispersed into alleyways and buildings. Some soldiers remained in the road behind defensive shields. They formed a line and waited. A few minutes passed before the first bottle landed at their feet and a spray of flame and fire erupted. Others followed. Gradually, around the corner a group of masked men and youths appeared. They ran from one side of the road to the other, calling to each other and shouting insults towards the soldiers.

One, not much more than a child, ran forward, a bottle in his raised hand, a small flame in its neck. There was a shot. He fell forward as the rubber bullet struck his chest and the bottle rolled on the road, where it exploded into flames.

Joe pulled back from the window.

My God, they're firing on them.

The troops stepped forward, maintaining a line. Behind them, another vehicle approached and more troops emerged. Some formed a further line behind the first; others disappeared down side streets. Another petrol bomb, another gunshot, flames leaping and slowly extinguished.

Then it was completely dark, the sky illuminated only by explosions and fires. Down on the streets, unnatural faces glowed strangely in the firelight or fled like shadows into the deeper darkness of lanes and houses. Helmeted faces appeared occasionally at fractured windows behind the muzzles of rifles. A fire erupted at the end of the street and a surge of flame and smoke rose and burnt a hole in the sky. Flames crept round the door of a house and a soldier vanished from a window above. He emerged a moment later on the street as fire crackled and spat around him and flames engulfed the interior.

There was nothing Joe could do except wait. Perhaps the violence would burn itself out. Perhaps the troops would clear the streets; perhaps the different factions would crawl back into their holes and lick their wounds. He crouched down below the sill and rooted in his pocket for his phone. It was Stone who answered but the signal was poor. He could barely hear. He repeated everything slowly.

'I'm okay. I'm safe.... Yes, I'll be back for the funeral...Listen, Stone, I want you to do something for me...contact someone...Sheila Jones...Hannah will tell you. Get her to come to the funeral...Can you hear me, Stone? Are you there?' The phone signal, after a valiant effort to remain connected, had raised its hands and surrendered. It would not fight any more. Joe rested his head back against the wall.

Despite the noise and the constant, gnawing fear of detection he could not help but slip into a light sleep. Overwhelmed by the physical and mental pressures of the day, he could no more fight off sleep than he could stand alone in the street and make the fighters stop.

Chapter 27

For three nights now Akmal had been out on the streets. He had slept very little, snatching an occasional hour when he could fight it off no longer. From early evening until dawn began to break over the rooftops, he led his forces against the barricades built by his enemies, and mustered forces behind those of his own construction. With unremitting energy and unwavering self-belief, he drew his followers together from all parts of the zone. The message was always the same and it was shouted with complete conviction.

'Take to the streets! Kill, kill and keep killing! They are nothing, these people – less than nothing! God is great!'

He called on others to do the same, in all the other cities and towns and wherever his people assembled. He called to them to come out into the eerie light of the burning streets. His voice was heard and many hundreds responded.

'Let them believe the assassination was ours if that is what they desire,' he told his followers. 'Let them believe that we have chosen this moment for insurrection if they cannot see the truth. We have no choice but to fight. We must venture everything now or we shall be destroyed. Trust in God! We must litter the streets with their corpses.'

Now he stood behind a barricade of cars and vans, burned-out and hollow, surmounted and surrounded by a wreck of furniture, timber, old crates and pallets, tyres and even wheelie bins dragged from the roadside. It looked like the detritus of a horrific storm cast on the shore of a strange sea. The road was a main thoroughfare and shops, once busy and thriving, lay disembowelled. Smoke and flames still rose from broken windows. Above the shop fronts, curtains waved a hopeless surrender from broken windows.

Akmal was calculating the effect of a hail of missiles directed at the troops, when the call came. It was a murmur at first but it soon became an anxious cry. Then he heard a gunshot and a young man close by him stumbled and fell. He lay there crumpled and motionless like the corpse of a dead dog thrown across tyres on the barricade.

There was a moment of panic. The shot had come from behind them and it wasn't a rubber bullet such as the troops used. It was live ammunition. There was another shot and another man cried out. He looked down at a gaping wound in his gut and raised and inspected hands of blood as if it belonged to someone else. He sat heavily on the road and rolled onto his side. His eyes emptied of life as Akmal watched.

'The Nationalists are behind us,' someone shouted and the cry was taken up by others. As each voice called the warning, panic spread through the fighters. They were trapped and they were vulnerable. They had little with which to protect themselves but stones and clubs, petrol bombs and a few knives and machetes. There had been no time to locate and distribute more than a handful of guns. Faces turned to Akmal. He paused only a moment and then sprang to the top of the barricade. He paced along it, shouting. He called for sacrifice, for martyrdom, he directed them to the enemy behind. It was the fascist supremacists they had to defeat.

'We are without fear,' he yelled. 'Death is martyrdom.'

Gunshots ricocheted about him but he paced on.

'Forget the troops,' he shouted. 'Our enemy lies behind us. Turn your back on the barricade and trust to God and to the justice of our cause. Death means nothing! It is only the beginning! Leave the barricades to the troops. God is greatest!'

He raised his hand and in rapid, confident words, roused his followers to a frenzy of fanaticism. A bullet crashed into his shoulder. He felt the bone shatter and the blood flow warm on his arm and hand. Pain seared through him and he felt weak and sick. His followers were numbed and motionless. On the edge of the group, some fled silently down the side streets or crept into the cellars and ruins from where they could escape into the alleyways and streets beyond. Salim watched his leader fall and slipped into the darkness. He did not plan to die that night.

Akmal crouched for a moment then, with an effort which revealed itself only in the tightening of his brow and the gritting of teeth, he clambered to his feet. His raised a pistol and cried out again.

'Follow me! Follow me and destroy the enemy. Leave no one alive. This hand,' he cried, raising it again, 'is the weapon which will break our enemies. It will destroy all it meets. I will never be defeated. Follow me!'

His cry was taken up by those around him and then it grew wider and wider until the streets were filled with the sound. He climbed down from the barricade and broke through the crowd. As he strode down the street, his followers gathered behind him, their cries drowning all other sounds.

'Allahu Akbar!'

'Allahu Akbar!'

'God is great! God is great!'

Behind them, the troops moved slowly towards the barricade. Ahead of them, emerging gradually from the side streets and collecting in the road, came his Nationalist enemies. Occasional shots were fired from the windows and rooftops and people fell, wounded or dead. Akmal walked on. He raised his pistol and fired. One man fell. He fired again and again and two more people fell and died.

'Allahu Akbar!' The cry went up.

'God is great!'

The fighting was hand to hand now and gradually the enemy were forced back. The troops could do little more than watch. Tear gas canisters fell among the combatants and momentarily separated them and cleared small areas. But they filled again as the gas drifted and dissipated. Only the arrival of the water cannon threatened to control the madness. By then the Nationalists had been driven back and were running to escape the remnants of Akmal's fanatical force.

Akmal did not see the temporary victory his words had inspired. Nor did he see the final destruction of his own forces. He did not see troops gather from another side street and block them in. He did not see the man who fired the bullet which ripped into him. He slumped to his knees and then forward in an attitude of prayer. The second shot penetrated his skull, emerged and embedded itself into tarmac.

High on a rooftop overlooking the barricade, a solitary figure dismantled a high-powered rifle and packed it carefully away. He was in no hurry. He was just one obscure figure, small, undistinguished, engaged in a fierce battle. In a few minutes he would join the others walking away from the violence, fleeing the savagery of Akmal's soldiers.

He had done his job, just as he always did. He was reliable; he never failed. Whether the target was up close, like the three men he shot and dumped in the sea, or a distant target like this, made no difference to him. He made no fuss. When he arrived at his rooftop location and levelled his rifle, he took out a few others just to get the sights balanced, but he knew who he was looking for.

His target was called Akmal, though that was unimportant. He was taller than the others, obviously a leader. It wasn't easy to see him at first but then he rose on the barricades and all those fools called his name. He took out another couple while he was waiting. He watched Akmal lead his forces down the street. It was like something from a history book – like the French revolution, stupidly heroic. It roused no envy or admiration in the assassin. He took aim carefully. The first shot hit the centre of mass. That was how he had been trained. The second was a clean head shot, his speciality, the mark of his genius. It was that easy.

The job concluded, he walked silently across the rooftop and back down the metal fire escape steps. Once on the street, he slipped into a deserted office. He stood by the door and checked up and down. The battle was raging a hundred yards away. People were stumbling past him, heading away from the carnage, heads bloodied and bruised. It meant nothing to him. He'd done his job. Akmal was dead. He joined the throng and disappeared.

Akmal's savage but foolhardy charge had brought a temporary victory over his enemies, but it came at an awful cost. When a misty daylight gradually broke, few people who looked on that scene did not wish that time would stop, that the sun would reverse its course and hide the horror it had unwillingly revealed.

Chapter 28

When Joe awoke there was an unnatural silence in the streets. Nothing outside was moving. It was a landscape of the damned. He stretched out aching legs and struggled to his feet. As he ran his tongue round his mouth, he was aware of thirst and hunger in a form which, since his incarceration at the hands of Akmal, was becoming regrettably familiar. This was not the thirst he was accustomed to, little more than a desire for that first coffee of the morning; it was a deep and physical need. The hunger too was deep and cried out for remedy.

How long was it since he had eaten anything? He tried to remember. He had eaten at the hotel the morning he left, but after that? He smiled ruefully. How often could you tell yourself that you had forgotten to eat?

A solitary jackdaw fled over the rooftops and cawed half-heartedly. Somewhere in that wilderness there must be trees, other birds, food. Life went on.

What time was it? He looked at his watch. Half past six. Normally, people would be on their way to work. There would be cars on the streets, people waking, curtains opening, shadows of sleep and darkness receding in the bustle of morning television, breakfast and chatter. Not today.

Usually, Joe liked the silence. It was nature's way of speaking to him, telling him that despite the bustle and the noise, everything was still alright, that deep down, perhaps almost invisible and unheard in the modern world, the stable core of life still pulsed with a steady heartbeat. In the silence, he could hear it.

This silence was different; it was ugly and it was empty. He thought of other skies like this, worse than this; he thought of the sky above the camp where his family had been herded and then slaughtered and he thought about the disembowelled cities of the Middle East. It was as if a heart had ceased to beat. He shuddered. He was relieved to hear a sound on the street and he looked down to see a car turn the corner and approach. Two men climbed out, father and son perhaps. They opened a door and vanished into a house further down. Life goes on, green shoots emerge and a flickering flame of green breaks through concrete and stone.

He went down to the kitchen, drew a glass of water and drank it like a man in a desert. He looked in cupboards and the fridge. There was no electricity, but he found a can of fruit with a ring pull. He paused before eating it. It felt like theft. Jival wouldn't resent it, but that wasn't the point. He wasn't there to ask. Joe had spent the night in his house, not as his guest but as an intruder. He brushed away the thought. There was no time for ethical niceties. Perhaps one day he would return and tell Jival, apologise, explain.

There was more movement on the street now. He could hear heavy vehicles clearing the wreckage. It was time he got moving. He finished the fruit and stuffed half a loaf of bread inside his coat, past its sell by date but still edible, still soft. Jival or Haasita must have bought it shortly before they left. He searched the drawer to find a pen or pencil and, since he had five pounds in his wallet – the last of his money - he decided to leave it with a message. On a slip of paper, he wrote just the one word, 'Joe.' He put the note with the money beneath the can.

As he turned back towards the kitchen door, a voice called out unexpectedly.

'Is that you, Jed? Are you there?'

Someone in the front lounge mumbled and swore.

'Is that you in the kitchen?'

Joe pressed his back against the wall behind the kitchen door. He was breathing fast; his heart was racing. There were people in the lounge, just now waking from their night time exertions. How many were there? He heard someone yawn and swear and then the sound of feet dragging along the hallway. Someone stopped in the doorway.

'You're fucking imagining things.'

He took another step forward.

Across the room, Joe could see the empty can, the money he had placed beneath it and the note he had written. He breathed slowly and he didn't move. Every muscle tensed and threatened to cramp. He waited. If he was seen, he would have one brief opportunity to disable the man and run for the door. He thought of Hannah and Jessica and Meg and his resolve hardened. He was ready.

The man paused and looked round but then he turned away and shuffled back to the lounge. Other people were moving now. Joe heard someone stumble to their feet and call out. Someone swore.

'Where's Al?'

'Dead – got his throat cut.'

'Fuck.'

Something smashed against the wall.

'Bastards.'

Joe crept round the door. Ahead of him, the front door lay open but he had to pass the lounge door and that too was open and there were at least three people inside. He looked back across the kitchen towards the back door, but at that moment another figure slouched along the carpeted hall and walked across the kitchen. He picked up the glass Joe had left there and filled it with water. Joe had no choice. Any second now he would be seen.

He slipped round the door and pulled up his coat collar. He would walk straight out of the door.

'Who the fuck are you?' someone shouted.

'Fuck off,' he shouted back. 'You don't own the place.'

They didn't move. He was just someone else, like them, taking shelter in the ruined house. He walked quickly away without looking back.

The daylight hurt his eyes so he shaded them as he looked up and down the narrow street between the rows of houses. He hoped Jival might appear around the corner but he didn't. Perhaps it was better he didn't. There were people in his house who wouldn't appreciate his appearance or his colour. Besides, Joe had little time now to stop and speak. He had to get through the city and the rest of the zone before the end of the day. The funeral was tomorrow.

He walked on through the wreckage. He soon stopped counting the number of times he was approached by troops checking his identification and his intentions. Police cars passed him and slowed down as the occupants studied his face and demeanour. Sometimes they stopped. One car passed him and then pulled to a halt. The door opened and a white officer emerged, clad in a protective vest, a pistol holstered at his side.

'Show me your identification.' His command was peremptory and distrusting.

Joe performed the usual ritual.

'Haven't I seen you before?'

Joe shook his head.

The officer looked at the card again and a flicker of recognition passed across his eyes. He tried to hide it, but Joe knew what it meant.

'Where are you going, Joe?'

It was too late to lie. There was no point.

'I'm going home. I'm going to a funeral.' He stared at the officer defiantly. There would be no more fear now. 'My father-in-law is dead.'

A flicker of light burned in those narrow eyes, a brief moment of elation. He handed the card back to Joe and returned to his car and his colleague. He watched Joe as he walked along the street and rounded the corner at the end of the block.

Joe didn't see what happened next but he knew, as clearly as if he'd been in the rear seat. The officer would make a call. Caine would answer.

'I've just seen Joseph Auer – Joe Savage. He's on his way home for the funeral. Yes, he's yours.'

Joe imagined he saw the listener smile and the ugly lines crease the livid scar in that white face. He stepped resolutely forward. He didn't care now. He was going home. It would all finish there. One way or another Hannah, Jessica, Meg – all of them – would be free.

Chapter 29

Joe's progress through the city was more difficult than he could ever have imagined. There were roadblocks every few hundred yards on every main street, some barricaded by Nationalists, some defended by assorted groups of Asian youths, often at opposing ends of the same streets. There were troops everywhere too, in vehicles, patrolling on foot, standing at street corners, watching from the windows of burnt-out houses. He was stopped frequently and the routine was always the same.

'Show me your identification.'

'Where are you going, Joe?'

'Why are you going there?'

The warnings were always the same.

'You can't go down here. Turn back, try the next right. Go to the main road if you can. Make sure you're not on the streets after dark. Keep to the main roads, it's safer. Don't stop.'

He smiled. Of all these instructions, 'don't stop' was the most difficult to obey. When he wasn't stopped by soldiers or the police he was obstructed by burnt-out cars and roadblocks. Sometimes he saw groups of sullen youths standing on the road. He turned aside to avoid them, recalling vividly his last encounter with Akmal and his group. Then his luck changed and he rounded a corner to find himself only a few metres from a small, grim-looking group loitering by a smashed and burnt-out car. He saw a figure he knew, the thin wiry youth called Salim, who'd been with Akmal. One of the youths saw Joe.

'Hey, Salim, look what we got.'

Joe stopped and backed away, but not before Salim turned and saw him. There was a flickering of recognition in his eyes. It lasted only a moment but it gave Joe the advantage he needed. He ran, ducking left and then right down obscure alleyways, crossing small side streets. At first, he heard footsteps and shouts as the group, roused from their boredom and lethargy by the prospect of a chase, pursued him, but gradually the sounds grew less and then stopped altogether. He paused at a junction and glanced back, breathing hard; no-one. He waited and listened - still no-one.

He took a deep breath and turned to walk towards a junction with a larger road, but before he reached the next corner, Salim appeared ahead of him. He was walking away, looking left and right down side streets and alleyways – alone now but still hunting. Joe ducked unseen into a cobbled lane with high, brick walls, and bins and wooden gates leading to small backyards. He tried a latch. The gate opened and he slipped inside and crouched beside a brick outbuilding while he listened for any sounds outside. He waited. Half an hour passed before he slipped quietly into the alleyway and the street. It was empty now. Salim had gone. He turned and walked quickly away.

Half an hour later still, he breathed more comfortably but only slowly did he emerge from the worst areas and even then, the destruction didn't end. It merely diminished in scale and extent. He reached a main road but almost immediately turned aside from it; another roadblock, more troops and a gaggle of youths idly lobbing bricks as if passing a boring day. He saw a sign for the railway and followed it around a corner into another housing estate with narrow streets and brick terraces, probably dating back to the 1950s, maybe even pre-war.

He smiled. They were strange phrases - pre-war, post-war. When you looked back, it seemed like war had never ended. When you looked forward....

He paused across the road from a small terrace. A door opened and some people emerged. An elderly couple lugged an old, torn mattress towards a skip on the roadside. The old woman wore a hijab from which her creased face looked out uncertainly. The old man stumbled and fell heavily under the weight of his burden. Joe stepped forward to help. For a moment, the old woman looked scared and a cry of fear broke from her dry lips. Joe bent down and helped the old man to his feet.

'It's okay,' he tried to reassure them. 'I don't mean you any harm. Can I help?'

The old man watched him uncertainly.

'I'm Joe.'

The old man didn't answer.

'Is this to go in the skip?'

The old woman recovered first. She nodded. Joe began to lift it from the front and to drag it towards the skip. At first, the couple did nothing. They just watched, waiting for the trap to be sprung. Then the man slowly took the other end and together they upended it and heard it fall heavily into the hollow interior.

'Those monsters,' he said. He waved his hand towards the empty street as if they stood there still. 'They soiled it. They found nothing to steal so they destroyed or fouled everything. The animals, they left us nothing.'

The old woman began to sob gently. Only her mouth was distorted in a shape of grief. Nothing else moved. There were no tears. She leaned back against the door frame and slid down to the ground.

Joe glanced at his watch. It was not much after midday. He could spare a couple of hours. The railway wasn't far and from there it would be six or seven miles before he would break into open country.

'I'll help,' he said.

'We have no money to pay you.'

'I don't want money.'

'Then what do you want? I have nothing.'

Joe didn't answer. He couldn't. He didn't even know himself. Perhaps he wanted to feel clean amidst all this filth, human amidst the inhumanity. He just knew...he smiled at the thought...he had no choice.

'Show me,' he said.

The house had suffered even more than Jival's. It had been ransacked in a frenzied attack and little remained unbroken. Items too large to be smashed had been upturned. The old man started to lift a sofa and set it back against the window. Joe looked around. It was difficult to know where to start. He lifted a television which lay shattered on the floor and carried it to the skip. He returned and gathered wooden chairs, the legs fractured and cast aside. He took them out and returned and the day wore on.

'Have you any cleaning materials?'

The old woman nodded towards the kitchen. 'Most of it was poured over the floor but there is some left in the bottles.'

Joe cleared the soiled areas and scrubbed areas of carpet clean.

Eventually much of the small house had been cleared and what could be salvaged had been set back in its place, the windows on the ground floor had been boarded up and the house, if not yet habitable, was clean and ready to be furnished again, ready for life to continue. It was another small victory.

It was late and Joe knew he had to leave. It was already getting too late to escape the zone before dark, and even then, it would take many hours to reach home.

'Thank you,' the old woman said.

'There's nothing to thank me for.'

'Yes, yes there is.' The old man grasped his hand.

'Is there anyone who can help you with the rest?'

'Yes, my son. He will come as soon as the roads are clear. He'll help us.'

'Where will you stay tonight?'

'Here., We have nowhere else. The vandals will not return. The police are in control here now. Soon the electricity will come back on and the shops will re-open.'

'The good guys will win.' Joe smiled uncertainly, 'Green shoots. I've got to go.'

'We won't forget what you've done for us.'

It was not long before Joe realised he had little chance of escaping the city suburbs before dusk and that his troubles were far from over. As well as the usual police patrols and soldiers, he saw larger groups of people gathering on street corners and outside houses and shops. An Asian family were standing outside a hastily boarded-up shop. They held clubs and hammers and looked determinedly along the street to where a group of youths gathered. They were fighting back, defending what was theirs. They didn't plan to move again that night.

Groups of young men were still heading into the city, carrying whatever weapons they could find. There were occasional gunshots and plumes of smoke rose again from distant explosions. Occasionally, a stone would be thrown at him and once, as he passed a menacing group, a bullet struck a window beside him. A dark-complexioned youth leered at him and took a step forward. He hurried on. The creatures of the night were emerging. It soon became evident he could go no further without help. Campfires had been lit at intervals, where groups gathered waiting for the darkness to thicken and obscure them. Some held rifles or shotguns, others machine pistols or knives or baseball bats. He returned to the main road and found a quiet corner where he slouched down to think.

He had one option. It was not an easy one and it carried risks of its own, but he had little choice. He rooted in his pocket and found his wallet. Inside it was the card Jackson had given him – Jackson, the detective who had taken him to Jival's house, Jackson who had recognised him and warned him of the dangers he faced, Jackson who said, 'Call this number if you need help. Consider it your Get Out of Jail Free card.'

Now he needed help.

'Can I speak to D.S. Jackson, please?'

'Who's calling?'

'Tell him it's Joe. He'll understand.'

A moment later, the hoarse voice of Jackson grunted a greeting.

'Where are you, Joe?'

Joe explained.

'You're lucky to catch me. It's bloody mayhem here. All leave has been cancelled. I've been out on the streets for the last twelve hours and I'll be heading out again soon. What can I do for you, Joe?'

Joe took a deep breath. 'I need help. It's the funeral of Martin Savage tomorrow. I have to be there.'

'I wish I could help you, Joe, I really do.'

Joe sighed.

'It's okay. I understand. It was a long shot.'

'It's so busy here. I can't get away. What will you do?'

'Keep going.'

There was a moment's silence.

'Hold on a minute, Joe. Let me call you back in five minutes. Just find somewhere safe and stay low.'

It was ten minutes before his phone rang.

'Someone's coming for you, Joe. I called in a favour from a couple of guys I know who're working that area. They're good men. I can vouch for them. They'll get you somewhere safe on the outskirts but you'll need to make your own way from there.'

'That's fine. Thanks.'

'No problem, Joe.'

'Are the good guys winning, Jackson?'

Jackson paused for a moment.

'We have to. Otherwise there's nothing. You told me that.'

It was an hour before an army Jeep rounded the corner. The window opened.

'Joe?'

He nodded.

'Climb on board. We're your taxi.' He clambered into the rear seat behind a second soldier and the Jeep slowly drew away.

'I'm Dave Jackson, DS Jackson's brother,' the driver said. He held a hand back to Joe. 'This is Solly.'

Solly held out a sturdy hand and gripped Joe's hand like a vice.

There wasn't much conversation. Jackson and Solly scanned the streets, occasionally reporting back over a crackling radio about groups they saw approaching the city. Sometimes they stopped and one or the other climbed out to check a casualty, to reassure civilians, or to dissuade stragglers from heading any closer to the centre.

'Sorry, Joe, we've got to finish our patrol. Sit back and enjoy the ride.'

As they drove into the suburbs and the outer approaches to the city, everything grew strangely quiet and the darkness was intense. There were no lights anywhere beyond their headlight beam.

'The Nationalists took out a power station last night,' Jackson said. 'We need to watch for looters.'

'It's quiet,' Solly muttered.

'I like quiet,' Jackson replied. 'Quiet is my favourite sound.'

Distant explosions momentarily brightened the sky like sheet lightning. They heard rapid gunshots in the distance.

'It's never quiet for long,' Solly said.

The patrol continued but the Jeep stopped less and less now and as they rounded each corner they were met by the same shuttered and closed emptiness. Caught briefly in the headlights, a fox loped across the road. It paused on the pavement and watched them before it was swallowed by the darkness. It was the only life they saw. The curfew, out here in the suburbs, was holding. The radio cracked.

'Quiet as the grave,' Solly reported. 'How's the city?'

He listened and then signed out.

'Maybe the worst is over,' Jackson said, 'maybe.' He looked at the time on the dashboard. 'Right, Joe, let's get you to safety.'

He turned the Jeep from the silent suburban streets and out onto a main highway and the strangely silent motorway. Soon they were leaving the city behind them and the suburbs they passed grew smaller and quieter. After a few miles they took an exit and joined another empty road. There were lights in windows here and streetlights illuminating the houses. Occasionally a car would emerge and join the main road for a while, and then slip away back into one of the towns. Soon even the suburbs disappeared and they emerged into open country.

'Can I ask you something?' Joe asked.

'Sure.'

'Why are you doing this? Why are you helping me?'

'My brother asked me.'

'Besides, it's not every day you get to meet someone who's dead,' Solly laughed.

Jackson brought the Jeep to a halt outside a small village store and reached a hand back. 'This is as far as we go. Good luck, Joe. I hope you make it.'

'I'll make it.'

The door closed and the Jeep turned. Jackson sounded the horn once, twice and they sped away, back through the suburbs and into the darkness of the city.

Joe looked round. There was a small recreation ground opposite the shop with a bench and trees and grass. A streetlight shone onto a war memorial for the dead of two wars. His mind drifted back to the streets of the city, the destruction and the death. For a moment he stood before the memorial, a marble cross inscribed with names on each side.

'Here's to all those who are left to pick up the pieces and restore their damaged lives,' he murmured. He raised an imaginary glass in salute. 'Here's to those who died and to those who survived – to Jival, to Mikhal, to all the others. Here's to them.'

He lay back on a bench and looked up towards the sky and the stars and he was overwhelmed by the pettiness of human conflict, by the confusing relativity of beliefs and values. It was all so complicated. Akmal and his followers, behind all the brutality and cruelty, thought they were right. Caine wasn't just some dumb psycho, some James Bond villain. He had beliefs and values and he probably believed he was acting for some greater good. And there *he* was, Joe Savage, and he was right too. What made Joe Savage so fucking special? Maybe there was no absolute right or wrong, no ultimate good or evil. Maybe he was no different from them.

But some things were better and some were worse, weren't they? Democracy was better than Nazism, wasn't it? Freedom kicked the hell out of slavery and tolerance was better than persecution, that's for sure. People could be wrong, couldn't they?

Maybe he had to get inside the heads of these people he called monsters, though, walk with them, talk to them and understand them. And maybe they had to be persuaded to walk with him. Maybe only then could they be reconciled, move on together.

Or maybe that was just another delusion.

Maybe...maybe...

He needed to rest, to sleep, but tomorrow was the funeral and first he had to speak to Stone. He checked his phone. There was just enough charge left. Then he would lie back on the bench and look up into the empty sky and think of Hannah and Meg and Jessica. Certainty was fragile and fleeting but he was certain of them in a way he could be certain of nothing else. He would fall asleep knowing that tomorrow he'd be home.

Chapter 30

The house where Hannah and Joe lived had belonged to Martin Savage. He had lived there after his marriage, when he could escape from his work in the city, and it was always a place he associated with the happiest years of his life. It was Hannah's childhood home. Martin had visited the house infrequently since his wife died, so he was especially pleased when Hannah and Joe agreed to move there and adopt his surname. Now he could visit again and enjoy vicariously the memory of the warm, family home it had always been.

Hannah was happy there too. She had attended the local primary school in the village and the secondary school in Dowlheim before her university years. The house was always 'home' to her and she felt it was the perfect place to bring up her own children in happiness and security.

Martin Savage's own childhood had been passed in another house not far away, and his family was well known in the area. It was understood by local people that he worked with Sebastian Steele in Zarten, but few understood the important role he played in the devolution settlement until the press coverage started to draw attention to it. That was how he wanted it. Like Steele himself, he had no desire for the limelight. He would have found his funeral something of an embarrassment.

Nonetheless, the whole village turned out to pay its respects to a private, family man and a significant public figure.

'He would have slipped away from the funeral as soon as he could and gone home to his study,' Hannah said. She smiled at Lisa through tears. 'He'd be sitting at home and no-one would realise he'd gone.'

'We can't prevent people expressing their feelings for what he achieved and for who he was.'

'I know. But I'm going to imagine he's slipped out. I don't want to think of him at the centre of so much attention.'

'Secretly, I think he would have been rather proud.'

'He wouldn't have let it show, and he would never have said.'

'No.'

'He would have hated the memorial service.'

'I doubt he'd have gone.'

'Still, it's good of Mrs Steele to insist he's remembered in the service.'

'The country needs an opportunity to honour Sebastian and Father. It'll remind them of what they risk losing. Stone thinks it may be a turning point.'

'I hope so.'

A field, mercifully dry, had been converted to a temporary car park and the village main street was closed to traffic. A loudspeaker would transmit the service to the people who had gathered outside and couldn't fit into the small, country church. Representatives of the Government would attend today but theirs would be a quiet and respectful presence. The press had agreed to keep a discreet distance. After the service, the mourners would disperse. The burial in the adjoining graveyard would be a private affair for family only.

'Where's Daddy?' Meg whispered as they climbed in the black car for the short journey to the church.

'Daddy may not be here in time,' Lisa whispered to her, 'but he'll be home very, very soon. You have to be a brave girl and help Mummy now.'

'But he promised. He said he'd be here.'

'I know and I'm sure he did everything he could. Sometimes...' She struggled to find appropriate words. 'I'm sure he tried his very best,' she said lamely. It was so easy to make promises, so difficult to keep them.

'He'll be at the church,' Hannah said firmly. She held the children close. 'He promised.'

'Even Joe can't...' Lisa began, but she stifled the words. It was better to say nothing. This was no time for recriminations. The next few hours would be difficult enough. 'I'm glad Adam's coming. I don't think I could manage without him.'

'Where's Inspector Stone?' Jessica asked.

'He's making sure everything is ready for us at the church.'

'Is Casey with him?' Meg asked.

'N, he's staying at the house.'

'Is he making sure no bad people break in while we're away?'

'He's looking after the house for us.'

'And Inspector Stone is watching the people in the church?'

'There'll only be good people today...only good people.'

The car pulled slowly away.

Inside the church, people were gathering. The Reverend George Stanhope, vicar of the parish, greeted them outside the ancient porch with its Norman arch. Hunched now and as grey as the granite of his church, he had been the vicar of St. Jude's as long as anyone could remember. Above him rose the heavy rectangular tower with its bell and clock and before him lay the pathway to the wooden, main gate and beyond that the long, narrow village street. The two remaining shops, the butcher and the general grocery, were closed for the day, as was the school.

A limousine pulled up and its passenger emerged and was greeted by Reverent Stanhope before she disappeared into the sombre interior of the church.

'She's a Home Office Minister,' someone murmured. Heads turned.

'What's her name?'

'Barbara Reid.' Someone supplied the missing information.

Another limousine drew up, shared this time by members of the Opposition. They too spoke briefly to the Reverend Stanhope and disappeared with the other mourners into the church. The streets were lined now by local people, who emerged from their cottages and stood waiting on the roadside.

A murmur arose as the funeral cortege approached. It moved slowly between the respectful onlookers. Someone threw flowers. A woman in a doorway wept. Hannah watched from the window of the car. She saw the flowers which lined the short path to the church and lay against the walls around the tower and wiped away a tear.

'Look,' Jessica whispered. 'There are my friends from school. And there's Mrs. Simpson from the bakers and Mr. Reynolds, the butcher and... oh look, there's my teacher.'

Hannah held her hand.

'You mustn't wave.'

'Why not?'

'Because there are rules about how to behave at a funeral and one of them is, "don't wave from the car window."'

'What are the others?'

'Say as little as possible and show respect,' her aunt told her.

'Do I have to cry?'

'Only if you want to.'

'Will you cry?' Meg asked.

'Oh yes,' her mother told her quietly.

'Are you crying now?'

'A little bit, just a little bit.'

'For Grandad?'

'Yes.'

The car moved slowly along the street and pulled up outside the church.

There's Adam,' Lisa sighed. 'I'm glad he made it.'

Meg sat up and stared from the window.

'Daddy,' she shouted, 'Daddy's there too.'

'Meg, sit down.' Lisa held her arm. 'Remember the rules. Show respect. You're mistaken. Daddy couldn't possibly get here in time.'

Meg sat back on her seat and waited for the door to open.

'I'm right,' she whispered to Jessica. 'I saw him; he's standing by the gate with Inspector Stone.'

She looked through the window and opened and closed her hand in a restrained wave.

Lisa glanced at Hannah and Jessica. One look was enough to confirm the truth. Meg was right. There was Joe, standing at the church with Stone and Adam, waiting.

'He's there,' Hannah murmured through her tears. She turned to Lisa. 'He promised,' she said triumphantly.

The door opened and they stepped from the car. The coffin had already been removed from the hearse and the bearers held it shoulder high. Joe drew in behind it, beside Hannah and the children, and Lisa joined Adam. Joe curled a protective arm around the children and with the other, gathered Hannah to his side.

'I knew you'd come back,' Meg whispered. There was a note of pride in her voice. 'I told Aunty Lisa you'd come back. I told everyone. You promised.'

'Whose clothes are you wearing?' Jessica asked. 'They're too big.'

'Uncle Adam leant me some clean clothes. Mine had got dirty. I came in the car with him.'

The Minister stood at the head of the procession and the awful, hopeful, hopeless incantation began.

Chapter 31

The only vantage points from which the funeral could be seen was provided by Dowlheim Lane, which ran through the centre of the village. The fields on either side rose to no great height and the church and graveyard were hidden from view by the surrounding houses. Only the great tower, reaching solidly and without aspiration, as if rooted to the earth, could be seen from any distance. Caine and Bull couldn't mingle with the throng of locals on the street. They would have been absurdly conspicuous. Nonetheless, it was important to have *someone* on the street. Hannah would have recognised him as the man from the pond but today he stood at the roadside and mingled with the crowd and no-on paid particular attention. As the cortege arrived outside the church, he saw three people approach the gate. He knew two of them from photographs he had been shown. The first was Stone. The second was Joe. He stepped back from the roadside and slipped into a corner beside the shop where he opened his phone.

'He's here.'

He said no more and there was no response from the other end. The phone went dead.

There were three men sitting in a bedroom in the Old Coaching Inn in the market town of Dowlheim, waiting for the call. Bull put the phone down on a glass coffee table.

'He's arrived. He's at the church.'

The others didn't speak. Caine barely raised his head. A vein in his neck bulged and throbbed more violently, but there was no other change. The third man was the burglar who had peered through the kitchen window of Hannah's home, only to find Stone staring back from the darkness. Lenny Smithers fidgeted anxiously and glanced at his watch as if he were late for an appointment. He wanted to be somewhere – anywhere - else.

'Go over it again,' Caine said.

'I've been over it time and time again.'

'I don't care. Go over it once more. Tell me again how we open the window.'

'You have two choices. If you plan to enter the house when there's no-one there you can smash the window and open the catch, but it might be a bit risky if they're in the house. Even at night and in their sleep, people hear sounds like that. It'll be even more difficult with *these* people. They'll be expecting something to happen. Their senses will be sharp.'

'Go on.'

'The alternative is to remove the glass. I've got a cutter you can use and I have a suction pad.' He lifted a small travel bag from the ground and placed it on the table.

Caine turned briefly to Bull.

'I want to be in the house waiting. We've got to choose the right moment.'

'What exactly are you planning?' Lenny knew his mistake as soon as he uttered the words. He stood up. 'Forget it. I don't want to know. It's time I was leaving.'

Caine caught him with a stare that gripped him more tightly than the hands that held the table. Lenny shuddered slightly and moved a step towards the door. Bull, as if reading his leader's mind, stepped quickly forward and blocked the man's path. He stood in front of the door, his huge arms hanging at his side.

'Sit down,' said Caine, leaning back and smiling. 'Go on. I'm hardly going to damage you here, in a hotel room in the middle of a wonderfully middle class, 18th century market town. I'd hardly be that foolish now, would I, Lenny?'

Lenny shook his head. He slipped onto the chair, sitting on the edge as if ready to lurch defensively sideways.

'Can I trust you, Lenny? I mean, can I really trust you?'

'Of course, you can. You know you can.'

'Do I? Do I really know that, Lenny?'

'I haven't let you down, have I? I wouldn't.'

'That's just words, Lenny, mere words. I mean, let's look at it rationally. You don't have a cause, do you? You don't actually believe in anything. This is just a business transaction to you. I hire you and I pay you and that's all. What if someone else were to offer you more money for a different job – say, to betray us? What then? You see my dilemma.'

'I wouldn't betray you. I've got values, principles. I'm loyal, I am. I don't let my friends down, not ever.'

'Are we you friends, Lenny?' He turned to Bull. 'Did you know we were Lenny's friends, Bull?'

'I didn't, Boss. I feel downright fucking honoured. I do, really.'

'I understand your sentiment, Bull. I feel the same – honoured.'

Bull stepped closer to Lenny and stared down at him. Caine continued to speak, his words as smooth as oil and as toxic as acid.

'The question, Bull, is do we trust him? Do we trust our new friend, Lenny, never to betray our little conspiracy?'

'I think we can trust him for as long as it takes that blood to dry.'

'What blood? I don't see any blood.'

Bull levelled a blow across Lenny's face with the back of his hand. Lenny fell sprawling on the ground. He was about to struggle to his feet but thought better of it. He wiped his lip with his hand.

'Ah, I see it now.'

'Look,' Lenny bleated from the ground, 'I've told you; I won't speak to anyone.'

'No matter what you hear?'

'No matter what.'

Caine shook his head. He stood up and paced to the window. He glanced out at the market square below, bustling with people shopping, cars searching for illusive parking spaces, children running between the trees and the black, wrought-iron benches where their mothers sat, and people walking dogs. Around the square, fine buildings with solid, 18th century facades looked benevolently on.

'You wouldn't think there was a war on, would you?' he murmured. 'Just a few miles away, people are dying for their cause.' He turned sharply back. 'You see, Lenny, me and the Bull have a cause. We believe. We are full of righteous fucking anger when we see our country taken over by foreigners. And when a Jew – a fucking Jew – defends those very foreigners and then testifies against my people and goes on television and is celebrated for what he's done, as if he's as patriotic as me and Bull here, it turns my righteous fucking anger into fury. I cry out for revenge. I insist that he pays. Do you understand me, Lenny?'

Lenny nodded. He was beginning to understand. He was beginning to wish he'd never taken this job on in the first place.

'I didn't know. I didn't understand,' he whimpered.

Caine's eyes flashed ominously. His fists were clenched until the knuckles were as white as his face. His scar bulged as if some alien creature were emerging from beneath his skin. That scar and the icy blue eyes were the only colour in that menacing, pale face.

'What didn't you know, Lenny? Didn't you know it was my kid brother he testified against? Or is it something else you didn't know? Is there something else you want to know? Do you want to know that my kid brother got killed while he was in prison, got knifed by a fucking Paki? Do you want to know that?'

'No, nothing, honestly, I don't want to know anything. You can trust me,' he ended lamely.

'Well, let me make it absolutely fucking clear what you don't know, just so there's no doubting our situation. You're an accomplice, Lenny. Whatever happens now, you are quite clearly an accomplice. If something unfortunate were to happen – let's say that either Bull or myself were accidentally captured, or betrayed – we would consider it a duty, yes, a duty, to make sure you were so implicated you would be sent down for a long, long time.'

Bull cracked his knuckles and stared through dull, menacing eyes at his hapless victim. 'Could we get him sent to the same prison, Boss, all nice and cosy, like? All of us together?'

Caine stared at the grovelling creature with contempt.

'I'd consider it a duty, Bull,' he said icily. 'Do you think you understand now, Lenny?'

Lenny nodded and didn't stop nodding. Caine indicated the chair and Bull dragged him back into his seat.

'In a day or two,' Caine continued, more calmly now, 'you will hear about another terrible event and it will have taken place in this very neighbourhood. You will, no doubt, be shocked, as any right-minded, God-fearing citizen would be. To hear of an entire family slaughtered in their own home – husband, wife and two little girls – is shocking. It's hard to comprehend. You'll hear it on the news. They'll tell you the whole county is in mourning, that every face within a vast area conveys shock and grief and that wreaths and tributes and, no doubt, a variety of soft toys, are accumulating outside the house. The images will be on every news bulletin. They will talk about mindless cruelty and indifferent savagery. They will exploit hyperbole until the crucifixion itself seems a mere act of spite beside it.

'When you realise that these people occupied the very house that you so recently inspected, the shock will, no doubt, take on a more personal quality. It's at that point that you must resist any urge to confess. Can you resist that urge,

Lenny? Can you assure me that you won't succumb to a momentary pang of guilt and conscience?'

Lenny nodded over and over again like some malfunctioning, mechanical toy.

'Can I offer you some advice, Lenny? You won't take it amiss? If I were you, I'd crawl back into whatever hole you emerged from and I'd stay there. I'd dig down deeper and deeper until I was so deep, I was sure I could never be found. I would stay there and I wouldn't emerge.'

Lenny understood. Oh, he understood. Caine paused.

'Look, Bull, Lenny has stopped bleeding. I recall you said we could only trust him as long as blood took to dry. Have you changed your opinion?'

'Do you want more blood, Boss?' He raised a fist and levelled it. Lenny squirmed and tried to turn away. Caine waved a hand impatiently.

'Get out.' He sounded bored now. He had nothing more to say. 'Get out, Lenny. Remember what we've discussed. You will remember, won't you?'

Lenny looked as if he would never forget, not for one moment. He stumbled to the door and the lift. In a few minutes, he was walking hurriedly along the street towards the bus station.

'What do you think?' Bull asked.

'I think Lenny understands,' Caine said calmly. He brushed a fleck of dust from his trouser leg and then ran a hand across his cropped hair. He checked his watch. 'I think I'll get some sleep. Tomorrow is going to be a busy day.'

Chapter 32

The funeral was over, the ritual of handshaking and the receiving of condolences at the church door had passed, the quiet, dignified private burial was over and those guests who were invited were making their way down to the hotel. Caterers, hired by the family, had provided a late buffet.

'I need to speak to Sheila Jones,' Joe whispered to Hannah. She had been in the congregation but during the funeral had maintained a respectful distance and was standing now beneath an old oak just beyond the end of the village, where a small play park had been erected. She was a thin, wiry woman made it seemed of nervous energy and not much else. Her hair was tidied out of the way to ensure it could not interfere with the subject of her scrutiny. Her glasses, perched on her thin nose, were narrow and perfunctory. She had the air of a woman with little time to waste. Even now she looked regularly at her watch.

Hannah nodded. 'Don't be long,' she murmured. 'All these people...'

'I know. I'll be half an hour, maybe less. I promise...'

'The girls are tired. It's been a long day for them. They need you.'

Jessica and Meg were standing beneath a yew tree beside a small wicket gate in the corner wall. They were playing idly with some leaves and flowers. Joe could see them talking quietly. Jessica saw him looking and waved. He waved back.

'As quick as I can. I wouldn't...but it's important...really important.'

'Okay, just be quick. Bring Sheila along if you want,' she added.

'I'll offer. I doubt she'll want to.'

Hannah walked to the girls and managed to draw a smile from the deep well of her emotions. 'Come on, let's go to the hotel. There's some food for us all and something to drink.'

'Is Daddy coming with us?' Meg asked.

'He'll follow us down.'

'He's not going away again, is he?'

'No, not ever, he just has to speak to someone before he joins us.'

'Is that the lady he has to talk to?' Meg pointed down the lane to where Sheila Jones was standing near the trees.

'Yes.'

'She looks cross.'

'She's a famous writer. She's very busy. She always looks rather cross.'

'I'm glad she's not my teacher,' Meg whispered.

'Me too,' her mother said secretly. 'She scares me.'

As Joe approached her, Sheila closed her phone.

'I thought I'd file a report while I'm here. "The whole village turned out to pay their respects to a great public servant and family man etc." I take it I can exclusively report that you've returned from the dead. It'll add a further poignancy to the event; death and resurrection and a very human scene at the church gate. I deserve an exclusive interview, don't you think, for being here this afternoon?'

'Yes, and you can report that there'll be no more hiding. I'm back to stay.'

'So, it's *High Noon* and the O.K. Corral rolled into one?'

'If you want to put it like that - you're the journalist.'

'It's not really my sort of headline – rather tabloid, don't you think? You said you need my help. Would you care to elaborate? But no, first of all tell me why you approached me and not someone else? My article about you wasn't the most flattering.'

'It was honest and I think I can trust you. You seem to have integrity and you don't have much time for the sort of people I'm dealing with.'

Sheila laughed softly.

'Honesty, trust, integrity – those are words rarely used to describe anyone in my profession and never before, in my experience, in the same sentence. If I didn't know you were incapable of deception, I'd suspect you of flattery.'

'What about Woodward and Bernstein? Edward R Murrow? Even Martin Bell? Your profession has turned up a good number of people with integrity.'

'That's very illustrious company you're placing me in, far too illustrious for a humble hack. Now I know you're after something. So, tell me.'

'Tomorrow night or the night after or one night very soon, someone will break into my house and try to kill me. Now that Martin Savage is dead, they may also be a threat to my wife and children. They've been following me, off and on, for two years. One is the brother of the man I testified against. He's called Nathan Caine. The other is his accomplice. So, I don't have time for flattery.'

'Why are you so sure they'll act now?'

'Sebastian Steele provided my wife with a bodyguard. Now Steele has gone, my father-in-law has gone, the bodyguard has been withdrawn - and I'm home for good and they know it.'

'I think you're over estimating your own importance, Joseph.'

'I need your help.'

'You think you're being set up?'

'I'm sure of it. I rattled a lot of cages. Now the doors have been unlocked, the hunters are free, and it's open season. The people who have been tracking me belong to a network of militant nationalists. They're powerful - much more powerful than I first realised. They have agents within every branch of government – the police, the civil service, every corner of society - and they're well organised. But even they're being steered from above.'

'Do you have a name?'

Joe hesitated before he spoke. 'Piers Goodwin,' he said.

It was Sheila's turn to pause and glance away. Her mind was working fast. She looked out across the play park towards the trees and fields beyond. Smoke rose from a distant chimney. A rook called. A vehicle changed gear as it turned a corner and moved along the village street.

'Everything changes,' she murmured, 'even in a place like this. It just changes more slowly, that's all. We can't prevent change, but we can try to make it palatable. Today's transition is tomorrow's normality. Piers Goodwin is like Canute, foolishly fighting off those things he thinks would erode our shores. In truth, he's condemned to failure. The future moves through us to the past. Was that James Joyce? I'm sure he wrote something like that. Of course, Goodwin sees himself rather differently. He thinks he's Alfred, fighting off the invaders and creating a new state.'

She turned to Joe sharply.

'Piers Goodwin is a substantial stakeholder in my newspaper,' she said. 'This would need to be watertight to get past my editor. There can't be even the smallest loophole.'

'I know.'

'Do you have proof – I mean real, substantial proof that won't get me sued, sacked and rendered un-publishable?'

'I can get it. That's why I need your help. I know these people were behind the assassination of Sebastian Steele and Martin Savage and all those others. I believe they did it cynically in order to foster hatred and anger and to provide themselves with the justification they needed to break the ceasefire. I think they hope to overthrow the Government. At the very least they want to bring an end the devolution agreement and all it stands for.'

Sheila Jones took a few steps away from Joe and sat down on a bench beneath the oak tree.

'You think it's just you and me against the bad guys,' she mused, 'Wyatt and Virgil Earp against the Clantons.'

'We've got Doc Holliday on our side too,' Joe smiled. 'He's called Stone. He's currently playing the renegade and offering us protection, despite orders from above. He works for the Security Services and he's our route to Goodwin and the other top people, if there is a route. He has the right contacts and he's well prepared.'

'Can I meet him?'

'He'll be at the hotel now if you want to come down there with me.'

'Alright, since I'm here I might as well hear your plan and meet your inside man. I commit myself to keeping everything you tell me entirely secret until you say otherwise, but other than that I can make no promises. I need to hear what you both have to say. Is that ok?'

'Yes, that's all I ask.'

'And somewhere down the line I expect an exclusive whether I help you or not.'

'You have my word.'

'Then that will have to do. Now, you can tell me your more recent adventures as we walk to the hotel – as a display of good faith. Then you can send your Mr. Stone out to speak to me. I'll book a room at the hotel for tonight.'

As they walked past the church and its graveyard and turned down Dowlheim Street towards the hotel, Joe sketched the details of the last two years and his recent, futile journey north. As they approached the hotel, Sheila stopped and turned to him again.

'One thing bothers me, Joe, I mean, really bothers me. We're talking about intrigue, high politics, corruption and civil insurrection and some very nasty people. Don't you think you should look after your family first, get them out of here?'

'My family will never be safe until this is over. I understand that now. Without Sebastian Steele and my father-in-law my family are impossible to protect. I can't let them out of my sight. If they stay with Hannah's sister or somewhere else, we'll have two places where we're vulnerable and we haven't the resources to defend both. If there's a chance to bring this to an end, I have to take it. It's the only way. Do you understand?'

'Yes, yes I think I do. I only hope you're right.'

Outside the 18th century inn with its solid granite facade and double doors leading to an inner courtyard, Stone was waiting on the cobbled path.

'I need to be with Hannah,' Joe said. 'Stone will explain everything. He knows what we need.'

As the outer door opened, a murmur of voices arose as if carried on a sudden breeze; then the door closed and all was silent again, the voices, like the warmth, locked inside, like safety.

'So, Mr. Stone, you have things to tell me.'

They turned aside and began to speak in low voices. Sheila asked questions, lots of questions. At times she turned away, as if inclined to leave at once.

'But that's madness,' she muttered. 'It's worse than madness it's suicide. If you think for one moment I can get this past my editor you are deluded...'

'But if it works,' Stone replied. 'Just imagine if it works...'

'Ridiculous. Just look at the risks regardless of anything else...' Sheila turned away again. 'I can't believe... I'm sorry, Mr. Stone, but I can have no part in it.' She took a couple of steps down the street.

'Wait, just give me ten minutes. Please, just listen.'

Sheila turned back and they spoke again.

'You know people I have no access to,' Stone said, 'people we can trust and who have access to resources we need.' He spoke firmly, controlling the anxiety he felt. Everything now depended upon his ability to persuade Sheila Jones to help them.

'That's not the point. For me to get involved in a harebrained scheme like this would be unprofessional. Even if – and I say this entirely hypothetically – even if I were foolish enough to go along with the scheme, there isn't a network or a newspaper which would touch it. It is utterly unimaginable. You need to put it out of your minds straight away.'

'Then we need your help to find an alternative.' Stone's tone was firm, resolute. Sheila was right, of course. The whole thing was madness. Someone in his profession, with his years of experience, should know better. The likeliest outcome was a house full of corpses, including his. But the stakes were high, so high that even his superiors might, just might, allow it to proceed – though not with either their blessing or their overt acknowledgement. His would be the professional neck on the line; he would be the human sacrifice. He was a lone wolf.

He could see Sheila was getting into her stride now. She turned on him with a glare that could melt glass. 'And you,' she snapped, 'you should know better. This is completely unethical. Joe may not fully understand the risks but you do. You should be pointing out to him the insanity of what he's suggesting.'

'Joe understands. He's gone through it time and time again. We've discussed it down to the smallest detail.'

'Impossible; there are contingencies you cannot possibly anticipate, details you cannot conceive, so many things that could go wrong. You can never fully predict how these people will react. And what about Joe's wife and his two little girls; do I understand correctly that they plan to remain in the house while all this Boys' Own nonsense is going on? It is absolute insanity. No, you can count me out.'

It was no use applying raw emotion with Sheila, Stone knew that. He had to reason with her, explain the significance of the outcome and the delicate balance of gain against risk.

'The house is the safest place for them.'

'How reassuring.'

'If this comes off, we'll be in a position to rid ourselves for once and for all of those people who are profiting from the current unrest. We can bring it to a halt and we can prosecute the people guilty of the assassination of Sebastian Steele.'

For the first time during their conversation Sheila Jones hesitated.

'You know people in television and radio.' Stone pressed home his advantage, 'People with the expertise to help us, journalists who would be willing to take a risk. Without your help we won't succeed. We need an outlet...'

'I think you overestimate my influence, Mr. Stone. No-one in the mainstream media will go near this plan of yours.'

'Yes, but imagine we succeed? What an exclusive that would be!'

Sheila glared at him sternly.

'Now you're trying to play me, Mr. Stone. That's most unworthy of you. You're offering me a poisoned chalice and telling me it's the Holy Grail.' She peered at him over her steel-rimmed spectacles. 'It's time I was going. I'm sorry to walk away but...'

'Will you help?' Stone asked. 'Please.'

Sheila sighed. She took a couple of steps and then stopped. She seemed to be thinking. 'If you are intent on going ahead with this plan,' she said at last, 'If I can call anything so utterly flawed a plan, I suggest you consider making some changes. Firstly, you need to use alternative and less conventional outlets. The regular, mainstream media won't touch this. They'll only come on board later when and if the outcome is edited *and clean*. No innocent victims and definitely no murdered children. I know a couple of people who work on internet-based news outlets, left wing liberal types, who may be persuaded, if they think it's in a noble cause. You won't get your worldwide audience, not straight away, but you have the connections, Mr. Stone, to ensure those who need to see it do. Besides, the last thing you want is to turn Mr. Caine and his henchman into martyrs, no matter what Joe Savage may think.'

'Thank you. Yes, yes, I think...'

'Never mind what you think, Mr. Stone. I can make no promises but I'll do my best. At the very worst I can console myself with the fact that if all else fails I will be first on the scene of a mass murder.'

'Let's hope not.'

Let's hope not indeed. Now, if I'm going to participate in this charade I must go to my room and commandeer a telephone. I don't suppose time is on our side.'

Stone nodded. 'We don't have much time. We need everything in place tomorrow.'

'Are your people ready to act?'

'Yes, at a moment's notice. It's all in place.'

'Can I tell that to my friends and, more particularly, my editor? I need to get something out of this.'

'You can tell them to have reporters and photographers on standby at locations I can give you. I'll let you know as soon as I give the order to move.'

'Well, that will have to suffice, I suppose. Where can I contact you when I have more information?'

'I'll be with Joe and his family. Here's my mobile number.'

Stone gave her a card and she turned and disappeared, shaking her head, into the hotel. Stone waited for a moment and looked up and down the street. It was empty now. In a few hours dusk would gather around the village and those who could, would sleep. He turned back to the hotel and joined the mourners in the log-fired lounge.

Chapter 33

'Are you sure about this, Joe? There's still time to change your mind. We can find somewhere for you and Hannah and the girls, somewhere safe...'

Stone lounged back on the sofa in the sitting room. The funeral was over, the mourners had gone home and a hush had fallen over everything. He held a glass in his hand and swirled the contents lazily. It was not the first he had had that evening and he had reached that easy, relaxed condition to which only a few drinks could bring him nowadays.

'Can you really find somewhere safe?'

Stone sighed and sipped, sipped and sighed.

'No, probably not.'

'Then I don't think we have any choice.'

'You could pack up and leave the country, courtesy of a grateful government, start again in foreign climes.'

'We don't want to leave. This is our home.' Hannah was sitting cross-legged in front of a small wood-burning stove, lit now to dull the late evening chill. It glowed, orange and yellow, behind glass doors. She turned towards Stone and Joe. 'The girls are happy here. I'm happy here.'

'You're taking a hell of a risk. What if they choose to shoot first and talk after? What then?'

'They won't.' Joe was trying to sound confident, maybe for Hannah, maybe for himself but his words lacked conviction. 'They've been waiting for this moment for a long time. They'll want to enjoy it – savour it, so to speak.'

'They still might shoot.'

'I trust you to prevent that, Stone.' Joe smiled.

Stone sighed and half closed his eyes. 'I'm too tired for this business. I should be in an office somewhere, waiting for my pension.'

'You'd be bored.'

'I could live with a bit of boredom right now. Do you mind...?' He indicated his glass and the open bottle on the table, 'Could I...?'

'Pour me one.'

'Me too,' said Hannah.

'This is a fine malt.' Stone held the bottle and looked at it. 'A peaty, island malt.'

'It was my father's favourite.'

'He was a man of fine taste and refinement. Here's to your father, Hannah.' He raised his glass. 'And here's to his favourite malt.' He sat down heavily beside Joe. 'What are your plans when this is all over?'

'Martin had a small cottage where the mountains meet the sea. It looks out towards the grey outer isles and the ocean. It's a blissful place. We went there once, a few years ago, before all this. It was one of the happiest weeks I can remember. We'll go back, try to be that happy again.'

'There's a small boat,' Hannah said. 'The outboard is kept in an old building converted into a storage barn. One day when the weather was calm, we took the boat out along the coast. We couldn't take the girls because they were too small then so my parents looked after them. I'd like to take them out around the nearest islands to see the birds, maybe even dolphins and whales.'

'It sounds idyllic.'

'It is – apart from the weather and the mosquitoes.'

They were silent for a few minutes.

'Casey has gone.'

Hannah looked suddenly pale and frightened. 'When did he go? Why didn't you say?'

'It didn't seem the right time, with the funeral and everything. He got his orders yesterday. He left when we got back after the funeral. He didn't want to leave but he had little choice.'

'Then it's beginning,' Joe murmured quietly.

'It seems so.'

Hannah stood up and moved towards the door.

'I'm going to check the girls.'

'Nothing will happen tonight. I've been round the house and secured all the doors and windows just to be sure, but nothing will happen tonight.'

'I'm still going to check them.'

The door closed behind her and they listened as her feet made soft sounds on the stair carpet.

Meg was awake. She stirred and turned in her bed as Hannah opened the door and a soft light from the stairs broke into the darkness.

'Mum?'

A soft, low sleepy voice, like a voice that had been waiting and hoping for someone, called to her.

'I'm here, Meg. I'm here. Could you not sleep?'

'I was thinking about Grandad and about dying. I don't want you and Daddy to die, not ever.'

She sobbed gently.

Hannah held her close and stroked her head; she was warm and safe and curled in a cocoon they had spun for her, to protect her from what lay outside. But how could they protect her from this? There were monsters beyond the windows, lurking in shadows.

'We're not going away. We're going to stay here with you and Jessica forever and ever. We're going to watch you grow up and be successful and happy and we're going to be part of that. When we are very, very old and we've had enough and we want a good, long rest, maybe then we'll die.'

'Grandad died. He wasn't old.'

What could she say that would make any sense to a child? It made no sense even to her. The order she had known had been destroyed and everything was in flux, everything was in chaos, as if evil had gained the upper hand. How could a few good people stem that tide? Even the hope she had for the future of her own tiny country was caught like a piece of straw in the wind.

'Grandad was a very brave man,' she said. She stroked Meg's hair softly, reassuringly. 'He always tried to do what was right, no matter what. That was what made him so special. Sometimes that meant he had to do things that bad people didn't like. They didn't like him because he was good and because he was right. They wanted him to stop. But Grandad did what was right, no matter what. Do you understand?'

'Did the bad people kill him?'

'Yes. They killed Grandad and they killed Sebastian Steele and some other people. They were very bad, evil people.'

Meg was quiet for a moment.

'Then the bad people won,' she said softly.

'Bad people will never win,' Hannah said firmly and for a moment she meant what she said. 'You must never think that, Meg. It may look like that for a while, maybe even for months or years, but in the end, good people will always win. People will always remember Grandad and Sebastian because they were good and because they were willing to give up their lives for other people and for what was right and fair. There are other good people who will step forward and take their place.'

'Like Daddy?'

'Yes, like Daddy. Daddy is a very brave man too.'

'The bad people might kill Daddy.'

'No, no, not ever.'

'They killed Grandad.'

'I know.'

'I don't want Daddy to die. I don't want him to be brave and to die.'

She was sobbing again now and the damp of her tears penetrated, warm, through to Hannah's skin. What could she say? She resorted to the old, heavy words, the words that weighed on them like a burden they could never drop.

'Do you remember what Daddy said? Do you? He promised you that he would come home and that we would be together and he wouldn't go away again. You believe Daddy, don't you?'

'Yes.'

'Daddy made a promise and Daddy always keeps his promises, doesn't he?'

'He promised to come home,' Meg murmured sleepily. 'He said he'd come back for the funeral and he did.'

'Just like he said he would.'

From the other bed, Jessica snored gently. Meg laughed quietly, a secret laugh between her and Hannah.

'Jessica always snores,' she said. 'Sometimes she talks. She says silly things that don't mean anything.'

'Are you okay now?'

'Yes.' She yawned. Her eyes would not stay open much longer. 'Mum?'

'Yes?'

'Remember when I was little and I was scared of the dark?'

'Yes.'

'Will you look in the cupboard for me?'

'Check for monsters?'

'Bad people.'

'Of course, I will but there's nothing to fear in our house. Remember we told you about the magic shield that closes over our house at night time? It keeps all the evil things away. If you imagine floating high in the sky and looking down at our house, surrounded by quiet fields and trees and rivers, you can see the shield that protects us.'

It was what they always told her, when the wind blew and she heard its lonely cry, when she feared creatures lurking in the darkness, when she looked out and saw the red eyes of death staring malignantly back.

Not here. Nothing can reach you here. We won't let it. Here, everything is safe and warm. We have a magic shield to protect us.

'That's just a story.'

Hannah checked the cupboard and looked under the bed – trainers, a crisp packet, an old handkerchief.

'No monster will go under here,' she said, 'it's a tip.'

Meg giggled softly. 'It's to keep the monsters away. Jessica's is worse.'

'I think you're the monster. Go to sleep.'

'Goodnight, Mum.'

'Goodnight, Monster.'

She closed the door gently and crept back downstairs. Stone was asleep, his head lolling back on the sofa, his mouth slightly open. An empty glass lay on his lap. Hannah took the glass and placed it on the table. Joe was staring into the embers of the stove.

'What are you thinking about?'

'The past, the present and the future.'

'All at once?'

'They're all here at once – tonight, especially. How are the girls?'

'Meg has the night terrors again. It's hardly surprising after all that's happened. She's asleep now.

'It's time for us to be in bed too, I think.'

'We have to hope no-one attacks us tonight,' Hannah said, nodding towards the sofa where Stone lay snoring. 'I don't imagine he'll be much help.'

A single eye flickered open and then another and a smile licked across the worn contours of Stone's face.

'I shall sleep here tonight,' he said, 'and you can be quite sure that if a pin drops inside this house I shall be on my feet quickly enough to catch it before it hits the ground. Sleep easily, my dear. You have nothing to fear.'

'Goodnight, Stone.'

'Goodnight.'

When he heard their bedroom door close, he walked through to the kitchen and rinsed his face in cold water. Then he came back and sat down.

'Well, Sheila Jones,' he murmured, 'it's up to you now. I just hope...'

Chapter 34

Daylight. The hours passed interminably. The postman brought a bundle of letters, redirected from the city office where Hannah's father had worked. Stone had phoned 'upstairs' and been granted authority to discretely open them, so that those of a poisonous nature could be removed. Those that remained, and they were by far the majority, spoke of the esteem in which her father was held, the courage he'd displayed, the importance of his work and of the example he set to others. Many spoke of the hope he had offered for the future. Joe and Hannah read them all and displayed the many cards around the house.

Then there were the flowers and other tributes. Sitting close to Joe and holding his arm she read the cards which accompanied the bouquets and wreaths and then, by arrangement, had the flowers delivered to the church and from there to the community at large.

'I don't think he would have understood this at all,' Hannah said. 'He always said Sebastian was the key figure in the negotiations. His own role was in the background. He preferred it that way.'

'It was inevitable his work should be acknowledged, I suppose.'

'He'd have been embarrassed by it.'

'Sebastian knew how important he was to the process.'

Late in the morning, Sheila arrived. Her car pulled up outside the door and she got out, dragging a bunch of flowers and a box wrapped like a present. A young man stepped from the passenger seat. He carried a camera, slung casually round his neck, and a notebook.

'Here, take these.' She thrust the package and the flowers into Joe's hands and returned to the car for her laptop and another package. She closed the front door behind her and dropped the package unceremoniously on the floor.

'Just in case anyone's watching,' she said sharply. 'I'm just a journalist bearing gifts and hoping for an exclusive interview. This is Marek. As well as being a very good photographer, he is extremely proficient where anything technological is concerned and he does a lot of work for internet news sites. Now, where are we setting up?'

She was abrupt and business-like and her sharp features seemed to have sharpened even more, as if just that morning she had applied them to a grindstone. Her glasses perched precariously and she stared above their steel rims, missing nothing.

'Ah, Stone,' she said as the officer appeared from the kitchen. 'I need to speak to you. Joe, take these packages to the room, the flowers too. Marek knows what to do.' She turned to Hannah, who was about to take the flowers to the lounge, where they could be added to the others. 'Sorry, it was a necessary subterfuge, if in rather poor taste, but there are some items which Marek requires hidden among the leaves and flowers. You can have them back in a moment.'

She turned and bustled Stone into the kitchen and closed the door behind her. Hannah returned to the lounge where the girls were reading cards and looking at the flowers. Joe led Marek through the house to the study.

'It must be like working next to a tornado.'

'Her colleagues tell me it's like working in a forge. Every now and then she spits, and someone gets burnt.'

Two hours later, they emerged from the study and went to the kitchen. Sheila had long since finished her conversation with Stone and they were sitting at the kitchen table. Stone had a coffee cup before him. Sheila sipped black tea. She stood up as Marek appeared.

'Are we ready to leave?' she asked.

'Yes, everything's ready.'

She turned back to Stone. 'Remember what I said. I'll have people stationed ready for your signal, people we can trust. I'll need no more than a few minutes to have them ready with cameras. Can you trust your people?'

Stone nodded. 'I know every one of them. Everything is battened down tight. There'll be no leaks.'

'I hope you're right.' She looked at Joe. 'You're a bloody fool. This is the most idiotic and hare-brained scheme I've ever heard of.'

'A desperate plan for a desperate situation; let's pretend it'll work.'

'Bloody fool,' she repeated. 'I don't often write obituaries, but for you I'll make an exception.'

Marek shook his fingers and blew on them as if they were burnt. He smiled slyly at Joe - sparks from the forge.

Sheila turned to go. 'Come on, it's time we were out of this madhouse.' At the door, she turned back. 'Good luck,' she said. 'You're a fool, but if this works, if this works...' She inhaled heavily through her teeth. 'Just imagine.'

As she walked to the car she called back, 'And don't forget my exclusive.' A moment later the car pulled out of the drive and turned down the lane. It accelerated away, leaving a silent vacuum behind it.

'I feel as if I've been slapped,' Stone murmured. 'Trampled underfoot and then slapped for good measure.'

They returned to the house and closed the door.

Hannah was sitting in the lounge with Jessica and Meg. Jessica was helping Meg copy a picture of a lion. Colouring pencils were scattered across the floor. The three adults sat back on the sofa and Joe picked up a newspaper. Photographs of the funeral of Sebastian Steele dominated the front page but inside, within the darkness and silence of an unturned page, were photographs of the funeral of Martin Savage in their own village church.

'He's where he would've wanted to be,' Joe murmured, 'tucked away in the inside pages, leaving the headlines for Sebastian.'

Nothing else happened that day. The girls grew restless. They wanted to be out in the garden but Hannah persuaded them to stay indoors. Only in the late afternoon did she relent for half an hour, and then she took them to the swing and the trampoline.

The next day passed in the same manner and, to make matters worse, the day grew dull and overcast and a light rain began to fall, keeping them indoors. The wind increased gradually and drove the raindrops against the window, where they hung for a moment before forming a channel down to the sill and the ground. In the garden, the rain dripped though the trees and the empty swing moved slowly in the gathering wind while the sides of the trampoline billowed.

In the late evening, the rain stopped and a star or two appeared through the trees, but the wind continued to grow. The branches of the silver birches bent forward as if checking the ground.

Darkness had just fallen and the last glimmers of light had faded from the west when they heard a distant sound, like a gunshot. The curtains were closed now and the lights were switched on in the lounge and kitchen. The girls had gone to bed an hour before.

Stone was immediately alert. He sat forward on his chair and then stood up and stepped towards the window. Joe threw the light switch and the room plunged into darkness. Stone eased back the curtain and looked out.

'Nothing,' he said after a moment. 'It was too far away, probably a poacher or a gas gun, or maybe a car.'

He spoke reassuringly but he couldn't hide his anxiety. He stayed by the window, staring out, scanning the drive and the deeper darkness beneath the trees. After a few minutes though, he sat back down, the lights went on again and they watched the television news. Conflict in the Far East, the Middle East and in Africa, floods and drought, earthquakes and high seas were driven from the broadcast by more pressing news close to home. The insurrection was continuing across several cities. The footage showed streets where Joe had recently walked, barricades he had passed, areas he had avoided. Mostly it showed scenes of destruction, where neighbourhoods had been ransacked and burned out. Footage from the previous evening showed the disparate groups fighting each other, the troops and the police. Young people armed with handguns, knives and rifles swaggered and postured and threatened.

Politicians and experts presented their advice and argued endlessly about the correct course of action. The Chancellor spoke reassuringly. The troops, she said, were gradually restoring order. It would take some time. People should remain calm. Already, several cities were quiet. The worst areas were quieter. She was calm and he did not smile. She expressed outrage and resolute determination. The country would emerge from this and it would be stronger. The people could believe her. She was their leader.

Then Piers Goodwin appeared, smiling, benign, like a jovial uncle, and he spoke clearly and with such lucidity he was hard to resist.

'Do you condemn the violence of white nationalists?' he was asked again and again.

'I condemn the actions of those who provoked this crisis, those who attacked our democracy and killed Sebastian Steele. I understand the anger and I understand the fear that ordinary people feel every day. The Government has done nothing to help them so these people - ordinary, working people like you and I, - patriotic people, have been forced to go out on the streets to defend their own homes. The Government has completely let them down.'

He was 'everyman,' the ordinary man on the street, the one politician willing to say what everyone was thinking, to express the feelings that everyone felt, to lay the blame where everyone wanted it laid.

'There are people in our cities and towns who do not share the values we cherish. They would change our country to reflect their own distorted views. The good people out there know that, even if the government and the media don't. They feel like strangers in their own land, as if *they* are the immigrants. Go out on the streets and talk to real people whose jobs have been taken, whose laws have been broken and whose values have been trampled underfoot. Ask them. I have. I know how they feel.'

He spoke smoothly and disguised his xenophobic hatred in a poisonous web of reason. It was hard to find a specific phrase or sentence that could rouse hatred in his followers but the words were there. The oil he poured so reasonably ignited like petrol.

'We have to *struggle* to reassert the values that have made our country strong. We have to *fight* against this new tyranny and *stand up* for what we believe. No one wants to see violence on the streets of our country but the reality is that successive, weak, liberal minded governments have allowed our people to feel like oppressed minority in their own communities. It has to stop. I understand how these people feel and where the urge to *rise up* has come from. I hate violence but I share their frustration. They have been let down by the very people who should have protected them.'

Hannah stood up and turned the television off.

'I'm sorry but I can't watch that man. I hate him and everything he stands for.'

She walked towards the table and started to gather together cups and saucers and plates.

It was then that she noticed something different out on the lane, a bright, flickering light in the distance between the trees, not far from their neighbours'. She drew back the curtains.

'My God, there's a fire,' she cried.

Again, the lights were dimmed and Stone drew her away from the window and peered carefully out.

'It looks like it's at your neighbour's house or just outside. It's hard to tell. Come here, Joe, but keep out of sight. What do you think?'

'It's on the road near the end of their drive. You can see the house lights to the left.'

'I need to get a closer look,' Stone murmured. He turned towards the door, then stopped suddenly. 'Do you have their phone number? Can you call them instead?'

Hannah ran across to the sofa and drew her phone from a bag beside it.

'Do you think it's them?'

'I don't know. I can't....'

He paused and glanced anxiously at Joe.

'Hello, Jane? It's Hannah. Are you and Colin all right? We saw the fire.'

There was a loud explosion on the lane and a plume of fire shot high into the air.

Hannah listened and relayed what she heard. 'It's a car. Colin has been out to see what happened. It looks like it crashed into the ditch by the roadside and hit a tree. He can't see anyone in the car, but the whole thing is engulfed in flame. They've called the fire brigade and the police.'

She listened again.

'Jane thinks it's maybe some drunk from the village trying to get home. Maybe they missed the corner and crashed.'

In the distance they heard sirens approaching.

'Okay, Jane. Thanks, so long as you're both alright. Let me know if you hear more. Goodnight. Goodnight.' She closed the phone. 'I'm going to the girls,' she said.

Stone nodded. 'Close the door and stay with them. Don't come out, no matter what. You know your role now. You look after the girls, nothing else.'

She fled quietly towards the stairs then paused and returned to the hall as if she'd forgotten something. A moment later, she slipped quietly into the girls' bedroom and closed the door. A key turned in the lock.

'You think it's beginning?' Joe asked.

Stone nodded. 'Are you ready?'

'Ready as I can be.'

'Take care, Joe, and good luck.'

'You too.'

Chapter 35

Jacob Tarvey worked for the Government - freelance. He had been recruited straight from the army, where his expertise with a rifle had earned him a specialist role as a sniper. He was good, probably the best. He had qualities that the others didn't have. He was devoid of any troubling doubts and he never betrayed the slightest emotion. Killing was all in a day's work for Tarvey. He got his orders and he obeyed them and that was all. He slept without any troubling conscience or unwelcomed dreams and when he awoke, he looked forward to each day.

He had few friends. His pinched, concentrated face and staring eyes repelled people, even those in his regiment whose lives depended upon his skill. His humourless, cold manner fitted badly with the joviality of his comrades. He shared none of their interests, - sport, films, women, – and he had little to say. Worst of all, he didn't notice the repugnance others felt. He didn't care that when, a few at a time, left the table or the bar where he sat in near silence, it was to escape him and his cold, fishlike eyes and emotionless stare. The chill and the calm that surrounded him reminded them of death. His hands were cold and thin and his lips narrow. Everything about him made them think of death, death, death.

When he left the army, he gave no-one his address or phone number. He didn't share email links or contact ex-colleagues through social media. He simply disappeared and his colleagues felt as if a weight had been lifted from them.

Occasionally, someone would mention him.

'I wonder what happened to Jacob Tarvey?'

Someone would shudder and others would feel an icy chill pass over their skin, like the touch of a ghost. Usually someone laughed uneasily, as if to dispel something they all felt.

'I heard he's working for the Government.'

There was a silence.

'I guess we know what that means.'

Another silence followed.

'Fucking psycho,' someone said.

The conversation moved on and the memories roused by the name of Jacob Tarvey slowly dissipated, like a damp mist in sunlight.

Tarvey spent his time alone now, but he cared about that no more than he cared for the company of his army colleagues. He sat amid the tools of his new trade and he was at ease whether he was in an apartment in the city, a tent on a hillside, a ruined building or, as now, in a smart, family-run hotel in a picturesque market town called Dowlheim. The job mattered - nothing else.

He was on a particularly intriguing mission at the moment. His order for this job hadn't come through the usual channels but straight from the top. He knew the man who contacted him by name but had never spoken and they had never met – until very recently. This man was close to the very top of the Service food chain.

Tarvey was in Zarten when he got the encrypted message on his laptop. *Meet by the river, on the embankment, six o'clock.*

The man was already waiting when he got there. He was wearing a dark overcoat and a hat, pulled down over silvery grey hair. His hands were in his pockets and he stood by the rail looking over the river. When Jacob walked up and stood beside him, he didn't even turn.

'Tarvey?' he asked.

Tarvey looked out at the grey water, moving sluggishly between the banks towards a distant bridge. He nodded. A wisp of hair fell forward. He ignored it.

'I've a job for you. I've been told you're the man to do it.'

Tarvey didn't answer. He knew his worth, his status.

'Your target is one of ours. Does that bother you?'

It didn't; a job was a job. Those who employed him made the decision. They could worry about reasons and consequences. His job was simpler. He did what he was ordered to do and that was all. He was still a soldier; he was still fighting for his country, albeit in a different way.

'He's not a man of any consequence, a minor cog in an inconsequential wheel.' The client waved a long-fingered hand slowly. 'He's...in the way, that's all you need to know. We need to remove him quietly and efficiently. There'll be no authorisation and no official approval. You'll deal with me and no-one else. Do you understand? If this goes wrong, no-one will know you. You'll be on your own.'

Tarvey nodded. He knew his position. He was necessary to the smooth running of the engine of state until he failed and became a liability. Then he was no-one. Tarvey had no intention of being no-one.

'You'll be paid accordingly, of course.'

Tarvey didn't talk money; it was distasteful, as if he were some common mercenary. He looked away.

'Should I anticipate any immediate repercussions; is there anything I should be prepared for?'

'We'll deal with the repercussions. You do the job and you disappear. The blame will be directed elsewhere. Can you do it?'

Something which, on another face might have resembled a smile flickered for a moment and was gone.

The man didn't look at Tarvey during the interview. His eyes didn't move from the river and the far bank, the outline of buildings rising and falling on the skyline like strange battlements. That was his world, over there among the fortifications of the city, the banks, the ministries, the offices. It was his job to protect it, to sustain it when it was under attack, to fight off anything that threatened its stability. It was under attack now. The establishment into which he was born was threatened like never before. Something had to be done. Why else would he be here, dealing with the likes of Jacob Tarvey? He grimaced and a frown of distaste flickered across his face. Suddenly he wanted to be gone.

He removed his hand from a deep pocket and handed Tarvey a card and a phone.

'Book yourself into the hotel on the card and wait. It's a place called Dowlheim – a busy, little market town but nondescript, - you'll like it. A photograph and address will be sent to this phone. Check out the location of the target but don't be seen. It's under guard, just two men. Can you do that?'

Tarvey didn't answer. He didn't need to.

'Will the guards be a problem during the operation?' he asked. He liked the word 'operation.' It had a professional ring; it was clinical, cold and impersonal, like him. Akmal was an operation, so were the men in the boat.

'The guards will be withdrawn before you're required to act. Once you're booked into the hotel, someone will contact you personally with details. He's called Caine. You can trust him.'

'How will I recognise him?'

The grey man laughed softly. 'You'll recognise him.'

Tarvey turned and walked along the embankment towards the bridge. For the first time the grey man looked towards him as he disappeared into the crowd of pedestrians, a thin, inconspicuous figure, drawn into the seething mass and lost.

'Not what I expected at all,' he murmured.

He opened a phone and spoke briefly.

'Goodwin? It's all set. Yes, completely safe. Okay. The next thing you'll hear will be the news on television.'

He closed the phone and then removed the sim and cast it into the river. He broke the phone in half and dropped it in a litter bin. Then he pulled the collar of his coat against the evening chill. He looked up and down the embankment and walked briskly away towards the city and the centre of government.

Tarvey had been in the hotel for three days before he met Caine. The town was buzzing with news of Martin Savage's funeral, but Tarvey knew all about that. He was there, on the village street, watching impassively as the cortege passed. He saw Joe and his family and he saw Stone.

Caine arrived one evening and knocked sharply on the door of his hotel room. The grey man was right; you couldn't mistake Caine, not even without that livid scar. For a moment he felt a tremor of repulsion, but it soon subsided. He'd seen worse.

Tarvey observed him closely, like someone sizing up an opponent. He was a tall man and well built; he looked after himself. He expected to be feared, you could see that. Those ice-cold eyes could hold you and trap you and draw your strength. He would terrify a lesser man. Not Tarvey; Tarvey was immune to such wiles. He watched curiously as Caine stared down at him, waiting for a reaction. Tarvey smiled softly to himself. He remained seated on his bed and continued to clean the barrel of a dismantled rifle. His eyes only returned to the pale figure when he strode casually across the room to the window, pulled back the curtain and looked out.

'Have you been followed?' Tarvey inquired, without interest, and when Caine said nothing, he continued, 'I guess not. You want to sit down? You're in my light.'

He indicated the shadow which had fallen across the bed and the gun barrel. Caine sat down on a chair set against the wall beside the door. Tarvey didn't look up, but he was acutely aware of even the slightest movement. Beneath his pillow a small pistol lay cushioned. He adjusted his position so his hand could reach and fire that pistol before Caine could reach his pocket, his waist or his leg. Tarvey took no chances. His life often depended upon fine calculations.

'Have you visited the location?' Caine asked.

Tarvey nodded.

'You know the target?'

He nodded again and his sharp eyes fixed on Caine. 'I watched him at the funeral. I joined the crowd. It was very touching, especially the family, a sad and tender moment. I didn't see you there.'

Caine ignored the taunt and stared coldly at Tarvey but the assassin was busying himself again with his task.

'There'll be other people in the house, two children, a woman and a man. Can you be sure you get the right man?'

Tarvey's fingers closed on the barrel; his lips tightened. For a moment he stopped. He looked directly at Caine and their eyes met. Neither of them flinched. A smile like a knife wound passed across his lips.

'Only we don't want you going off half cocked and killing the wrong man,' Caine said smoothly. He checked the nails on long, pale fingers and then looked at Tarvey again.

Tarvey resumed his task. There was no point wasting effort rising to Caine's taunts. He knew his job and he knew his target. He had studied Stone closely. He had watched him as he spoke to a group of people at the church gate, measuring and weighing him, identifying his silhouette, calibrating his gestures, his way of walking, of standing. Then he'd ventured out of the village and he'd chosen the best location and trained the rifle on the window and the door. He was ready.

Caine was watching him closely. Evidently, he didn't like Tarvey. Maybe he was angered or even unnerved by the indifference the assassin showed towards him. He was a man who was used to being feared.

'They say you're the best. You don't look particularly special to me.'

Tarvey glanced up but his expression betrayed nothing. 'You want to try me? Go ahead.'

Caine rose to his feet but before he had moved a step Tarvey had reached under the pillow, removed the pistol and pointed it at Caine's chest. For a moment Caine stared angrily, then laughed a dry laugh and sat down.

'Is there anything you need from me?'

'Respect,' Tarvey said.

Caine laughed slowly. 'You've got to earn that.'

'What about you? Have you ever done anything except posture?'

'Just do your job. The real work starts when you leave. Don't get under our feet and don't get caught.'

'Worry about yourself.' Tarvey replaced the pistol beneath the pillow.

'Is there anything else you need, *apart* from respect?'

'You know someone who can crash a car, set fire to it and get away without being seen?'

'That can be arranged. Just tell me where and when.'

'No amateurs; this has to be done right. I want the car in the ditch outside the neighbours' house, just west of the gate. I want it nose first and blocking the lane. I want it doused in petrol and set alight. And I want your driver to disappear into the woods and not get caught. Can you do that?'

Caine nodded. 'I know just the man. What time?'

'Ten o'clock precisely - make sure your driver can tell the time.'

'What do you want it for? It'll draw a lot of attention.'

Tarvey didn't answer. Why would he? It was obvious. It would be helpful to have the road blocked. It would draw Stone to the window or outside onto the lane and it would cast at least a little light on the house.

Caine was thinking fast.

'I have plans of my own,' he said. 'I have to get into the house. I may take advantage of your fire.'

243

'Fine by me, but don't get in the way.'

'I won't.'

Caine stood up to leave. It was time to reassert his authority and make Tarvey respect his power.

'Don't let me down,' he said. 'A lot is riding on this. You're just a pawn in a bigger game. If you fail, we'll come looking for you.'

Tarvey was packing the rifle back into its case. He laughed softly. Jacob Tarvey was no-one's pawn. 'Be careful you don't get in my line of fire,' he said. 'I don't want to waste a bullet.'

As Caine walked along the corridor to the stairs, he heard a soft, tuneless whistle. It accompanied him like irony. He hit the banister angrily with his fist.

Chapter 36

Stone didn't hear the glass fracture. Nor was he certain what caused the searing pain in his shoulder and chest. He slumped back against the wall and felt the hot sticky fluid ooze through his fingers. He looked down at the blood with disbelief. One minute he had been looking out through a crack in the lounge curtains, watching the front garden and the lane beyond. He saw the fire engine approach and stop and heard its siren die away. The next moment he was staggering back from the window and reaching out to the table and the chairs. He stumbled back and slid down against the wall. There was no strength in his arms or legs.

He breathed quickly and painfully and tried to stem the flow of blood and control the burning pain. He could do neither. The blood poured steadily through his fingers and gathered in a widening pool on the floor. The pain was merciless and unrelenting. His eyes dimmed, he could no longer focus, he couldn't think. It was like slipping into a deep, unwelcomed sleep. He shivered as if a cold hand had passed over him.

'Shit,' he murmured and then, 'Joe,' and then his eyes closed.

Out beyond the front garden and beyond the road, part way up a field which rose gently towards the west, a solitary figure rose to his feet. Tarvey moved in a calm, professional manner as he quickly and efficiently dismantled the rifle and packed it into a bag. He slung the bag over his shoulder and then slipped down towards the road. He felt no remorse; this was the job he was trained for, the job he undertook in order to keep the ignorant population safe. Six hundred yards further along that road, now blocked by the fire brigade and the wrecked car, his motorcycle was secreted in a small parking area beside a stream. It took him a matter of minutes to reach it and a few minutes more to disappear. They would never find him, never trace him, never know he had ever been there. He disappeared as quickly and as easily into the darkness as he had disappeared into the crowd on the bridge in the capital. This was what he did. This was his profession. He was the best.

A strange stillness fell over the house. Outside, the restless wind stirred the branches of the birches and moaned as it passed hurriedly around the shrubs and flowers and between the outbuildings and the house. A momentary squall sent rain spiralling through the air and the moan grew to a howl. Then it stopped and the wind drew back into the trees and brushed the leaves as if to soothe them.

Stone didn't know how long he'd been lying there; perhaps it had been a minute, perhaps an hour. He listened but there was no sound from the rest of the house. Perhaps there was still time. He knew how much depended on him now. He reached slowly, painfully into a pocket and gasped as the pain shook him and tore at him, a storm striking a foundering ship, ice crushing the life from it.

'You've got to press those two keys,' he told himself. 'That's all you have to do... Let Sheila know... Then lie back...Sleep... Everything depends...'

He tried to raise the phone to his eyes but his arm fell helplessly at his side and now he heard a sound outside the door. It was the clear, distinct sound of someone breathing, someone silently edging round the door and into the room. He hid the phone with his arm and lay still, his eyes shut, trying not to breathe. He had to pass for dead, he had to. He could show no reaction to the surging pain. He lay still and waited.

Someone stood in the doorway. He imagined them looking down at him and saw himself as they saw him, lying dead in a pool of blood coagulating over the carpet. He saw the gaping wound in his shoulder and the deathly pallor on his face. It felt as if minutes passed before the figure turned and quietly left the room.

He raised the phone again and fumbled for the buttons. It was already primed. All he needed was a moment more...just a moment...just...

Hannah sat on the edge of the bed in the silence of the girls' room. They slept undisturbed, unaware of the danger which surrounded them, unaware of the fragile thread by which so many lives were held. She sighed anxiously and lay down.

Jessica had taken her words seriously. 'Look after Meg,' Hannah had told her. She had knelt before her on the landing as Meg prepared for bed. She held her shoulders as she spoke to her. 'I have to rely on you now, Jessica. I can't say this to Meg. She's too young and she'd be afraid. I need you to be brave. If you hear anything in the night, no matter what, you must stay in your room. Don't open the door and don't leave the room. Everything will be all right if you do what I say. Can you do that, Jessica?'

Jesssica nodded.

'We all have our jobs tonight. Yours is to look after your sister and to keep her in your room, no matter what. I'll try to be with you but if I'm not, I have to know you're both safe. Do you understand?'

'Are the bad people coming for us?'

'Daddy and Mr. Stone are ready for them. You trust Mr. Stone, don't you?'

Jessica nodded earnestly.

'And you know Daddy won't let anything happen to you.'

'Yes.'

As soon as the door closed and Hannah returned to the lounge, Jessica had slipped into bed beside Meg. That was how Hannah found them, sleeping together. The warmth radiated from them; she could hear them breathing softly, regularly. Better they should sleep on a night like this. She lay on Jessica's empty bed and listened through the darkness for any sounds, any cries, any movements. But the house was still and dark and eerily silent. Even the light from the fire could not penetrate this side of the house, and the moon was locked for a while in a cage of cloud. A squall of wind and rain drove against the window and then faded.

Ten minutes passed, then twenty; perhaps they weren't coming tonight. Perhaps the accident on the lane was simply that – an unfortunate accident, a misjudgement on a narrow bend in the dark, resulting in a ghastly livid fire, maybe injury, maybe even death.

Thirty minutes.

Perhaps she should go back downstairs. Perhaps by now Stone had turned the light back on and Joe was sitting with him by the fire. Perhaps they had left her, imagining that she had fallen asleep beside the girls. She began to uncurl slowly so as not to wake them.

It was then that she heard the first sounds. Quite clearly, from the room below hers, she could hear voices. She recognised Joe but whose was the other voice? It wasn't Stone. She knew Stone's voice. This was deeper, more abrupt. This voice had something of oil or slime about it. Even through the floor, she could hear it.

She could hear something else too, something that caused her flesh to chill as if a cold hand had passed over it, something that froze her with dread. It was a scraping, brushing sound, soft in the darkness, accompanied by controlled quiet breathing. It was close, very close. Something was rising from the floor behind her, ghostlike. She shuddered, conscious of the fearful beating of her heart, knowing the children were there, lying near her, sleeping peacefully as this monster emerged from beneath the bed and rose, spectre-like in the darkness. She rose slowly, oh so very slowly, trying not to make the slightest sound. There was someone standing behind her, beside the bed, looking at her.

Before she could face the apparition, a hand pressed against her mouth and pulled her back. She felt the weight of a heavy chest and broad shoulder behind her. She wanted to struggle, to cry out, to bite and kick but most of all she wanted to protect the children. Suddenly she knew just how true that old cliché was; at that moment, she knew she was willing to die for them.

A face came close beside her, hot breath against her ear and neck, lips close.

'Shh,' a voice said quietly. 'Shh.'

Chapter 37

As Lenny drove the stolen car through the slumbering village and past the church, and Tarvey took up his position in the field beyond the lane, two figures crossed the meadow and climbed over the fence at the side of the house. They ran hunched and low across the garden towards the shed where they rested for a moment, breathing heavily. A soft light flickered from a window on their side of the house but the rear was in darkness. They crouched down, unseen.

A small moon, not much more than half full, emerged from behind charcoal clouds and caught the two men in a glint of silver. The clouds didn't linger but covered and uncovered the moon as if some strange tumult was driving them on. Down below, it was still; there was barely a tremor. The earth held its breath.

The two men waited a moment then, as the moon emerged, they slipped towards the corner of the house. In a matter of seconds, they found the pantry window. It took no more than a minute to remove the single pane of glass and reach a gloved hand through it to ease the latch. The window opened silently and a rush of warm air fled from the invading cold.

Bull clambered clumsily through the narrow space and dropped heavily behind the closed pantry door. He opened it very slightly and peered out and listened. The kitchen, which lay beyond, was empty and dark. Beyond it, the door lay open into a wide hallway. No-one had heard him. He closed the pantry door. Behind him, Caine slipped through the open window and closed it quietly.

Bull opened the door again, very slightly; still no-one.

'Go,' Caine whispered and Bull crept across the kitchen floor towards the door to the hallway. He paused and listened again, his back pressed against the wall. He could hear voices in the front lounge now, just down the hallway to his right. A warm light broke through the half open door and cast a glow on the carpeted floor. He slid into the hall and turned up the stairs, silent on the thick carpet.

Caine waited in the pantry, his pallid face now more ghostlike than ever. A minute passed, and then another. Where the hell was Lenny? Where was the fire on the lane? He checked his watch and swore. It was just past ten. Where was he?

It was another minute before Caine heard the sounds he had been waiting for – a dull, distant explosion, the cracking of glass and an eruption of sound approaching him like waves. There was a sudden movement in the room at the front of the house. He could hear voices.

Lenny had done his job just as they had planned it. He had approached along the lane from the village, not going fast, taking no risks. He'd pulled up just down the lane and dimmed the lights. Then he'd eased the vehicle forward until it dropped heavily into a ditch and against a tree. He'd climbed out and removed a petrol can from the back of the car, scattering the contents through the interior and on the ground all around. He had opened the petrol cap and inserted a soaked rag then scattered the remainder of the can and stood back.

The lit match engulfed the car in vivid flames. Lenny watched for a moment and then slipped into the darkness beneath the trees. He would make his way back to the road and be away before anyone approached.

What Caine heard was the explosion as the petrol tank ignited. His body tensed and he watched closely through a slit in the pantry door. His hand reached down to the pistol by his side and he slipped like a pale shadow towards the hallway. He heard voices, three voices, Joe, Hannah and Stone. Then he heard Hannah speaking as if on a phone.

Perhaps she was calling the police. They wouldn't come, of course – he'd seen to that. He waited.

The hallway was suddenly illuminated as the lounge door opened. He pressed his back against the kitchen wall and waited. Whoever it was paused for a moment as if distracted, turned back and then turned again and hurried past the kitchen door and up the stairs. A moment later, someone else passed the door and walked along the corridor towards a room at the back of the house. He heard a voice call back to the person now alone in the lounge. Caine recognised it at once; it was Joe.

Caine still waited. He listened intently. Where the hell was Tarvey? What was he doing? Would he have to deal with Stone himself? He grimaced irritably. Then he heard a crack and the sound of glass fracturing, barely any sound at all, like an ornament from a Christmas tree trodden underfoot. Someone stumbled and slumped against a wall. He heard a muffled groan then everything was silent.

He held his breath and listened.

The house was still. No-one else had heard the sound, no-one had moved, so he stepped across the kitchen floor and checked the hall and the stairs - no-one. Even more slowly now, he edged towards the lounge door. He slipped round the door with his gun raised, his back to the wall, and he checked the room. At first, he saw nothing. Then, in the shadow behind the door, he saw Stone slumped against the wall. He saw the gaping wound, just off centre, near his left shoulder, and he saw the blood. There was no sign of movement and Stone's face was pallid and grey, like death. He edged back to the hall, passed the kitchen door and the stairs and crept towards a back room, from which a subdued light shone like an invitation. The door was open.

He paused before it, his back against the wall, then turned and stepped into the doorway, his gun levelled, ready. A small lamp on the study desk illuminated a figure seated on an upright office chair, reading a small magazine.

Caine glanced around the room. His eyes took in a wall-mounted television, switched off, a laptop on a desk, a bookcase, nothing more. As he stepped into the room, the seated figure lay down the magazine and looked towards him.

'I've been waiting for you,' Joe said. He turned the chair to face Caine. 'Come in.'

Caine took another step into the room and pushed the door closed behind him. With his elbow, he pressed the light switch. He wanted to be seen and he wanted to watch the fear spread across Joe's face. He wanted to count the seconds as the blood drained and the slow realisation of the inevitability of death gradually dawned. Everything had gone according to plan. It couldn't have gone better. He had waited a long time for this moment. There was no need to hurry. It was time for Joe to understand the power of his enemy, to know that he wasn't just some thug but a man driven by principle, someone who would stop at nothing to make his country great again.

Chapter 38

Far to the north in his lime-washed cottage, Alan yawned and looked at his watch. The book he had been reading had fallen on his lap and his hot, bedtime drink lay cold beside him. It was nearly half past ten. The fire in the stove lay subdued and dully glowing. Outside, a strong breeze played in the trees and a sudden squall rattled against the window. He clambered to his feet. It was time he was in bed.

He was just picking up his book when a message arrived on his phone. He picked it up and checked it. It was from an old family friend.

Have you seen this? There was a link to a web address. *Isn't that Joe? What's going on? I thought he was dead?*

Another arrived a moment later and then another.

Just got this link; what's happening, Alan?

Have you seen? What should we do? Where are Hannah and the girls?

Then his phone announced a message on his social media account.

What can we do? He's going to be killed.

Alan was scared. He ran through to his study, turned on the laptop and followed the link to "fromleftfield.org," a left leaning internet news outlet, new to him. It took a moment for him to absorb what he was watching.

'Jesus, Joe, when you said you had a plan, I never thought...'

He was looking into the small study at the back of Joe's house. Joe was sitting on the hard-backed office chair. His back was to a camera which was filming from some point on the wall. Alan tried to remember the room. Was there a wall light there or a picture? Standing before Joe and facing the hidden camera was a tall, pale figure with a livid scar on his cheek and blond, close-cropped hair. He had a gun at his side and he was staring, almost nonchalantly, at Joe. He spoke in a slow drawl. Alan shuddered. He recognised that tall figure immediately; he knew what he was capable of.

'I've been expecting you,' Joe was saying. He gestured towards the front of the house and the lane outside. 'That was a bit melodramatic - a car exploding on the lane. You could have just knocked.' He stood up slowly and walked past Caine towards the curtained window. A heavy blow sent him sprawling back. He sat down again and rubbed his jaw ruefully.

'Stay right where you are,' Caine snapped.

'Still, it is a bit melodramatic, don't you think, a car fire? It'll have every policeman for miles heading this way.'

'They won't be coming here, Joe. Nobody will be coming here.'

Joe smiled. He looked relaxed, almost casual.

'They'll come sooner or later,' he said. 'You can't control them all.' His hand reached out for the magazine and flicked a few pages. Only someone who knew him well, like Alan, would notice the tension in the shoulders, the speech emerging too, too slowly, the effort that controlled each word he spoke, each gesture he made. Alan could see him thinking, planning each word, each move. He knew, just as Joe clearly knew, that one false word, one bad move would precipitate a sudden and painful death.

Christ, Joe, what are you doing?

But he knew what Joe was doing. He had run as far as he could, he was exhausted and he had nowhere else to turn except back. There were few people he dared trust so he had to act alone. It was a last, desperate roll of the dice. If he couldn't push Caine, goad him and draw him on to reveal what he had done and for whom, if he couldn't provoke him to boast of his influence and his connections then all would be lost and he would be just one more victim of the conflict.

But what of Hannah and Jessica and Meg, where were they? What had Joe done? They would all be killed. How far would he get before a wrong word drew an inevitable response? Caine wasn't a fool. He wasn't some brainless lout driven by self pity and envy. He was intelligent, manipulative and cunning.

He picked up his phone and called Lisa.

Write this down,' he said. 'www.fromleftfield.org. Have you got that? No, I can't explain, just log onto it. You'll understand... Oh, and Lisa...?'

'Yes?'

'Make sure you're sitting down when you see it.... It's not good. No, I've got to go now... Speak later... Bye.'

Then he began to message family, friends, colleagues, even clients. He was pretty sure Joe wanted an audience, no matter what the outcome.

Share this link. Share it now. Don't wait. Share it.

'I hope you know what you're doing,' he muttered, 'you bloody fool.'

Then he leaned forward, his eyes fixed on the computer screen, and he watched.

Sheila Jones was sitting in her editor's office staring impatiently at a blank screen. She glanced towards Trevor's haggard, unshaven face as he stood beside her and then towards Marek, co-opted by Sheila to help her, now sitting directly before the monitor, his face concentrated and excited. Trevor looked at his watch, turned and paced the room, then looked at his watch again.

'For goodness sake, stand still,' Sheila snapped.

'I'm too old for this,' he complained. 'I need my sleep.' He turned away again and sipped from a mug of cold tea. 'I don't like watching these internet news sites. It's like sleeping with the enemy. As for you...' He gave Marek a hard stare. He looked at his watch again. 'I'll give it another half hour and then I'm going home. You can call me if anything happens.'

Nonetheless he remained, watching. It was twenty past ten when the link from the Home Page of fromleftfield.org flickered and a grainy image appeared. They saw Joe enter the study and turn on a lamp.

'It's started,' Sheila said.

The editor pulled up a chair and insinuated himself beside Marek, all thoughts of sleep gone. They watched as Joe picked up a magazine and sat back on the office chair.

'He doesn't look like a man who's about to be murdered,' Trevor muttered. 'Is that confidence or arrogance, I wonder?'

'The jury's out on that,' Sheila replied. 'Time will tell.'

Sheila's phone rang, a single loud note, stunning the silence like a shockwave. It was the pre-arranged message from Stone. She read it then turned to Trevor and nodded.

'That's it,' she said. Her usually steady voice trembled slightly. 'Tell everyone, it's cameras at the ready.'

Trevor reached across Marek, picked up the office phone and called a number.

'They're on their way. Are you in place outside Goodwin's flat?' he snapped. 'No, I don't want you in the cafe down the road and I don't care if it's raining...I want you out there now...You're paid to get wet. If you miss this, you'll be lucky to get a job selling papers on a street corner. Where's your photographer? With you? Wonderful, that's bloody wonderful. Get off your arses and get down there now!'

He slammed the phone down, picked it up and started again.

The message was repeated with few alterations.

'Where are you? They're on their way. Miss this photograph and I'll have you skinned and hung from the biggest bloody bridge I can find. Are there any other reporters? None? Good, that's good. They'll be there in droves before you know it. If we're lucky they'll arrive just too late.'

He phoned again and again.

While he was distracted, Marek looked at Sheila and then at the screen.

'Shall we invite everyone to the party?' he asked, 'Put it on your home page?'

She shook her head and gestured towards Trevor. 'He'd never allow it and I can't blame him.'

'We could go live right now.' Marek mimed pressing a few keys. 'That's all it would take,' he said. 'There's a three-minute delay; if anything goes wrong, we have time to cut the broadcast before any of your more sensitive viewers get upset by an encounter with brutal realism.'

'Sorry, but no, this is as much as we can do. Besides, it's enough. We're just capturing evidence, nothing more.'

She stood up and paced the room. Something wasn't right. Why had Stone set things in motion before Joe had got anything from Caine? The plan was to wait until something was said - something to incriminate Goodwin or the others. If Caine heard of these arrests now Joe's life wouldn't be worth the gossamer thread by which it hung.

'I think Joe was hoping for something more, something like a public exposure on screen to the entire nation,' Marek was saying. Sheila barely heard him.

'Joe must be grateful for what he gets,' she murmured. 'If he survives, he can lodge a complaint.'

Marek glanced at her. 'Can we at least put a link for people to follow to take them to the leftfield website?'

'Ask him.' She glanced towards Trevor who, his phone calls completed, now joined them in front of the screen.

'No,' Trevor said.

Marek sighed and they watched as the screen revealed Joe and Caine facing each other.

'My God, he's one big, ugly son of a bitch,' Marek murmured. 'I wouldn't want to meet him on a dark night.... like this.'

'It would be a mistake to think of him as nothing more than that,' Sheila warned. 'I hope Joe isn't making that mistake. Mr. Caine, from my enquiries, maybe a fanatic, he may be a callous, desensitised and totally unpleasant man, but he's intelligent, shrewd and single minded and he's totally committed to his cause. Joe won't find it easy to manipulate him.'

'I wonder how long it'll be before the other papers and television channels pick up on the arrests?' Trevor was distracted. He was thinking about those exclusive photographs and video sequences.

'It'll hit the newsrooms within minute now.'

'Let's hope Joe lasts that long.' Sheila picked up a laptop from beside her and opened it. 'I can't watch. I'm going to start writing the optimistic version. Maybe it'll bring him good luck.'

Trevor stood up and paced to the office door. He flung it open. 'Switch the televisions on, check the web,' he shouted to no-one in particular in the newsroom. 'Call me when something interesting happens, like news bulletins or hoards of journalists heading across the city.'

He shut the door and returned to the screen.

Sheila had started typing but after a moment she stopped, unable to do anything but watch.

'Are you sure you don't want to stream this on your Home Page?' Marek asked again. He saw Trevor's face. 'Okay, okay, but you don't often get chances like this. It's the ultimate exclusive.'

Trevor's eyes flickered. He looked at Sheila and at the screen. He shook his head. 'Impossible,' he said. 'Even if...'

His phone rang and he grabbed it and listened closely. His face brightened in a wide smile. 'We got it,' he said. 'Goodwin has been arrested and there was no-one there but us.' He beamed triumphantly. Marek laughed. Only Sheila's face betrayed doubt and fear.

'Something's gone wrong,' she said.

Alan was right about Joe's frame of mind; beneath a relaxed exterior, his heart was pulsing and racing. He felt moisture forming on his forehead and brushed it quickly away. He watched Caine and saw the pale, blue eyes assessing the situation, taking him in, measuring him. He felt their chill and their icy, inhuman, xenophobic hostility. For a moment he felt a tremor in his limbs and he fought off a shudder of revulsion and fear.

'What now?' he wondered.

Caine raised his gun slowly. He stepped towards Joe and levelled it at his head. Joe didn't move. He stared along the barrel of the gun to those penetrating eyes. He fought to prevent his own eyes closing; he struggled to stop himself blinking. Caine's long finger slowly eased the trigger. It snapped. There was no bullet; Russian roulette. Caine laughed without humour.

'That's too easy,' he said.

'If you're going to kill me, you'd better do it now. You can't keep the police away for long.'

'There'll be no police.'

'You don't have that much power. They'll be here.'

'I have more power than you could ever imagine. I work for people who...' He paused. 'You may not wish to believe it, Joe, but we are alike in many ways, you and I. We both have beliefs, principles.' He raised an elegant hand as Joe began to protest. 'Oh, I know what you think of me. I'm a violent, brainless thug, aren't I? I'm easily manipulated, swayed by the xenophobic propaganda of bigoted media, too stupid to think for myself. I suppose you believe that every intelligent being, presented with rational argument, would inevitably be drawn to one conclusion – that only you, Joe Savage, represented the true path. The rest of us are too ignorant and stupid. That's a very arrogant position, Joe, and one I find offensive.'

'You sound like Piers Goodwin.'

'Oh, I differ from Piers in many respects but I think the country would be a better place if he were in power. Aren't entitled to that view? Isn't that democratic?'

'Snake oil,' Joe laughed. 'The devolution agreement will be democratic. The assembly will be democratic. Besides, you're standing there pointing a gun at me and that's certainly *not* democratic.'

'We must fight to preserve what we love, and protect what we value. We just fight in different ways, you and I.'

'Why are you telling me this?'

Caine smiled coldly. 'I wouldn't want you to go to your death thinking I was just some irrational, Jew hating bigot. I have influence, Joe, and when this is over, I'll have the power to help rebuild a country free from weak, liberal minded leaders who lack strength and commitment.'

'Maybe the weak, liberal minded leaders will stop you. They still have more support than you.'

'Support means little without power. We have people in top positions all over the country. We've been planning this for years.'

'Is that how you knew I wasn't dead? Is that how you always managed to find me?'

Caine laughed. 'There are a lot of people who believe in our cause; some of them are police officers. You could never get far.'

'I got far enough. You never caught me.'

'I've caught you now.'

'Maybe I've caught you. Maybe the police are already here. Maybe this is a trap and you've walked into it. Maybe you're not as clever as you think.'

'That's not really the point is it, Joe? The point is that I'm holding the gun which makes me much cleverer than you would like to believe.'

Lisa sat with her husband, Adam, in their lounge. The children lay asleep upstairs. She watched the computer screen with trepidation and growing anger.

'While Joe is playing silly games, where are Hannah and the children, that's what I want to know? Are they safe? And where are the police? I'm going to call them.'

'Don't be silly. The police will be on their way. My God, he's one scary bastard, isn't he?'

'He doesn't scare me. I'd tell him what I thought of him.'

'Joe's staying pretty cool though, even with a gun pointed at his head. I thought it was all over when he pulled the trigger.'

'Stop talking about it as if we're watching some cheap police drama. There could be old people watching this - it isn't right. I don't want my brother-in-law dying on screen like some cheap American film. I'm going to phone the police.'

Adam drew in his breath sharply. He shuffled on the chair and pointed at the screen.

'Be careful, Joe. Don't goad him. My God, he's raising that gun again. He's going to...Lisa, quickly, I think...'

Caine stared down the barrel of his gun and then lowered it again.

'You think Stone will come to your rescue?' he asked and an unpleasant sneer licked his face like the tongue of a snake. 'Stone is dead. He's lying on the floor of your lounge and his blood is spoiling your nice carpet. He's calling no-one. You're on your own. There's no happy ending for him or for you, Joe.'

For the first time Joe's face betrayed some doubt, some fear. Caine saw it and sneered again. 'Don't feel bad,' he snarled, 'he didn't feel a thing. A shot fired from a distance straight through the window. Thud – that was it. What were you thinking, Joe? Did you really think we'd leave you alone? Did you really think we'd let some Jew flaunt his liberal humanism by rescuing a couple of Muslims, and get away with it? Did you really think we'd just sit there and watch whilst your testimony saw my brother sent down? Did you think I'd let them treat you like some fucking hero whilst my brother was knifed to death in prison? Did you really think we'd just forget? You never had a chance. The police aren't coming. No-one is coming. Our people are everywhere. We've infiltrated every corner of the nation – patriots reclaiming what's theirs. This is their country, my country. Look at you; look at your half-Jew children. Do you really think we'll let you live?'

'No,' Joe said. He sat back in his chair. 'I guess I knew it was hopeless. I just got sick of running. I suppose I thought if I'm going down at least I'd die knowing you lost. Stone's people are out there now, you know, making arrests, cleaning up the mess. There are still some good people at the top. You don't have them all in your pocket.'

Caine raised the gun again.

'Commissioner Meadows and Chief Superintendant Whitely are co-ordinating a move against you even now. Even Goodwin will be arrested.' Joe carefully fed the names Stone had given him.

Caine laughed. He leaned forward and whispered in Joe's ear. 'They're ours, Joe. They're doing nothing.'

Joe was silent, as if the dying embers of hope had been extinguished.

'Then I guess you've won.'

'Of course, what did you expect?'

'I know it was you who assassinated Sebastian Steele and my father-in-law,' Joe said.

Caine raise his arms in protest. 'Really, Joe, such unfounded accusations; I was here in your pretty little town, in a hotel. There are numerous people who can vouch for me.'

'It was your people.'

Caine leaned forward again and whispered. 'You would hardly expect me to confess to such a thing, would you? Who knows who might be listening?' Aloud he said, 'It was Muslim terrorists, everyone knows that. Now, Joe. It really is time I was making a move.'

Joe was thinking quickly. There was no way Caine would incriminate himself. He was too suspicious, too clever for that. It was time for one final, desperate act. He reached across for the television remote and pressed it. The screen on the wall above them flickered, an Asian face appeared, not a regular news presenter, probably a political correspondent. He was speaking from Altwelt Park outside Greyminster. Beneath his face a banner rolled across the screen.

Police raids are taking place across Zarten. Piers Goodwin, Police Commissioner Irene Meadows and Chief Superintendant Jack Whitely of the Metropolitan Police Force have been arrested and are helping police with their enquiries.

The banner rolled past again and again.

The correspondent spoke calmly, measuring his words. *'I repeat - news is reaching us of several police raids across Zarten and the cities of the Zone in what looks like a carefully co-ordinated plan. Senior members of the police, the army and the judiciary have been taken to police stations to be questioned. Official sources are saying that these arrests are linked to the recent riots and the assassination of Sebastian Steele.*

Joe raised his hands and gestured round the room. He stood up. 'Why the fuck would anyone be listening to you,' he said, 'with that going on?'

For the first time a surge of doubt coursed across Caine's face. Joe turned and quickly switched off the television.

'Did you really think you'd get away with killing all those people and blaming a Muslim group? Really?' He laughed. 'Piers Goodwin is going to hang you out to dry,' he said. 'He'll do anything to save his self-important neck. For fuck's sake...'

The blow which struck him sent him reeling back towards the wall where he lay, doubled up and gasping for breath.

'Why'd you do it?' he managed to groan, 'all those people killed...and for what?'

'Those weren't people – they were Blacks, Poles, Romanians, Asians, Muslims, Jews. They were vermin.'

'There were whites too – a mother, a child, an old man, people in cars, on the bus...'

Joe struggled to the chair and sat down, his face grey with pain, his eyes glazed, his breath oozing in uneasy bursts. He couldn't stop now. He couldn't give Caine time to think. How long would it take him to recognise the tell-tale signs, the flickering of the film when the television was switched on and the film kicked in, the unfamiliar correspondent, the time of day, the wrong weather, even the carefully used words, 'I repeat...', just in case the film overran.

It was a clever plan of Stone's, scripted by Sheila and presented by Karim but it would fool nobody for long. It was a last resort, *if all else fails.*

'There are always casualties in a war - collateral damage. Goodwin knew that.'

'Goodwin? So, he knew it wasn't the Asians?'

'Of course he fucking knew. It was his plan.' He span around and stared at the TV screen. 'Turn it on,' he shouted. 'Turn the fucking thing on. This can't be happening. We had top men. Even the troops would soon belong to us. 'Harvey, Warner, Henry...'

Joe shook his head. He rose to his feet and stepped forward. His eyes too blazed with anger.

'You've got a few top men, just a very few, but not the soldiers out there on the streets, not their officers. I saw them. I saw the people there too. They might be frightened at the moment but they won't stay frightened. They'll come back to their houses, they'll build them back up again and they'll be out on those streets, reclaiming their lives. People like you will always lose.'

Caine raised his pistol again and Joe knew it was the third and final time. It was over. All he had to fight for now was his life. He took another step forward until the gun was touching his forehead. Still he did not flinch.

'You think you're the great white hero, the man who could bring down governments, the leader of the supremacists, the nationalists. But I can see you now. For all your intelligence and your clever words, you're just a murderous thug. You think you have power? You've got nothing because most of the people out there don't want you. You're finished. You want me to turn on the television?' he yelled. 'Okay, go on! Look at what they're all watching out there.'

He picked up the remote and pressed a different button and the television on the wall flashed into life and this time a famil face looked out. The news was the same. Goodwin arrested, others arrested, in Zarten, and the cities of the Zone; for Caine it was all falling apart. He looked at the screen and then at Joe and then at the screen again.

In the distance, Joe heard sirens wail.

'You think that's bad? Look at the wall up there. See the wall light? Yeah, well, you were right. There are people out there watching and listening – lots of them.'

'You're bluffing.'

'You think?' Joe hadn't moved; he hadn't flinched. 'They heard your confession, loud and clear. They heard you name names.' He turned away and sat down on the chair. 'You're finished. Give up, Caine.'

Caine looked to the door as if measuring his escape route and weighing it against the time he had available. Suddenly, he stopped and he laughed. He raised the handgun and pointed it.

'Is that how you want to play it, Joe? Is that what you want?'

'It's over,' Joe said quietly.

Caine laughed.

'It'll be over when I say so,' he said. His voice was cold and his eyes flashed dangerously, like a blade. 'You remember my brother, Joe? Remember? He was knifed, died in prison like some common thug. And where was the fucking press when he died? He wasn't even worth a headline, whereas you - weren't you the fucking hero? The fucking Jewish, Muslim-loving self-righteous fucking hero of the liberal fucking left. Oh, the press and TV loved you. They were all over you while my brother, the real hero, bled to death in a prison cell. That was down to you. Well now you're going to pay.'

He reached slowly into his pocket, pulled out a phone and opened it. He looked jubilant. The scar on his cheek pulsed and his eyes flashed a cold, empty blue.

'Kill them,' he said into the phone. 'Kill them now.'

He held the phone towards Joe. 'There'll be no victory for you, Joe. You don't even get to say goodbye.'

A gunshot echoed from the phone and through the house. A child screamed.

'That's one,' he said.

There was another gunshot.

'That's two.'

Chapter 39

Lisa sprang to her feet, screaming at the television, as if the characters on the screen could hear her.

'Hannah!' she cried. 'Meg! Jessica! No! Please, no!'

She gripped her hair and stared. She couldn't move. Adam stood beside her and held her tightly to him.

'This is your fault, Joe, your fault,' she screamed. 'And where's Stone? Where is he? They should have been here with me where they'd be safe. They should've been here. I told Stone. I told Joe. I'll never forgive them for this, never.'

She watched Joe push Caine from his path and spring to the door. He was screaming their names. Over and over he was screaming their names.

'Hannah,' he shouted, 'Jessica! Meg! Hannah! Jessica! Meg!'

He flung the door open and disappeared from the room and the screen. Caine looked slowly towards the camera and those pale eyes in that bleached, scarred face looked out at his audience. Lisa and Adam felt a cold chill across their necks and shoulders and fear ran through them like a wound opening.

Alan, in the darkened room of his cottage in the north, felt a wave of repulsion and dread and shrank back in his chair. Those eyes were looking at him, just at him and they told him what everyone knew. There could be no victory over a man like this. It was futile to resist him.

Caine looked at the camera, raised the gun and coolly blew across the barrel then turned and walked out of the door. The noise of police sirens grew louder. In a moment they would be outside the house. Marksmen would position themselves in the garden and on the lane. Then they would wait; they would begin the process of negotiation or maybe they'd storm the house. Either way, it wouldn't matter to Joe or Hannah, Jessica or Meg. They would be dead.

Chapter 40

Bull slowly released his hand from Hannah's mouth. She felt the cold, steel barrel of a gun pressed against her cheek. She held tight to the duvet and watched the children in the adjacent bed, curled round each other, breathing softly. Her greatest fear now was that they would wake up from that soothing sleep and find themselves in a nightmare.

'Now we wait,' Bull hissed in her ear. His breath, as foul as the mind behind it, repelled her but she could not move. She dared not.

'Not the children,' she begged, 'Please, not the children.'

His hand moved across her cheek and through her hair. She shuddered. Then the hand grasped her hair and tightened. He pulled her head back until she could see his small, mean eyes and his unshaven jaw.

'Make one sound, just one, and the kids die first.'

'They're just children,' she pleaded, her voice no more than a whisper. Silent tears formed in the corner of her eyes but she drove them away. This was no time to show fear. 'They're just children. They have nothing to do with this.'

His hand gradually released her and he wiped the palm across his chest as if in distaste. His small, empty eyes stared at her without feeling.

Hannah lay down, her head resting on the pillow. At all costs now the children must not wake. This was not the world she wanted for them. This was the world only adults should know, where their warm, secure home could be blown down like a house of straw. I'll huff and I'll puff and I'll blow your house down.

Jessica stirred and moved.

'Mum?'

'Go to sleep, darling. Mummy's here.'

She spoke quietly, hiding the fear in her voice, while inch by inch she moved her hand towards the pillow. She saw Bull glance at his watch and the dial illuminated. He was waiting, but what for? How long did she have before the final, ugly conclusion? She inched her hand further towards the pillow but the weight of her body on the duvet made it difficult. She eased her body gradually away. Somehow, when she slipped her father's gun from the locked cupboard in the hall, she had imagined she would have more time. She pictured herself standing between her children and the men who would hurt them - a final, desperate act of love to save their lives and keep them safe. She hadn't told Joe or Stone when she took it. They would have told her to stay with the children, that they would take care of everything. But Hannah knew that things could go wrong and that she would never, never let those men hurt her children. She'd die first.

She had tucked the pistol safely under the pillow of the empty bed as soon as she came into the room. The safety catch was locked and she'd had loaded a bullet but she wasn't sure if it was in the barrel. She wished now that she'd listened more closely to her father when he'd tried to explain its use.

'You may never need it,' he said. He held her hands and looked in her eyes. 'I hope you don't. But you need to know how you load and fire it. Watch me.'

'I don't want to. I don't...'

'Hannah, look at me. You need to know – just in case.'

She watched unwillingly. He held the gun towards her.

'Now you,' he said.

She pulled away. 'I can't.'

'You must,' he said gently. Slowly he opened her hands and pressed the gun into her grip.

'Now load it and show me how you take off the safety catch and how you aim and fire. Go on, show me.'

She did as she was told, just once, then handed the gun back.

'I'll never use it,' she said, 'never.'

'I'll lock the gun in the wall cupboard in the hall,' he said patiently, 'where the children can't reach it. I'll put the key on top of it.'

'I don't like it in the house. I hate guns.'

'You may never need it but I'll be happier if I know it's there. Do it for me, Hannah.'

Now she wished she had taken more time to rehearse its use. As she lay on the duvet and gradually eased her hand under the pillow, she went over and over in her mind the actions she needed to take - how she must grip the gun and quietly release the safety, how she must hold and point the gun and ease the trigger.

'But only if...' she told herself, 'only if...'

She listened now for sounds from the room into which Joe planned to draw his adversary. She thought she could hear subdued voices speaking but she could not be sure.

'You'll never get away,' she said quietly, without raising her head.

'There's no-one to stop us.'

'They could be out there, even now, just waiting. And Stone...'

'Stone is dead,' he said. 'Now shut up.'

Her heart beat rapidly and she breathed deeply and slowly to calm herself. No use losing control now. Her hand inched closer to the gun.

'And Joe?' she forced herself to ask.

He just laughed a low unpleasant growl.

'Soon,' he said.

Hannah's hand moved again, imperceptibly. She felt the coarse grip of the pistol and slipped her hand around it.

A phone rang. Bull stood up and reached into his pocket. She heard the words as if they had been spoken in her ear.

'Kill them now. Kill them all.'

In the other bed, disturbed by the ringtone, Jessica stirred and opened her eyes. It took a moment for her to understand what was happening, that there was someone in her room, someone ugly and scary, someone menacing, someone who now smiled unpleasantly at her and licked his lips – the wolf and Red Riding Hood.

'Mum!'

Jessica buried her head in her pillow and cried. Meg slowly opened her eyes.

'What's happening?' she murmured, 'Mum?'

She saw the intruder and the alarm on her mother's face and she heard Jessica's smothered cries. Bull was distracted. It was only for a moment but it was long enough. Only Meg saw how her mother moved her hand quickly from the pillow; only Meg saw the glint of a pistol in her hand and heard the soft movement of the safety catch. Only Meg saw the look of surprise and shock on the face of the figure before her. He raised his gun quickly. There was a loud explosion, she screamed and then there was another. Both girls heard the gunshots but only Meg saw the man look down and raise his blood-soaked hands as if to show her. Only Meg saw his eyes grow fearful and then pale as they emptied of light. She watched, terrified, as he slumped back and fell heavily on the floor.

Hannah still pointed the gun at the dead man. She shuddered and her hands trembled. She could feel blood on her sleeve where a bullet had grazed her arm and embedded itself in the wooden headboard but she felt no pain. She couldn't take her eyes from the dead man's. They looked at her accusingly.

Meg sat motionless, a freeze frame of terror. Jessica sat up and stared at the body and then at her mother.

'Mum,' she cried.

Hannah moved, as if awoken from a trance. She clambered over to their bed and pulled the girls to her and drew them to their feet.

'It's okay,' she said. 'It's okay. It's over. You're safe.'

They stumbled towards the door. With trembling fingers, Hannah turned the key in the lock and threw it open. The light from outside flooded the room. She pulled the girls out into the light just as Joe ran up the stairs towards them. He caught them in his arms and held them close.

Below him, at the foot of the stairs, Hannah saw Caine emerge like some evil spirit. He raised a gun towards them. She hugged Joe close and hid the children from the eyes of the creature at the foot of the stairs. She did not take her eyes from him. She would not allow him that satisfaction. She would look into those cold eyes to the very last. Outside the sirens stopped. The police had arrived too late.

Then behind Caine she saw something else too. Stone was lying in a trail of blood at the lounge door.

'I'm sorry,' Joe murmured, 'I'm so sorry.'

He tried to push them back towards the room but they had barely moved when the gunshot rang out. She winced as if she felt the pain of a wound and the moment of death. She felt Joe sag and his weight dragged at her. His head fell forward on her shoulder.

There was another shot and Hannah knew it was all over. She opened her eyes and stared defiantly. But it was Caine who stumbled forward and lay face down on the stair. Behind him, beside the door, the gun now lying helpless by his side, lay Stone.

He motioned weakly to the door.

'Watch you don't get shot by them,' he said, smiling thinly.

Joe, his arm trailing blood, stumbled down the stairs. He turned on the outside light.

'We're coming out,' he shouted. 'We're safe. Don't shoot. I'm bringing the children.'

He drew Hannah and the girls to his side and enfolded them.

'We're safe. Do you hear me?' he whispered. Then he shouted again. 'Don't shoot! We're coming out!' He kissed their heads and hugged them close. 'It's all over,' he murmured. 'It's all over, I promise.'

He opened the door and stepped out into the glare of headlights.

Chapter 41

They were sitting in the back of an ambulance. Joe's arm had been temporarily bandaged and the flow of blood arrested. His face was ashen. They watched as Stone was taken out on a trolley, his face grey but uncovered.

'How is he?'

'Not good, he's lost a lot of blood, but I think he'll live.'

It took minutes for Stone to be hooked to the equipment in the ambulance. Then the doors closed and it drove from the house and, siren blaring, moved more rapidly away towards the town and the hospital.

'Is Mr. Stone okay?'

It was Meg's voice, tremulous and soft. She sat opposite her father, beside Hannah, and she shivered as if from the cold.

'Yes, he's tough,' Joe said.

'Say, "I promise." Meg's voice seemed to emerge as if with difficulty and from a distance, a voice piloting itself from great depths, barely audible.

Hannah hugged her close. They'd wrapped a blanket round her and she peered out now through questioning eyes, like through a misted window.

'I can't, but I think he will.'

They watched as another trolley was wheeled by. The body was covered this time.

'I've got blood on me,' Meg said.

The paramedic handed a wipe and Hannah pulled away the blanket and took her hands. 'Here, let's clean them.'

'Are the bad men dead?' Meg asked.

Another trolley was pushed by, another corpse covered by a sheet.

'Yes.'

'I'm glad.'

'Me too.'

Joe managed a smile. Beside him, Jessica held her blanket loosely over her shoulders. She sat without speaking, her head resting on him, his arm wrapped around her. He looked at Hannah sitting opposite him but her eyes focussed above his head, looking at nothing. Her hand stroked Meg's hair. Joe reached across and held her hand and her eyes met his and they exchanged brief flickering smiles like a fire re-awakening.

Joe stood up. He lifted Jessica and set her beside Hannah.

'Look after Mummy for me. I'll be back in a few minutes.'

'Don't go,' she cried, 'not again, not ever.'

'There's something I've got to do,' he said. 'It won't take a minute. There are people out there... it's an opportunity...'

'Can't it wait, Joe?' Hannah's voice was tired. 'Just phone Lisa and Alan, let them know we're okay.'

He shook his head.

'It's got to be now. Tomorrow will be too late.'

'For God's sake, Joe, can't we come first just once? I just want a life like other people now. Don't you understand? It's over. Leave it to them.' She waved a tired hand towards the police officers performing their rituals within the house and outside. 'I don't want any more of this. I want my house and my family and my friends; I want school for the girls, trips to the shops and holidays. I want us to go out to work and come back in the evening and sit down and talk and watch shit on the television.'

'Don't go back in the house,' Meg murmured. She looked from the back of the ambulance through frightened, little eyes. 'There'll be ghosts.'

'You don't believe in ghosts,' Jessica reminded her. 'You said so.'

'I do really,' she whispered. She shivered.

Jessica moved to her side and put an arm round her. 'There's nothing to be scared of now. It's all over. Daddy and Mr. Stone won. The bad guys are gone forever.'

'What if they come back?'

'They won't. They're dead.'

Hannah looked at Joe and then turned to the girls. 'Daddy's going back in the house, just for five minutes. He'll tell everyone that the bad people are dead and that everything is going to be okay. It's over. We're safe.'

'Promise?' Meg asked.

Hannah looked at Joe but she couldn't speak and the words she longed to say died on her tongue.

Joe knew what he had to do. He thought of Mikhal and of Jival and Haasita and their two bright eyed children. He thought of the Asian couple restoring their ruined home, of D.S. Jackson and his brother and Solly and the other good people he met on his journey. He thought of the mother and her little girl on that crashed bus and of the injured man crawling towards him on the tarmac. He thought of Alan and Lisa and Adam and of all the people out there looking for nothing more than a chance to live, to raise their families, to reach out a hand and touch a fragile, gossamer web of happiness. He could talk to them now, to all of them. Sheila would ask her editor to let him speak and he would nod to Marek who would press a few keys and Joe would have an audience he could never reach again. Maybe later it would be taken up by the news channels and the whole country would hear. He had to tell all those people that the cities, the towns, the villages and all their streets and lanes, all that rich, interconnected web, was theirs. The future was theirs.

'I've got to go,' he said.

'I know.'

'But do you promise, Daddy?' Meg asked.

He looked at her and at Jessica and Hannah, and he smiled.

'I promise,' he said.

Turbulence